MANAGING TO

KEEP

THE

CUSTOMER

ROBERT L. DESATNICK
DENIS H. DETZEL

MANAGING TO
KEEP
THE
CUSTOMER

HOW TO ACHIEVE AND MAINTAIN SUPERIOR CUSTOMER SERVICE THROUGHOUT THE ORGANIZATION

REVISED EDITION

Jossey-Bass Publishers
San Francisco

Substantial discounts on bulk quantities of Jossey-Bass books are available to corporations, professional associations, and other organizations. For details and discount information, contact the special sales department at Jossey-Bass Inc., Publishers. (415) 433-1740; Fax (415) 433-0499.

For sales outside the United States, contact Maxwell Macmillan International Publishing Group, 866 Third Avenue, New York, New York 10022.

Manufactured in the United States of America

 The paper used in this book is acid-free and meets the State of California requirements for recycled paper (50 percent recycled waste, including 10 percent postconsumer waste), which are the strictest guidelines for recycled paper currently in use in the United States.

Credits are on page 291.

Library of Congress Cataloging-in-Publication Data

Desatnick, Robert L.
  Managing to keep the customer : how to achieve and maintain superior customer service throughout the organization. — Rev. ed. / Robert L. Desatnick, Denis H. Detzel.
      p.   cm. — (The Jossey-Bass management series)
  Includes bibliographical references and index.
  ISBN 1-55542-415-5
  1. Customer service.   2. Customer relations.   I. Detzel, Denis H., date. II. Title. III. Series.
HF5415.5.D47   1993
658.8'12—dc20   93-6842
                                                                       CIP

FIRST EDITION
HB Printing   10 9 8 7 6 5 4 3 2 1   *Code 9320*

THE JOSSEY-BASS
MANAGEMENT SERIES

CONTENTS

PREFACE

It is becoming increasingly difficult for organizations to differentiate their products and services from those of their competitors. While every organization claims to treat the customer as king, and most recognize that they fall short of this ideal, few know how to conceive and implement change.

Yet service supremacy is definitely achievable. It begins at home, with the recognition of an organization's internal customers and the realization that customer relations mirror employee relations. Our willingness to settle for mediocrity is the result of underinvestment in our human resources. This malaise can be remedied, however, and the cure results in an enormous return on investment.

Genesis and Scope of the Book

The stimulus for *Managing to Keep the Customer* was a major initiative sponsored by Citicorp when the senior author, Robert L. Desatnick, was corporate vice president of human resources for McDonald's. It featured seventeen acknowledged service superstars, including McDonald's, from a variety of businesses (both service and manufacturing). The study clearly illustrated the management practices that all shared in common.

Since 1981, the date of the study, we have tested and refined those characteristics to determine whether they apply equally to small, medium, and large organizations, regardless of the nature of the business. This book is the result of that practical field research and testing with more than five hundred organizations. It is a how-to book.

Although bookstores deluge readers with brochures announcing new books on customer satisfaction, we do not know of any book that has been as thoroughly tested as *Managing to Keep the Customer*. More than five hundred organizations have embraced the management practices of this book, and they have produced extraordinary results: they have created a perceptible difference between themselves and their competitors.

The first edition of *Managing to Keep the Customer* was published in 1987. How is this second edition different from the first? We have had six additional years to implement the management practices described in the first edition; consequently, there are many more practical suggestions in this edition. Also, since 1991, Desatnick has acted as an examiner for the Malcolm Baldrige National Quality Award. His exposure to world-class quality leaders has reinforced what we already knew about the importance of exceeding customers' expectations in a quality-driven world. Finally, we have been fortunate in assisting many client organizations to create and implement change, and our measures of customer satisfaction have become more precise and sophisticated.

Audience

Managing to Keep the Customer provides a proven, time-tested step-by-step process leading to service supremacy. It tells how to exceed customer expectations. Its premises are equally valid for all organizations — public and private, profit and not-for-profit, small, medium, and large. Whether the reader's organization is in sales, service, distribution, manufacturing, or all of the foregoing, this book will exceed expectations. Every manager, supervisor, teacher, consultant, and professional will benefit from its how-to contents. After all, we are all in the business of service, and all of us are in the service business.

Whether the reader owns a small bookstore with five employees or is a manager in an organization with thousands of employees, the practical, easy-to-apply ideas expressed in the book will increase sales, profits, and market share (in for-profit organizations) and strengthen customer satisfaction. Its focus is on building, maintaining, and reorienting the entire work force, from the top down.

Managing to Keep the Customer takes the reader beyond the ongoing service revolution — what might be called the "customer rebellion" — by providing a blueprint for building and maintaining a customer-oriented work force. It contrasts the financial rewards of superior service with the costs of mediocre, inattentive service. It shows the reader how to select customer-oriented employees and managers and then deals with their orientation, performance standards, training, motivation, development, evaluation, rewards, recognition, and retention — in particular, as each affects customer satisfaction.

Overview of the Contents

Chapter One provides an overview of the service revolution. It highlights common mistakes that organizations make and suggests ways to avoid them. It defines the high cost of unhappy customers, provides a successful formula for how to do the right things at the right time, and reveals the secrets of McDonald's phenomenal success in the marketplace.

Chapter Two spells out the role of the chief executive officer (CEO) in prevention-based management. This role includes personally monitoring select measures of customer satisfaction. The chapter also describes how management, by establishing the highest standards of service excellence, can create a culture that worships the customer. It then discusses the importance of the mission statement and tells how to develop one. The chapter goes on to explain how to recognize the need for change and then, specifically, how to make needed changes. Because employee participation facilitates the implementation of change, the authors include specific measurements that readers can use to evaluate quantitatively the degree to which their organization provides a participative management style.

Chapter Three describes how to put one's own "house" (in this case, the organization) in order, on the premise that customer relations mirror employee relations. It notes the factors to be dealt with in establishing service supremacy through effective leadership of the work force and offers a survey that readers can use to measure the climate for customer satisfaction in their organization.

Chapter Four tells how to create within an organization an awareness of the importance of the customer, beginning with hiring the right people and proceeding through all the steps necessary to create empowered, self-directed work teams. The key is in the participation of the work force through ongoing, two-way communication and the establishment of self-directed management and floor-level teams. The subject of customer service performance teams is also covered.

Chapter Five discusses how to establish behavioral performance standards that involve the entire work force through a highly participative approach (and reveal the unpleasant consequences of *not* involving the work force in the establishment of their own performance standards). Performance standards are described for newly hired employees, existing employees, and managers and supervisors, with examples drawn from McDonald's and other organizations. Performance standards specific to internal and external customer satisfaction are also included. Finally, the chapter highlights the importance of training and discusses various kinds of training and the best methods for evaluating training effectiveness.

Chapter Six describes for the reader how best to measure employee performance against standards established to benefit the organization and the customers. It highlights four kinds of surveys that organizations can use to evaluate the management climate, employee opinion, customer satisfaction, and internal client satisfaction. It also tells the CEO how to get started, how to get the best results with an outside consultant, and how to use survey results based on the four quantitative assessments.

Chapter Seven describes the differences between reward and recognition systems, emphasizes the importance of each, and tells the reader how to use both for maximum impact. Specific examples of each are highlighted for both the manufacturing and the service sectors. A pay-for-performance merit system that was designed and facilitated for a hospital is described in detail, and a number of other pay-for-performance examples are given more briefly. The unpleasant alternatives to implementing a pay-for-performance merit system are also presented, and the manager's role as leader, coach, and cheerleader is noted.

Chapter Eight discusses how managers can maintain enthusiasm in employees and customers through consistency and predictability. It stresses the importance of top-management visibility in this endeavor and presents detailed suggestions to improve staff meetings. In addition, it recommends that the idea of continuous improvement in all that an organization does be brought home through training designed to build and sustain enthusiasm. A number of specific steps for sustaining enthusiasm are described, along with methods by which the service superstars manage continuously to exceed customer expectations. The unpleasant alternatives to continuous reinforcement of customer-oriented values are discussed.

Chapter Nine tells how to plan for tomorrow through the use of today's trend analyses. The work force of the 1990s (and beyond) is described in terms of its growing diversity and what the people will be doing. It tells what a coping organization will need to do to get and keep talented employees. Untapped sources of talent are shared with the reader, along with how best to benefit from these sources. The importance of career ladders is highlighted, along with flexibility in procedures, pay, and benefits. The message is this: adapt or evaporate.

Chapter Ten suggests how to plan for the unknown in

an increasingly competitive global environment based on what we know today. It highlights the importance of innovation and the keys to survival and prosperity, which include preparation for the new work force, a shared cohesive vision of the future, and a plan for implementation based on present knowledge.

Acknowledgments

For giving of their precious time to meet with us and share their thoughts about and experience with building and maintaining a customer-oriented work force, our special thanks go to the following:

- The Dartnell Corporation, Chicago, Ill.
- John A. Young, president and CEO, Hewlett-Packard, Palo Alto, Calif.
- Steve Watson, chair and CEO, Dayton Hudson, Minneapolis, Minn.
- Joseph J. Melone, president, Prudential Insurance, Newark, N.J.
- Ken Garrett, senior vice president, AT&T, Trenton, N.J.
- Harvey Lamb, president emeritus, Subaru, Cherry Hill, N.J.
- Pat Leamy, owner and president, EconoPrint Shops, Madison, Wis.

March 1993   ROBERT L. DESATNICK
Chicago, Illinois   DENIS H. DETZEL

THE AUTHORS

ROBERT L. DESATNICK is president and founder of Creative Human Resource Consultants, headquartered in Chicago. He received his B.S. degree (1954) with honors from Franklin College in liberal arts and political science and his M.B.A. degree (1956) with distinction from Washington University, where he was a Weinheimer Fellow.

For more than thirty years, Desatnick has worked at home and abroad in all fields of human resource management and business planning. Currently, his consulting work focuses on assisting organizations to exceed customer expectations in a quality-driven world, improving productivity through performance management, enhancing staff effectiveness, and designing behaviorally oriented selection systems and management skills training programs. During his career, he has worked with McDonald's (as corporate vice president of human resources and worldwide senior human resource officer), Chase Manhattan Bank (as vice president and group executive for human resources), Indian Head (as corporate director for business planning and executive development), Booz, Allen & Hamilton (as a consultant for professional personnel services), General Electric (as MBO coordinator, management development director, seminar leader, and plant and division human resource manager), and Otis Elevator (as director of worldwide human resources).

Desatnick is affiliated with several universities and frequently participates in national and regional conferences of the American College of Health Care Executives, the American Society for Personnel Administration, the Human Resource Planning Society, and the American Society for Training and Development. He was one of the business leaders selected from around the world to participate in the first World Symposium on Business Achievement held in Niort, France, in October 1986, and is a member of the board of examiners for the Malcolm Baldrige National Quality Award.

Desatnick has written numerous articles and several books on human resource management, including *A Concise Guide to Management Development* (1970), *Innovative Human Resource Management* (1972), *Human Resource Management in the Multinational Company* (1977), *The Expanding Role of the Human Resource Manager* (1979), *The Business of Human Resource Management* (1983), *Managing to Keep the Customer* (1987), *Keep the Customer* (1990), and *The Business of Service* (1991).

DENIS H. DETZEL is a vice president of the Hay Group, a director of the Hay Group's Research and Organization Development Practice, and a member of the firm's Quality Council. He has experience in organization planning, organization culture change, employee involvement and total quality management processes, and organization, market, employee, and public opinion research. He received both his B.A. degree (1967) in English and his M.Ed. degree (1969) from the University of Cincinnati. His Ph.D. degree (1980) in administration and policy studies is from Northwestern University.

Before joining the Hay Group, Detzel was director of public policy for McDonald's, where he created and managed corporate projects and functions in the public affairs, public relations, marketing, corporate contributions, corporate communications, and human resources areas. Since joining the Hay Group, Detzel has served more than one hundred clients, including Amoco Oil, Cincinnati Gas and Electric, Contech, Hyatt Hotels, the Mercy Healthcare System, Secura Insurance, McDonald's, Hilton Hotels, and Glidden.

Detzel has served as chair of the board of the Cosmopolitan Chamber of Commerce and on advisory boards for the Fund for the Improvement of Post-Secondary Education, Northwestern University's Center for Urban Affairs and Policy Research, and the U.S. Commission on Civil Rights. He has also served as chair of the board for Lyon Coachworks and Show Car, Inc. Over the years, he has written about and presented papers on a variety of research and policy issues and has studied at research institutes in the United States, Canada, and Mexico.

MANAGING TO

KEEP
THE
CUSTOMER

PART ONE

SERVICE: THE REAL BUSINESS OF ORGANIZATIONS

Keeping the customer—ensuring customer satisfaction—is big business, no matter what size the company. In Chapters One through Three, we provide background information useful to all organizations in their quest to keep their customers. We emphasize the necessity of service excellence and the dissemination through corporate culture, via the CEO, of the attitude that the customer must come first. In addition, we discuss the importance of employee relations, examining the direct connection between customer relations and management's attitude toward and treatment of employees.

Chapter 1

THE BASICS OF
SERVICE QUALITY

Customer satisfaction starts with the CEO as a role model—talking, listening, responding, respecting, creating, and living the environment and having an open door to all employees at all times.
— Steve Watson
Chair and CEO
Dayton Hudson

The 1980s were clearly a decade of customer rebellion and sovereignty. It does not take a crystal ball to foresee that this trend will continue through the 1990s. Consumers, having rightfully insisted on getting what they paid for—whether that be a clean glass, an impeccable hotel room, a decent meal in the hospital, an on-time delivery, or courteous treatment at the point of purchase—are not likely to relinquish their rights. Further, dramatic changes in demographics, economics, politics, technology, and social values—changes that are still ongoing—point to continuing changes in the business field, both domestically and internationally.

The business organizations that will succeed despite these changes are those that recognize today's customer revolution and are fully prepared to meet the challenge with the highest standards of service. For any business or institution — public or private, for-profit or not-for-profit, service-oriented or product-oriented — now is the time to seize the competitive advantage.

It is time for every business to reassess how well it manages its relationships with two key groups: internal customers (employees) and external customers (those who purchase their products or services). Both are essential; in fact, the two are inseparable. Any business that fails to take this preventive initiative before market share, sales, or profits decline may well find itself unable to reverse the downward trend.

It matters not whether a company is large or small — or whether its business is manufacturing, sales, service, or distribution. Trying to compete solely on the basis of product or price is insufficient, primarily because product differentiation is becoming increasingly difficult. Look, for example, at airlines, hotels, fast-food restaurants, hospitals, banks, and auto rental agencies. How can they create a perceptible difference that sets them ahead of the pack? The distinguishing factor is rarely product superiority. Instead, the key is service: attention to the customer. Service is now the standard by which customers are measuring an organization's performance. It is not *a* competitive edge; it is *the* competitive edge. And, according to futurist John Naisbitt in *Megatrends,* it is rapidly becoming our nation's most marketable commodity.

The Service Revolution

The fastest-growing segment of our economy is the service sector, a factor that helps give service its status as *the* competitive edge. Already, the service sector accounts for two-thirds of our gross national product. More than 60 percent of all people employed in this country today work in service jobs; by the year 2000, this figure is expected to reach 90 percent.

These numbers signify a heightened awareness on the part of customers, who in all likelihood work in service-oriented positions themselves. The numbers also signify that service is here to stay. We are all in the service business; we are all in the business of service.

Quality service must be each organization's primary goal, as well as its most important market strategy, because it is the key to survival for the next decade. Superior service will increase sales and market share as well as reduce costs. What will it take to be one of the nation's most rapidly growing businesses? In our opinion, it will require a total service orientation, a service-oriented organization culture. The challenges facing any business will change over the years, but they will remain focused on increasing the level of service and customer satisfaction.

What is needed is a genuine, corporate-wide commitment to the customer. Ted Levitt, marketing guru from Harvard University, notes that a company should approach the relationship with the customer as if it were a lifelong one. But all too often the promises made by sales and marketing arc not fulfilled by the service delivery system, just as marriage vows are often broken. As a consequence, after a sale is made the relationship often goes sour and the customer is lost. How can this happen?

Most of us encounter poor service with distressing regularity. On a typical business trip, the only thing worse than the service may be the response to your complaints:

What You Experience	*What the Service Provider Says*
Your radio alarm fails.	We only sell it. Read your warranty.
The trunk of your airport limo is full of water and greasy tools, and your garment bag and its contents get soaked.	Did you buy our optional personal-property insurance?
You try to check in to claim your assigned seat on the plane.	Sorry, this line is closed. Please move on.
You pick up your rental car at your destination.	We're all out of compacts, but we can rent you a minivan once the mechanic is through with it.

You check into your hotel with a supposedly guaranteed reservation.	Sorry, but we have no record of your reservation, and we're full.
Breakfast is a half-hour late.	Sorry, it went to the wrong room.
Your secretary calls. Back at the office, the photocopier is down. •	We'll need a few days to get it fixed.
The hotel telephone is making funny noises.	We'll have to schedule a service rep, but I can't say for sure when he'll be out.
Your answering service abruptly says, "Oops, hold on," and you get cut off from a long-distance call.	This happens all the time. It's nothing to worry about.
You order a hot sandwich for lunch, but it arrives cold and greasy.	Our chef is out sick today, so an assistant is cooking.
You check out of the hotel — or try to. Your bill is wrong; the breakfast charge was not included.	I'll fix it for you as soon as I track down my supervisor.
When you finally pick up your baggage after the flight home, it's torn and broken.	Fill out a claim form, but I'll warn you: our liability limit is low.

The Dangers of Growth

A big part of the service problem is corporate America's love affair with marketing. It is hard to pick up a newspaper or magazine without being deluged with information on marketing. There are many articles on such issues as mature-brand strategy, marketing innovation, advertising, product improvement, and product differentiation. But what about service to the existing customers? If customers were valued as highly as most companies allege they are, more firms would have a vice president of customer service along with the vice presidents of sales and marketing.

Aggressive sales and marketing can get too far ahead of an organization's ability to provide required services on time. The mistake many service companies make when times are good is to get so caught up in adding new customers and new services that they lose touch with the existing customer base. In their eagerness to grow, they take on more new accounts than they can service properly. Anxious to capture more market share, they neglect their old accounts and eventually lose part of that business to competition.

What is the next effect? Research on customer service conducted by Technical Assistance Research Programs (TARP) in Arlington, Virginia, indicates that it is five times more expensive to get a new customer than it is to keep an old one. Put another way, the cost of losing a repeat customer is approximately five times the value of that annual account.

Organizations will spend literally hundreds of millions of dollars to attract new customers while their old customers slip out the back door, never to return again. What drives people away is rude, discourteous, inept, incompetent service, often the result of mere apathy or inattention.

Now it would seem logical that if an organization is willing to spend $100 million or more annually on advertising and sales promotion, it should be willing to spend $20 million to keep its present customers. That lesser sum is money well spent: outstanding service and its ensuing word of mouth will not only keep present customers but attract new ones as well.

The High Cost of an Unhappy Customer

In today's fiercely competitive market, no business can long survive without satisfied customers. Let us look at some significant findings from recent studies conducted by TARP:

- Ninety-six percent of consumers who experience a problem with a small-ticket product (for example, small packaged goods) do not complain to the manufacturer. (Of these, 63 percent will not buy again.)
- Forty-five percent of consumers who experience a problem with a small-ticket service (for example, cable television or local telephone service) do not complain. (Of these, 45 percent will not buy again.)
- Not surprisingly, only 27 percent of unhappy consumers of large-ticket durable products (for example, automobiles,

computers) do not complain. (Of these, 41 percent will not buy again.)
- Thirty-seven percent of unhappy consumers of large-ticket services (for example, insurance, loans, MHO) do not complain. (Of these, 50 percent will not buy again.)

These numbers alone are significant and can make a major dent in future sales. But TARP has confirmed that negative word of mouth can create an even more formidable problem. Unhappy consumers share their experiences with others. A dissatisfied consumer with a small problem typically tells ten other people; those with large problems tell sixteen others. Further, 13 percent of dissatisfied consumers tell their experiences to more than twenty people.

The news is not all bad, however. Each consumer whose small problem is satisfactorily resolved can be expected to tell five other people. Each consumer whose large problem is satisfactorily resolved can be expected to tell eight other people. Of these people, some will then become new customers.

Further, most consumers whose complaints are satisfactorily resolved go on to buy again. These figures range from 92 percent of purchasers of small-ticket products to 70 percent of consumers of large-ticket services.

Consider the following price tags on customer loyalty. The automobile industry believes that a loyal customer represents a lifetime average revenue of $140,000. So why fight over an $80 repair bill or a $40 replacement part? In banking, it is estimated that the average customer represents at least $80 a year in profit. In appliance manufacturing, brand loyalty is worth more than $2,800 over a twenty-year period. Your local supermarket counts on you for $4,400 within a given year. So why quibble about some little something that the customer thinks is not right? People who believe in service superiority make things right, they want their customers to be satisfied—and to return.

Customer Satisfaction

Clearly, customer satisfaction is vital to a company's success. But what *is* customer satisfaction? Here is our definition: *Cus-*

tomer satisfaction is the degree of happiness experienced by the customer. It is produced within and throughout an organization — among all depart- ments, all functions, and all people. Customers include external purchasers of goods and services from the organization, suppliers, the local commu- nity, employees, managers, and supervisors (and shareholders, if the or- ganization is publicly held).

Whatever the definition, the facts show that customer satisfaction warrants every company's attention. Consider the following information:

- According to the Strategic Planning Institute (SPI), revenues of companies with high levels of customer satisfaction (what SPI refers to as "relative perceived product or service qual- ity") grow an average of 12 percent annually, compared with no growth for companies with lower levels of customer satis- faction. Further, profits of service-oriented companies grow an average of 10 percent a year, compared with 1 percent a year for those perceived not to have superior service.

- According to our research, 91 percent of retail customers will avoid a company that served them poorly. Of those, 80 percent will go out of their way to find a comparable store that offers superior service and 70 percent will pay more for that service.

- A customer with satisfactorily resolved problems provides three times the revenue of customers who have not had prob- lems. In addition, customers request adjustments that arc reasonable in relation to what the company is willing to offer 90 percent of the time.

Given these rewards, clearly the goal should be to do right by the customer, to cultivate customer satisfaction.

Doing It Right

Some companies understand this and have incorporated a full commitment to service superiority. Past and current customer- oriented practices include the following:

- Procter & Gamble has toll-free numbers to handle customer questions about many of their products.

- Neiman-Marcus has a no-questions asked refund policy.
- Management consultants often offer a money-back guarantee for customers who are not satisfied.
- Holiday Inn proclaims, if it's not right, it's on them.
- McDonald's provides refunds or replacements to dissatisfied customers.
- IBM has an army of repair technicians to take care of its computers.
- Frito-Lay potato chips are delivered even in a blizzard.
- Rolls Royce makes service calls anywhere in the world.
- Johnson & Johnson voluntarily accepted great financial loss on the recall of Tylenol, as did the Perrier Group on the recall of bottled water.
- Herman Miller does a customer survey, and the results of the survey determine employee bonuses.
- Motorola has a participative management policy.
- Dayton Hudson holds free public seminars on such topics as the changing role of women and the problems of the aged.
- Weyco Group employees put their names on products they make.

All these firms know that their major strategic weapon is added value to the customer through superior service. They are willing to admit an error, and they immediately take steps to correct it. They clearly recognize that customer relations mirror employee relations. They are all open to change; in fact, they have institutionalized the process of change to avoid stagnation.

But what about organizations that do not yet have this cultural value of service? Can they manage to become customer-oriented? To redefine their key values in terms of the customer? And then to get all their executives, managers, supervisors, and employees fully committed to achieving those values? Can they profit from the successes of those at the top while avoiding the mistakes of those who did not survive?

The central thesis of this book is that they can. We are privileged to be living in an information age, when shared knowledge and experiences are readily available. Thus those in customer-oriented organizations have immediate access to the successes and failures of those who came — and went — before them.

Doing It Wrong

Most organizations *say* that they are close to the customer, but few are. This is evidenced over and over again in battles that are won and lost at the simplest level of customer contact — the point of purchase — which frequently is staffed by minimum-wage employees. If we could do a complete postmortem on all businesss that fail, we would almost certainly find that one of the most prevalent causes of failure is inadequate or discourteous service.

And just talking about service is not enough. Consumers know the difference between words and action. How often have you seen situations like the following?

The Promise	*The Delivery*
Our warranty has teeth.	You'll have to send it to the manufacturer, and repairs will take six to twelve weeks.
We want to know how well we did.	That's not what you ordered? Are you sure?
Ours is a no-excuses guarantee.	You must have mishandled the product.
We'll give you satisfaction or your money back.	No sales slip, no return.
We really try harder.	Gift wrapping is in the basement, and it's extra.
We pride ourselves on the highest standards of customer service.	We don't have your reservation, and we can't give you a room without it.
We stand behind our products.	We only sell it; we don't service it.
No one delivers faster than we do.	Sorry, we lost your package.

Why does the delivery so often fail to fulfill the promise? Because companies, large and small, relegate the customer service function to the lowest levels of the organization. Then they proceed to staff those levels with entry-level and unskilled people.

The Success Formula

By way of contrast, the essence of McDonald's success has always been its focus on the customer. Its corporate values are quality, service, cleanliness, and value. After more than forty years, these values have not changed. McDonald's found the success formula.

It is important to recognize that Kentucky Fried Chicken and White Castle System were on the scene long before McDonald's became a major player, but they were surpassed. Why? Because McDonald's fully understands that superiority in customer service is really superiority in "people" practices.

Businesses wanting to apply this success formula must remember to count their employees among their customers. If a company's own house is not in order, it is not possible to achieve customer service superiority. We have long known about the direct impact of employee relations on productivity and participative management. But we are just beginning to recognize the magnitude of that impact on market share, sales, costs, profits, and customer relations.

When Business Is Good, Make It Better

The rapid pace of the times in which we live results in constant change as a way of life. This virtually mandates that we do things differently from those who preceded us. In *Managing in Turbulent Times,* management authority Peter Drucker strongly suggests the need to "slough off yesterday." The time to change and reassess, to question every aspect of our operation, is not when we are in trouble but while we are successful. If a company waits until it is marginal to look for improvement, it goes down proportionately more when the economy goes down and comes up disproportionately less when the economy recovers. Once marginality sets in, it is almost impossible to recover market share and reverse the downward trend.

Drucker notes that it is particularly important to reassess management strategies and tactics after a long period of relative calm and predictability. In these turbulent times, every service, both internal and external, every process, and every activity needs to be put on trial every few years. Drucker suggests that all institutions — public and private, for-profit and not-for-profit — examine how their customers define "value" and how they perceive the institution in relation to its competition.

Service Superstars as Role Models

There are a number of organizations whose service success has set new standards of superiority. Two case studies of service superstars will help illuminate the importance of service.

Exceeding Expectations

In a 1990 interview with R. L. Desatnick, Joseph J. Melone, president of Prudential Insurance, said that his company's objective is to give more and better service than the customers expect. This is a thorough commitment to service excellence — excellence that retains customers, causes repeat sales, and attracts new customers.

As an example of the extra care Prudential provides, agents often take older people to Social Security offices and help them apply for their benefits. As another example of this extra care, when an eighty-two-year-old woman wanted to change a beneficiary of a $5,000 insurance policy, her agent personally drove out to see her.

The company also gives the customer the benefit of any doubt surrounding a claim. For example, one of Prudential's claims people questioned the coroner's certification that the cause of an insured's death was suicide. Based on the insurer's reassessment, the coroner deemed the cause of death an accident and the company paid double indemnity to the beneficiaries.

According to Melone, service is the most significant competitive advantage in a marketplace with too many suppliers and narrowing profit margins. And that service pays off. For example, the eighty-two-year-old woman's son — a very successful contractor — was so impressed with the level of service given to his mother that he and his partners bought considerable amounts of insurance from Prudential.

Paying Attention to Detail

As another example, in McDonald's restaurants all over the world, millions of customers are greeted cheerfully and sincerely, as if they were personal friends of the employees. And remember, these are minimum-wage employees, ranging in age from sixteen to seventy. Most of them are part-time, with no benefits and no tips. How does McDonald's do it?

McDonald's success is partially the result of spending hundreds of millions of dollars on advertising and sales promotion each year. However, the main reason for the success is meticulous attention to detail. It is much more an operations-oriented than a market-oriented company. This is not apparent to the consuming public, however. They see only the results: the cheerful smile.

McDonald's commitment to service and to good human resource management begins at the corporate level and extends to all the regions, districts, offices, and restaurants. The organization's customer-focused values are reinforced by its policies toward its own people.

Components of a Service Superstar

Our conclusions concerning what makes a company a superstar and what distinguishes a superstar's service record come from our combined experience in working with companies across the country and around the world. Individually and jointly, we have conducted interviews with senior officials of large, medium, and small companies — from companies with fifty employees and an annual volume of several million dollars to organizations with many thousands of employees and tens of millions in sales. A number of these companies have been evaluated as candidates for the Malcolm Baldrige National Quality Awards.

The businesses we have examined are widely diverse. They include manufacturing, service, sales, and distribution firms in both the public and private sectors; they include for-profit and not-for-profit, union and nonunion firms. A representative sample of the organizations with which we have worked directly includes Avis Rent-a-Car, Banc One, Dayton Hudson, EconoPrint Shops, Federal Express, FTD Association, Glidden, Good Shepherd Medical Center, Hewlett-Packard, Hyatt Hotels, ICMA Retirement Corporation, Johnson Controls, Mercy Health System, Northern Illinois Gas, Northrup Aviation, Otis Elevator, Prudential Insurance, Walt Disney Corporation, and Whirlpool.

So just what do service superstars have in common that makes them so exceptional? What management policies and values produce the highest standards of service quality, timeliness, and delivery? And will those same values still hold true in the future? That is what this book is all about. It tells not only what selected role models did, but how they managed to do it. It shares their management strategies and operational tactics.

Specifically, it is possible to distill ten characteristics that service superstars share. (These characteristics will be discussed in considerable detail in the chapters that follow.) Each of the superstars did the following:

1. Recognized the fact that customer relations mirror employee relations. Knew that they had to be superior in their relationships with their employees if they were to be superior in customer service.
2. Created an awareness of the importance of customer service in the minds of their employees. Taught the need for satisfied customers from an employee's perspective: the customer is the ultimate paymaster.
3. Developed and implemented support systems needed to teach and reinforce the expected behaviors.
4. Recognized that everything that happens in an organization has an impact on customer service. Established interconnecting support systems throughout their organizations.

5. Defined and implemented precise and demanding performance standards, coupled with high performance expectations, to translate concepts to behavior.
6. Trained managers, supervisors, and employees to reinforce and maintain those desired behaviors once they had been established.
7. Defined carefully the roles of managers and supervisors in promoting continuous service superiority.
8. Provided tangible and intangible recognition and rewards for exemplary behavior. Made employees feel important and appreciated.
9. Used quantitative measures to monitor the effectiveness of service and of personnel policies, practices, programs, and procedures.
10. Built in strong, continuing reinforcement to sustain customer-oriented value systems and management practices.

In short, these superstar companies developed human resource policies and practices that produced an outstanding commitment to service excellence. We give you a preview of these polices here and elaborate on them throughout the book.

Personal Accountability

To build personal accountability among all employees — to help them believe that "each of us is the company" — these companies have adopted various combinations of the following:

- Formally indoctrinate employees about accountability.
- Reward actions beyond the call of duty.
- Commend employees for formal customer compliments.
- Back up decisions their employees make when interacting with customers.
- Route customer feedback to appropriate employees.
- Route errors and problems back to the specific employees causing them.
- Frequently appraise individual performance.
- Practice justified firing in the context of a responsible grievance system.

As a result of these actions, the companies' employees understand the scope of their personal responsibility and the importance of every service interaction. In addition, they take pride in their jobs and in their professionalism.

Service Teams

To create a service team, these companies took some or all of the following steps:

- Commemorate formation of the team, and the addition of new members, with special events.
- Hold informative and motivational team assemblies.
- Broadly define and satisfy employees' need to know.
- Inform employees how their jobs fit into the entire organization.
- Quickly disseminate information.
- Frequently assess work-group performance with employees.

Through these steps, the companies minimize buck passing, strengthen their capacity to respond to change, and develop group trust.

Open Communication

We found that superstar service companies have built open communication in some or all of the following ways:

- Use employee attitude surveys.
- Promote suggestion programs.
- Require frequent staff meetings within work groups.
- Train employees in transactional analysis.
- Share customer reactions with the entire organization.

As a result, the companies have opened multiple communication channels and strengthened their employees' abilities to communicate effectively. These channels and increased communication abilities are then used to identify problems and expedite their resolution.

Personnel Investments

To make major investments in human capital, the companies have attempted some or all of the following:

- Professionalize service personnel in a multiphase process.
- Promote employees from within the organization.
- Use a structured, in-house program for management training.
- Recognize and reward outstanding service to customers with meaningful incentive systems.

As a result of these actions, employees have both the necessary service skills and continued allegiance to company goals and standards.

Business Teaching Business

Service superiority begins with a restless dissatisfaction with the status quo. It starts at the top, with those who say, "We can and will do better." By designing the corporate value system so that this belief is built into every aspect of the employment contract, managers then disperse their ideals throughout the organization.

The process continues with a hiring system that uses patterned interviews to select those individuals who share management's values. And it never stops.

The question this book addresses is, Can every organization achieve comparable results? The answer is yes! If senior management is committed to establishing and reinforcing new standards of service superiority in all that is done, the dream can become a reality. Best of all, the trial-and-error approach is no longer necessary, because through a process of compressing the collective experience, business organizations are able to distill and synthesize those ingredients that have worked well in building customer-oriented management systems for other companies.

In our observation and experience, those organizations that strive to be the best at everything they do seem inevitably to lead their industries in productivity, service superiority, cost-effectiveness, employee morale, and loyalty. Not to mention profits!

Chapter 2

SERVICE EXCELLENCE
FROM THE TOP DOWN

If you can't measure it, you can't improve it, and what gets measured gets done.

> —John A. Young
> President and CEO
> Hewlett-Packard

It is hard to overestimate the importance of the CEO and the CEO's attitudes about customer service. As we will see in this chapter, the attitudes developed and transmitted by the CEO are critical to both the direction of the company and the attitudes of its employees. As John A. Young, president and CEO of Hewlett-Packard, noted in a 1990 interview with Desatnick, service excellence is "easier in a smaller company because people have more fun, the CEO is closer to the employees, and it is easier to generate enthusiasm and make them feel that they are part of a team." The customer service pointers that we offer in this book can be applied in any size company, however.

If the highest standards of service superiority are to be maintained in the marketplace, there must be no tolerance for mediocrity in any of an organization's operations, internal or external. This zero tolerance for mediocrity must have a positive — not a punitive — basis. It requires a customer-oriented organization culture in which people genuinely want to come to work, enjoy the work, work well with other employees (both up and down the chain of command), and will do their best.

The service superstars provide many examples of this positive, proactive approach. Take, for example, EconoPrint, a small chain of retail outlets based in Madison, Wisconsin. EconoPrint is in the highly competitive market of fast, quality printing. The owner and president, Pat Leamy has instituted virtually all of the steps we recommend in this book, from formulating a mission statement to total emphasis on employee and customer satisfaction. As he emphasized in a 1990 interview with Desatnick, "We are only as good as our last job." Further, his policy with his customers is this: "If it's not on time, it's on us." Leamy's secret to success is no secret: it is prevention. He constantly surveys employees and customers to ensure that their expectations are met and that problems are avoided.

The best-managed organizations continuously strive for perfection in everything they do. They know that even once they achieve a superior level of customer service, they cannot relax. Top-quality service needs to be sustained and reinforced, never allowed to slip; it is an ongoing, never-ending *process*. All supervisors, all managers, and all employees at every level are continually reminded of the organization's customer-oriented values.

This process must reach every single employee, and it must start at the top. Management actions set the example. Employee awareness of the importance of customer service is influenced by the degree of importance management attaches to customer service, through its collective manifest behavior and the total budget it allocates to customer service.

The Role of the CEO

The role of the CEO is to provide the overall service direction, write (or at least endorse) the organization's service policy, define the customer service objectives, and direct the overall integration of the organization's service efforts. Once the overall strategy and plans are formulated, the CEO provides the necessary funding, conducts quarterly service progress reviews, and evaluates service accomplishments against plans.

Noel Tichy, in his book *Managing Strategic Change,* tells us that in order for CEOs to create an environment that focuses on the customer, they must ensure that

- The process is CEO driven.
- There is a recognition of the need to change, coupled with knowing where to change.
- Management has the capacity and willingness to make the required changes.
- Skills training is provided in order to effectively implement the change.

Indeed, the CEO's official recognition of the importance of customer service is critical. Hewlett-Packard's Young recommends that companies "have the customer service function report as high up as you can in the organization." In our interview, he noted that companies should "make sure the person responsible is part of the management council or management committee."

The CEOs of successful companies, our service superstars, for the most part are deeply and personally involved in the customer service function of their business. They send constant signals throughout the organization that say, "We are and will continue to be a service-oriented company. We are in the business of service." They personally read complaint logs and letters, take phone calls, and are highly visible and available to the rank and file. They both teach and attend training seminars, participate in orientation sessions for newly hired managers to talk about customer-oriented values, and speak at banquets celebrating employee graduation from in-house programs. In the early part of Desatnick's career, for example, the general manager of the Hotpoint Division of General Electric opened a training session with words of welcome and later passed out certificates at the graduation banquet. He said, "If this weren't important, I wouldn't be here."

The credibility of the service commitment is the biggest single problem for top management; it has to be reinforced all the time. Management has three basic tasks to perform: (1) establish the standards that employees are required to meet, (2) supply the wherewithal to meet those standards, and (3) spend time encouraging and helping employees to meet those standards and requirements.

At McDonald's, top management provides encouragement to everyone through its frequent visits to as many units as possible, both in the offices and in the field. During these visits, managers talk with as many people as possible, stressing the importance of both the employee and the customer. At Levi Strauss, top executives frequently work as salespeople in the stores of their major accounts. They want to test consumer reactions firsthand. At McDonald's and Herman Miller, there are no closed private offices; in fact, at McDonald's there are not even any doors! These practices are designed to encourage employees to take advantage of management's availability and willingness to listen.

In short, service leaders share a healthy sense of restless dissatisfaction with the status quo and feel an ongoing need to improve.

Implementing a Customer-Service Orientation

A CEO's efforts to implement a customer-service orientation fall into four major areas: preventing service problems, monitoring service measurements, changing the organization's culture, and setting a higher standard.

Preventing Service Problems

Service problems are caused primarily by disenchantments, carelessness, and lack of concern on the part of employees, and poor training, imprecise service standards, lack of service measurements, and poor follow-up on the part of management. These things can be prevented. But prevention takes time and attention — top-management attention.

We must place the responsibility for service superiority squarely on top management's back. If management does not provide clear performance standards, for example, employees will develop their own. Yet too often management does not know, or denies, that it is the cause of the problem. As a result, employees get turned off to the company and to its customers through the normal operating practices of their supervisors and managers.

Monitoring Service Measurements

But how does management know if the company has service-related problems? The simplest way to find out is through first-hand observation. Indirect observation is also useful: mystery shoppers—management appointees portraying customers—can assess the level of service they are given on the floor. Another way is to continually and selectively monitor and audit service policies, practices, and procedures. Still a third way is to ask, using telephone, mail, or in-store surveys, customer panels or focus groups, direct interviews, and exit interviews of customers who have not come back (if you know who they are).

There is yet one other way that is particularly appropriate for the CEO: look at business results—the bottom line. Here is a checklist for the CEO to use in measuring customer satisfaction (or the lack thereof):

- Compare your market share with the competition's. Are you gaining? Losing? Holding your own?
- Compare your sales growth against your own history and against the growth of the total market.
- Compare yourself against yourself in terms of operating results and earnings as a percentage of sales.
- Has turnover—of management, supervisors, and employees—decreased, increased, or remained the same?
- Can you and do you measure the impact of service on the following: return on investment, return on assets, earnings per share, new business, and lost business?
- What percentage and how many dollars of your total budget

are devoted to creating and maintaining service superiority, as contrasted with marketing and new sales?

Additionally, the CEO needs to pay close personal attention to the following:

- Customer complaint logs, letters of complaint, and phone calls.
- Reports of mystery shoppers.
- Survey data on outside customers, employees, supervisors and managers, and inside customers.
- Programs for communicating, accepting, and enforcing precise service standards for both internal and external customers.
- Service goals and their degree of attainment.
- Service budgets.
- Productivity per employee.
- Sales per employee.
- Employment costs as a percentage of total costs. (Are they increasing, decreasing, or stable?)
- Profit per employee.
- Costs of service complaints.
- Interval between the time a customer registers a complaint and the time it is satisfactorily settled.
- Grievances, strikes, sabotage, absenteeism, sitdowns, slowdowns, and walkouts.
- Performance appraisal reviews and discussions.
- Rewards for customer service excellence. (If rewards are financial, do the best performers receive the highest pay increases? Is the margin of difference significant?)
- Field service and field sales reports.

Changing the Organization's Culture

If service-related problems continue to be a major source of concern, if survey results are disappointing at best, and if customers are slipping out the back door, never to return, a company may need to change its culture. In other words, to improve customer relations significantly, a company may need to eliminate the causes that produce nonconforming products or services.

Changing the culture is possible, but it takes time. Jan Carlzon, president of Scandinavian Air System (SAS) changed his company's culture to give primary emphasis to service superiority, including service quality, service timeliness, and service delivery. On-time flights became the rule, and in just two years, the airline moved from a loss to a handsome profit.

Management attitudes are key to changing the culture. In order to successfully change the culture, management must possess at least the following three attributes:

- Recognition of the need to change, coupled with knowledge of what to change, based on appropriate diagnosis
- Capacity and willingness on the part of the CEO and other top management to make the needed changes
- Skills and competencies to manage and implement the needed changes

Culture changes do not come easily. As Young indicated in our interview, "The absolute involvement, understanding, and commitment of the CEO and the management team" are critical to a culture change. "This means talking to customers and employees. It means engineering some quick success stories, then merchandising them throughout the organization. It will take enormous perseverance."

The skills needed to manage culture changes normally include the following:

- Ability to change management style and direction
- Ability to create demanding performance standards; zero tolerance for mediocrity at all levels of the organization
- Skills in total performance management, including precise goals, strategies, standards, appraisals, and feedback systems
- Effective negotiation and communication skills
- Counseling and progressive discipline skills
- Ability to make difficult "people" decisions

Setting a Higher Standard

To avoid slippage and the necessity for subsequent culture changes, companies must continually test, refine, and improve their existing standards of service superiority. They must reward lavishly those who meet and then exceed their standards for quality of service. And once a standard is being consistently met, the CEO must set a new, tougher one.

CEOs and other managers in the service role models never let up for a moment. They continue to reinforce and reward the correct behaviors, and they constantly develop and introduce new programs and new means to reward outstanding service to customers. They make liberal use of service audits to monitor service policies and practices. They emphasize (and reemphasize) the ongoing, lifelong nature of training as a means to achieve and maintain service superiority. The high level of expectations that management — especially the CEO — sets for employees can be even more important than the actual training received.

Participative Management

George Odiorne, a management analyst and an authority on management by objectives, has identified what he calls the "Seven Deadly Sins of Supervision for the 90s." We restate them in a positive-action sense here:

1. Be sure to allow and encourage full participation in the decision-making process.
2. Clearly define and communicate to all the objectives of the organization and how each person can contribute to those objectives. Obtain agreement with each of your people on specific objectives.
3. Be consistent and predictable.
4. Encourage and personally practice objectivity in distributing work assignments and relationships with your people.
5. Take a good look at your perks. Be sure that they are related to the job and necessary to the business.

6. Be open to and welcome change.
7. Help employees achieve their full potential.

What these guidelines have in common is a respect for the opinions, values, and abilities of employees. Why is that respect so crucial? Articles and books on organization culture tend to validate that a "strong culture"—one that encourages the participation and involvement of employees in shared decision making—is a tremendously vital asset.

An organization's culture is reflected in its management style, and that style dictates how management by objectives, for example (or any other system of performance management), is to be introduced and implemented if desired results are to be obtained. Management style strongly affects at least the following five aspects of corporate life: leadership processes, motivational forces, communication processes, the interaction influence process, and decision-making processes.

A research study by Daniel R. Denison of thirty-four large U.S. corporations over a period of five years confirms that "cultural and behavioral characteristics of organizations have a major effect on a company's performance." Denison found that organizations with a participative management style—for example, with shared decision making—actually outperformed their competitors by as much as two to one in such key measures of financial performance as return on investment and return on sales over a five-year period.

The Research Institute of America (October 1987) confirmed that participative management pays off in many ways. In thirteen of fourteen measures of financial achievement, firms practicing variations of participative management come out ahead of those managed more traditionally. Of the 101 large U.S. industrial companies surveyed, those with participative management rated better on turnover, absenteeism, grievances, pay, and benefits. These results confirm what many managers have observed in their own organizations.

We have seen the benefits of participative management, but just what is it? The five criteria considered here are not an all-inclusive list of the characteristics associated with participative management. Instead, they are representative of some key values believed to motivate and empower employees to deliver superior service to the customer.

1. When a group is *goal directed,* its members have a context in which to channel their participation. Goals help distinguish the relevant from the irrelevant issues.
2. A *group orientation* improves the quality of decision making and the ease of implementation. It also helps improve morale and develops a commitment to the work unit and organization.
3. When management is *input-seeking,* it both gathers and uses the ideas of relevant parties to aid decision making. This improves the trust in management and also aids the quality of decision making.
4. *Shared decision making* involves reaching a gradual consensus prior to actual decision making. The most obvious results of this practice are commitment to goals and decisions, increased acceptance of change, and improved implementation.
5. Finally, *information openness* is a key to effective participative management. Well-informed employees can give more relevant and useful feedback than their uninformed counterparts. They are also likely to trust management when it is clear that management places faith in them.

You might take time now to rate your company's management style (see Exhibit 2.1).

Exhibit 2.1. Measuring Participative Management.

How would you rate your organization's participative management style? If you are a manager, respond to each question as you think your people would rate your style. If you are an individual contributor, respond in terms of how you perceive the management style of the organization.

For each statement, circle *T* for true or *F* for false—whichever best describes your situation.

Exhibit 2.1. Measuring Participative Management, Cont'd.

1.	Members of my work unit receive regular feedback about their service performance in relation to goals.	T	F
2.	There is more independent effort than teamwork in my work unit.	T	F
3.	Members of my work unit are encouraged to think for themselves and suggest ways to improve the internal climate for service.	T	F
4.	Major decisions affecting my work unit require group consensus before they are adopted.	T	F
5.	Management often makes decisions without explaining why.	T	F
6.	Members of my work unit are committed to achieving our goals of service quality, timeliness, and delivery.	T	F
7.	When a service-related (internal or external) problem needs to be resolved, we all pitch in and work together.	T	F
8.	Members of my work unit are seldom asked for their opinion before decisions are made.	T	F
9.	My work unit helps make decisions about important issues that affect us.	T	F
10.	The rumor mill is often a better source of information than our managers.	T	F
11.	Members of my work unit meet regularly to review how we are doing on our goals.	T	F
12.	There is little sense of cooperation and teamwork in my work unit.	T	F
13.	Management appreciates and uses our suggestions on how to improve the internal climate for service.	T	F
14.	The authority and power for decision making clearly rests with management in this organization.	T	F
15.	I feel free to go to management to find out about decisions that are being made.	T	F

Of the fifteen questions you just answered, three were used to tap each of the five major criteria for participation. To score your work unit on each factor, use the following key.

Factor	Item	Points
Goal-Directedness	1	T = 1; F = 0
	6	T = 1; F = 0
	11	T = 1; F = 0
Input-Seeking Orientation	3	T = 1; F = 0
	8	T = 0; F = 1
	13	T = 1; F = 0
Shared Decision Making	4	T = 1; F = 0
	9	T = 1; F = 0
	14	T = 0; F = 1

Exhibit 2.1. Measuring Participative Management, Cont'd.

Group Orientation	2	T = 0; F = 1
	7	T = 1; F = 0
	12	T = 0; F = 1
Information Openness	5	T = 0; F = 1
	10	T = 0; F = 1
	15	T = 1; F = 0

Adding across the five dimensions gives you an overall participative management score. These total scores can be summarized as follows:

13–15   *High participation.* Scores in this range indicate that participative management is definitely making headway in your work unit. Look at the five subscores to identify problem areas.

10–12   *Moderate participation.* Scores in this range indicate the emergence of some participative values. Examine subscores to see which areas are developing and which ones need work.

7–9   *Some participation.* Scores in this range indicate the need to place more emphasis on participative values.

4–6   *Low participation.* Scores in this range indicate a lack of appreciation for the values of participation. Major organizational or personnel pressures may be required before a shift will occur.

0–3   *No participation.* Scores in this range indicate that if the work unit is to survive, values need to be reexamined.

Having tabulated and averaged the scores in terms of the five components of a participative management style, develop some specific action plans to improve your management style. For example, what could you do to empower people at the lowest levels of the organization to make important decisions regarding customer satisfaction?

Source: Building Customer Satisfaction: A Blueprint for Your Business. © 1990 Dartnell Corp., Chicago, IL. Used by permission.

Now, having evaluated your organization, you may well see that you need to push toward a participative management style, but how do you begin? Odiorne has suggested a variety of ways to make participative management work:

- Keep an open-door policy and mean it.
- If you do not have an employee suggestion system, initiate one.
- Train your managers to listen. Listening is a very active, not a passive, process.
- Hold regular biweekly staff meetings at all levels of the or-

ganization. Have employees contribute their input to each meeting in advance.
- When an important job that requires innovation and/or change needs to be done, organize a task force to solve that particular complex problem.
- Conduct annual employee opinion surveys.
- Consider initiating employee involvement with a pilot project in quality circles.

The Mission Statement

To excel in service superiority, an organization must have a work force from top to bottom that shares a commitment to providing superior service. This entails the establishment of customer service as the number-one priority and the number-one goal.

Such a commitment begins with a clear mission statement. In organizations both large and small, we have seen a great deal of confusion over what constitutes a good mission statement, how it differs from a statement of values, and what each contributes to the goal of service superiority.

A good mission statement simply states what the organization plans to do, and for whom. It is based on a long-term (three- to five-year) strategic plan and encompasses at least the following main points:

- What is important to us?
- What kind of organization do we want to be — and to whom?
- What business are we really in?
- What business do we really want to be in?
- What are our management principles?
- What is our operating philosophy?

The purpose of the mission statement is to provide a common vision for the entire organization. The statement ensures clear and consistent direction from the top and serves as a point of reference for strategic and operational planning. It also engenders total work-force commitment by clearly communicating what the organization is all about. It seeks support and understanding from all of its stakeholders, including employees, managers, suppliers, customers, shareholders, local community members, government officials, and the financial community.

Once the mission statement is in place, each and every management decision must meet the test of compatibility with the organization's mission. Otherwise, conflicting and misaligned objectives will result.

In their *Executive Guide to Strategic Planning,* Patrick J. Below, George L. Morrisey, and Betty L. Acomb make the following points about the mission statement:

> Developing a Mission Statement for an organization is one of the most important steps in the planning process because it forms a foundation from which all other management decisions must be made. It requires careful thought and preparation on the part of the planning team with ample time allowed for refining the various points of view that team members are likely to express. Once such a statement has been clearly established and approved, it should remain constant for an extended period of time unless there is a major change in the nature of the business or of the organization's overall philosophy. Organizations should review formally their Mission Statement at least once a year as a part of the strategic planning process, as this is a prerequisite to any other planning activities.

Developing a Mission Statement

In his discussion of mission statements in the *Training and Development Journal,* Morrisey describes a CEO who visits his parking lot monthly to ask employees at random if they understand and can articulate his company's mission and objectives. Through these discussions, he gets excellent grass-roots feedback and encourages in the work force a thorough understanding of and commitment to the overall direction and objectives of the company.

Morrisey then offers some specific suggestions for organizations formulating a mission statement. He recommends that the top-management team work together at an off-site meeting to develop the mission statement. Each person at the meeting should, in advance, write down answers to the following questions.

- What business should we be in?
- Why do we exist; what is our basic purpose?
- What is unique or distinctive about our organization?
- Who are our principal customers, clients, or users?
- What are our principal products and services, both present and future?
- What are our potential market segments, present and future?
- What are our principal outlets or distribution channels, present and future?
- What is different about our business from what it was three to five years ago?
- What is likely to be different about our business three to five years in the future?
- What are our principal economic concerns, and how are they measured?
- What philosophical issues are important to our organization's future?
- What special considerations do we have (and will we have in the future) with regard to our various stakeholders — for example, external customers and employees?

Then, at the meeting, all team members read aloud their answers to each question. The answers can then be posted for later review. If meeting time is tight, answers can be forwarded to the facilitator beforehand and tabulated prior to the meeting. In either case, at the meeting, all team members are encouraged to express differences of opinion, to generate additional ideas, and to brainstorm. The team then agrees to a consensus on each key factor and decides which items will appear in the actual mission statement. The process normally takes from a half to a full day to complete.

Structuring a Mission Statement

The mission statement itself should be no longer than one page. It normally includes an umbrella statement of fifteen to thirty words that identifies the conceptual nature of the business in which the organization expects to be engaged in the future. After the general umbrella statement, there may be a series of "how" statements that open with something like, "In support of this mission, this organization is committed to . . . " These statements apply the philosophy of the organization to its actual operation. (See the sample mission statements that follow.) This section becomes the basis for how the organization will function and how departments or units within the organization can determine their own roles, missions, and objectives. The two sections together serve as a clear statement of the organization's perspective and of how it wants all of its various stakeholders to perceive it.

A word of caution: do not include anything in your mission statement that you are not willing to back up with action. If an employee perceives any item in a mission statement as not reflecting the way you do business, that discrepancy will destroy the credibility of your planning efforts. This is why dialogue among planning-team members is especially critical to formulation of the mission statement.

Beyond the Mission Statement: Clarifying Values

An organization's culture is the sum total of its beliefs, values, philosophies, traditions, and sacred cows. Culture is, in fact, the totality of the organization's characteristics — its personality. It is strongly influenced by the values of the CEO.

In order to deliver customer satisfaction, it is vital that a company communicate its values as well as its mission. Values are deeply held beliefs that evolve from experience. Culturally induced and broadly held, they are very slow to change. They represent what is important to us and, and as a consequence, they influence all that we do.

Unfortunately, an organization's cultural values are frequently neither understood nor shared by its employees, despite what the president and CEO choose to believe. Because the organization's real values are seldom articulated, many managers and employees try to second-guess the CEO and are frustrated in their trial-and-error search for goal attainment. Thus it is not surprising that many people fail to measure up to their boss's expectations. Although many executive failures are attributed to poor interpersonal skills, such failures seldom stem from an unwillingness or inability to do the job — or even from a lack of technical competence. The real issue is usually a lack of understanding of the organization's undefined value system.

In organizations, people behave in accordance with their understanding of the organization's cultural norms and values. These standards of expected behavior determine how decisions are made and problems solved. People's perceptions of the organization's real values affect the management team's performance, the individual's motivation, and the business unit's collective performance. Small wonder that many organizations are desperately trying to define their corporate culture on the basis of a shared set of values.

One organization that we have worked with, The Executive Committee, consists of cells of CEOs throughout the United States — approximately 2,000 CEOs in cells of ten to twelve each. Members are primarily from small to medium-sized organizations, and their intent is to learn from each other. Each cell is chaired by a member of The Executive Committee, who facilitates the group that he or she personally recruited and put together. Below is the mission statement of this organization, along with its statement of values.

The Executive Committee (TEC) is an organization committed to accelerate the learning and leadership ability of Chief Executive Officers of success-oriented companies. Our process is focused on improving the performance of members, simplifying their perspective of business, and broadening their ability and insights in serving others.

TEC Values

  We believe . . . in personally identifying the member needs and seeking feedback and solutions for practical business application.

  We believe . . . in providing members with a better decision-making environment to seek wisdom and discernment through the wise counsel of their peers.

  We believe . . . in presenting members with the in-depth knowledge from outside experts and peers through an exchange of ideas and discussions.

  We believe . . . TEC helps CEOs seek purpose and vision for their life and business.

  Exhibit 2.2, to be used in conjunction with the preceding discussion and example, is a worksheet to guide organizations through the writing of a mission statement and the clarification of values.

  Remember that if employees know what their company stands for and what standards they are to uphold, they are more likely to feel that they are an important part of the organization. Likewise, they are more likely to feel motivated if life in the company has meaning for them.

Changing Direction

Once a company has examined the questions involved in developing a mission statement and clarifying its values, then it is time to face the next steps. The goals and current status of the organization — as well as any discrepancy between the two — have been illuminated by the mission/values task. Now change must be implemented (from the top down) to bring the two into closer alignment.

Seeing the Need for Change

The most direct measure of the need for change is an organization's performance. An organization that is performing poorly — either in absolute financial terms or in relation to its own goals — may generally be said to be in need of constructive change. For

Exhibit 2.2. Mission Statement and Values-Clarification Worksheet.

Mission Statement

of

_____

(Company Name)

Umbrella Statement

_____

_____

_____

_____

"How" Statements

1. _____

2. _____

3. _____

4. _____

5. _____

Values Statements

1. _____

2. _____

3. _____

4. _____

5. _____

Communication Plan
Decide how you plan to communicate your mission and your values throughout
the organization. Record your plan in the space provided.

_____

_____

_____

_____

Source: Building Customer Satisfaction: A Blueprint for Your Business. © 1990
Dartnell Corp., Chicago, IL. Used by permission.

such an organization, the primary question becomes one of what
to change and how best to change it.

The reverse of this axiom may *not* be true. An organization that is performing well may in fact be in *more* need of change
than an organization that is performing poorly! Performance
differences may be directly related to the amount of internal
change that is occurring: an organization that is performing well
may be doing so because rapid change is always occurring. For
most firms, following the principle of "If it ain't broke, don't
fix it" guarantees that when change occurs it will be in a crisis — a
time when most organizations and their people are least able
and least disposed to radical change. Remaining at rest seems
to be appropriate only if an organization's internal and external environments are also at rest.

According to Noel Tichy, the conditions pointing toward
the need for change fall into four categories: environment, diversification and growth, technology, and people.

- *Environment.* Change to the environment can be summed up
  briefly as increasing competitive pressures, new legislation,
  and new competition. As competitive pressures mount, costs
  increase, and prices are squeezed, different approaches to
  management are mandated. When these changes are coupled with legislative issues and a potential loss of market
  share, a new executive approach is essential.
- *Diversification and growth.* Whether the company is entering
  new areas of business (related or not to the current business), acquiring (or merging with) another business, or making multiple use of existing facilities, these changes will require special attention.
- *Technology.* Changes in technology often require major investments in high-cost equipment, computerization, micro-
  processing, and communication systems. As technological
  conditions change, management must lead and manage the
  concomitant internal changes. New skills and abilities must
  be introduced into the organization.
- *People.* In today's business and industrial world, people's
  needs and expectations are on the increase; employee dis-

content remains high at all levels. People are more loyal to their professions than they are to their companies. Security is no longer requested; it is demanded. The "right to fire" is in question. Terminations are costly, and career expectations are high. These conditions imply a totally different, more highly participative management style.

Given the existence of any one or more of these four conditions, strategic change becomes necessary for survival. Indeed, within today's social and economic context, it is almost impossible to conceive of "holding the line" as a fruitful endeavor.

Making the Change

With any major change in an organization, success depends on laying the proper groundwork to shape the corporate culture. The CEO must be wholeheartedly — and very visibly — involved. But even with superhuman effort, the CEO cannot do it alone. Because change requires addressing a host of issues, the CEO must push the responsibility and enthusiasm for change down through the organization. Whether by empowering the right people on staff or by hiring from the outside, the CEO must ensure that the cause is taken up.

Bringing in an Outside Change Agent

Making the decision to bring in an outside change agent is a difficult one and should not be undertaken lightly. Without the support of key people, no outside change agent can bring about change, while *with* that support, outsiders can bring about dramatic change. (Tips on using an outside change agent and qualities to look for in such a person, as well as points to aid the agent in the assigned task, are set forth as Appendix A.)

With or without the help of a change agent, there is a lot to undertake in bringing about change. The CEO, other top managers, and the change agent (if one is hired) must learn and teach a number of new skills, such as communication techniques, how to facilitate a group session, and how to effectively conduct a meeting. They must also get involved personally in establishing performance standards for all levels of the organization to ensure consistency and predictability, in restructuring the compensation system to make it reflect a participative management style and to reward performance, and in training the entire organization in new human resource management skills. Further, new ideas stimulated by the new participation must be championed, and employees' and supervisors' fears and concerns must be brought to the surface and alleviated. These tasks are discussed in some detail in Part Two. As the change is begun, however, there are two points to keep particularly in mind: motivating employees and encouraging worker loyalty.

Motivating Employees and Encouraging Loyalty

Ernest Rudia, plant manager for Goodyear Tire and Rubber in Lawton, Oklahoma, presented a seven-point approach to employee motivation. His application of the following seven steps has resulted in a 99 percent attendance record in a plant with 1,800 employees and a productivity rate double that of its competition.

- Learn exactly what your people's capabilities are.
- Find ways to match employees to jobs that are best suited to their talents and abilities.
- Encourage workers to come up with their own solutions to work-related problems; then listen, encourage, and adopt their suggestions to the maximum degree possible.
- When hiring, look for team players with enthusiasm.
- Spend 85 percent of your day dealing with employee relations issues. Remember that good communication creates an atmosphere of mutual trust, respect, and mutual concern for satisfaction.
- Be fair, but be firm. Uphold your standards at all times.
- Treat your employees the way you wish to be treated.

This last point, a restatement of the Golden Rule, can go a long way toward motivating employees and toward strengthening their loyalty to the company (even in a time when worker loyalty is on the decline).

Motivating employees and encouraging loyalty are easier done in a small company. But there are, as we will see, ways to accomplish these tasks even in a large corporation. Integral to both is a recognition that the employee is vital to the bottom line and that how the employee is treated will carry over to how the customer is treated — and will thereby directly affect the company's success or failure.

Chapter 3

CUSTOMER RELATIONS MIRROR EMPLOYEE RELATIONS

Take care of your employees and they will take care of your customers. There is a strong correlation between employees' perceptions of how they are treated and customers' perceptions of the quality of service they receive.
— David E. Bowen
Arizona State University West

Well into the 1990s, and perhaps through the entire decade, the single greatest source of profit growth will come from better management of human resources. Organizations that fail to recognize this and to prepare properly may well fall behind in the profit race — perhaps even disappear. Our research suggests that 80 percent of the opportunity for productivity and profitability improvement lies in effective management of the work force. A work force committed to excellence in customer service — internally and externally — will provide most of that opportunity.

Managing an organization's human resources equates with managing its customer services. To put it another way, employee relations equal customer relations. The two are inseparable.

42

Personnel and human resource executives have for some time been aware of the relationship between motivated employees and productivity. Only recently, however, have they been able to quantify this impact. Now they have begun to position themselves as part of the senior management team, and in the process they are addressing a broader range of business needs—customer service and customer satisfaction, cost containment, and management of the work force.

David E. Bowen examined the notion that taking care of human relations equates to taking care of the business. His sample population consisted of two groups of branch banks; one group had twenty-three and the other twenty-eight. Here is what he found:

- There is a strong correlation between customer and employee views of service quality and the internal climate for service.
- When employees view favorably an organization's human resource policies, customers view favorably the quality of service they receive.
- A positive work climate directly affects customer service for the better.
- The area of human resources is an excellent vehicle for satisfying both employee and customer needs.

Many organizations are just now becoming aware of the impact that employee relations have on customer service. This chapter addresses that impact and provides ideas on how to ensure that the impact is positive.

Put Your Own House in Order

As a first step to improving customer relations, a company must have a good sense of its employees and their attitudes toward the organization and its customers. The brief survey presented in Exhibit 3.1 can help the company assess the current climate for customer satisfaction.

Why is an understanding of employee attitudes crucial? Because to enjoy the highest standards of service superiority,

Exhibit 3.1. Survey of the Climate for Customer Satisfaction.

	Strongly Agree	Inclined to Agree	Undecided; Don't Know	Inclined to Disagree	Strongly Disagree
1. All our employees are knowledgeable about our products and services.	___	___	___	___	___
2. Management treats its employees the way it wants the employees to treat the customers.	___	___	___	___	___
3. Customer service is management's number-one priority.	___	___	___	___	___
4. There are financial rewards for exemplary customer service.	___	___	___	___	___
5. We have excellent performance standards in our work unit.	___	___	___	___	___
6. We periodically measure customer satisfaction.	___	___	___	___	___
7. We have an excellent system for training people in quality of service.	___	___	___	___	___
8. Customer satisfaction is the employee's most important goal.	___	___	___	___	___
9. Our organization is well known for keeping its promises to customers.	___	___	___	___	___
10. We take pride in our work.	___	___	___	___	___
11. Customer complaints are resolved quickly.	___	___	___	___	___
12. I'm proud to work for this organization.	___	___	___	___	___

Source: Building Customer Satisfaction: A Blueprint for Your Business. © Dartnell Corp., Chicago, IL. Used by permission.

organizations must have motivated employees. But to have motivated employees, they must have motivated supervisors and managers. To have motivated supervisors and managers, organizations must first put their own house in order. To complete the loop, putting one's own house in order requires exceptionally cordial relationships between management and labor. This is the key. If it is ignored — as all too often it is — relationships break down and a disastrous strike may occur, wreaking havoc on customer service. Even short of a strike, when relationships of openness and trust degenerate, the customer suffers as much as management and labor.

As an example of what can happen if employee relations problems spill over into customer relations, let us look at a set of employee problems we confronted — and solved — at McDonald's. We were worried about slippage in service timeliness and service quality at six restaurants in the Midwest. The restaurants were earning low profits and suffering from high employee turnover, and customers endured a three-minute average wait for a meal — exactly twice the company standard.

Upon close inspection, we found the following:

- Employee turnover was more than 300 percent annually in each of the stores.
- There was a 60 percent annual turnover of the stores' managers.
- Stores were often understaffed.
- There were few crew meetings.
- New-employee orientation was minimal at best.
- Training manuals and procedures were not being followed closely.

A survey of the restaurants' employees indicated a high level of dissatisfaction with jobs, work hours, and working conditions. The end result: the employees were unhappy, the service deteriorated, and the customers were unhappy.

In the same geographical area, there were six other restaurants that had high profits and negligible employee and management turnover. In all six of these positive cases, service times were closely watched and enforced, staffing was slightly above the norm, and great care was taken to follow the policies, procedures, and practices laid out in the training manuals. The managers took a great deal of time over employee selection, orientation, and training and over sales; and profits continued to soar.

As our first step toward improvement at the problem sites, we introduced behaviorally oriented interviewing—that is, using a candidate's job and life experiences to predict how that person will perform in a given position and organization. We instituted formal orientation processes, conducted regular surveys of employee job satisfaction, and invested more time in training manuals and procedures, as well as certification processes. We also ensured that crew meetings, generally lasting twenty to thirty minutes, were held (and paid for by the company) at least once a week.

As a consequence, employee turnover decreased to less than 100 percent (versus the more normal 200 percent) in less than a year. Management teams were stabilized, and service timeliness quickly went back to normal standards. Best of all, sales, profits, transaction counts, repeat visits, and average size of check began to approach those of the six successful stores in the same area.

By these steps, management reinforced an atmosphere of respect for the employees' dignity. This respect was then reflected in increased customer satisfaction and, as a consequence, in the bottom line.

Factors in Employee Relations Superiority

If we accept the premise that superiority in customer service starts with superior employee relations, how do we put that into practice? What does it take to cultivate and maintain outstanding employee relations?

For many years we have correctly identified the relationship between levels of productivity and satisfaction of employee needs, wants, and expectations. Now it is time to relate these needs to their effect on the customer—the ultimate paymaster. To have motivated employees who will satisfy motivated customers and bring in new and repeat business, employers must successfully address these major areas of employee concerns:

> Supervision
> Communication
> Policy and administration
> Job security
> Working conditions
> Involvement
> Participation
> Advancement
> Achievement
> Recognition for achievement
> Compensation

Unfortunately, relatively few companies have paid more than lip service to these basics, and as a consequence their employees have responded with poor service to the customer.

Let us look at these concerns individually, particularly as they relate to customer service.

Supervision

Desatnick designed and conducted management skills training sessions for hourly and exempt nonsupervisory employees of a leading producer of household consumer goods. For the most part, these were high-potential people who were being prepared to assume broader responsibilities, including supervision. Over a period of two and a half years, each group was asked to define a good boss. Here is the composite they came up with:

- Someone who cares about me and my progress
- Someone I can trust to teach and develop me
- Someone who supports me
- Someone who corrects me when I need it
- Someone who shows me how to do a better job
- Someone who recognizes and rewards my achievement
- Someone who keeps me informed about what's going on

- Someone who consults with me on decisions affecting my job
- Someone who trusts me by delegating real responsibility

To further test what employees want and expect from a good boss, Desatnick conducted twenty-nine focus groups (a total of 150 people) as part of an assignment to design a selection system and management skills training program. More than one half of the participants (employees in a service business) agreed on the following description of a good boss:

Considerate	Treats me with respect
Fair	Gives me recognition
Honest	Appreciates me
Just	Uses tact and diplomacy
Caring	Has stature in the organization
Impartial	Maintains high standards of
Communicative	discipline and work
Interested	Sets a good example
Calm	Empathizes
Friendly	Does not scream or yell
Available	Delegates
Consistent	Is a problem solver
Trusting	Is a good listener

Communication

There are two major aspects of the internal communication processes that exert a tremendous influence on customer service: (1) what employees want and need to know to do their jobs, and (2) the messages passed through the organization from top management.

To do their jobs well, and to be committed to superior performance, employees need to know the following:

- Exactly what is expected of them; a clear definition of their specific assigned duties and the activities for which they will be held responsible and accountable

- Where their jobs fit into the total picture and why those jobs are important
- How their jobs affect other jobs within the organization (and vice versa)
- How their mistakes affect others within and outside the organization (and vice versa)
- The specific factors and criteria, behavioral as well as technical on which their performance will be judged (for example, service, courtesy, quality, quantity, cost, innovation, accuracy, and self-development)
- Exactly how performance will be measured — quantitatively, qualitatively, and behaviorally (against a series of statements describing the conditions that exist if each job responsibility has been adequately performed)
- For each area of responsibility, what constitutes below-standard, standard, and above-standard performance in both quantitative and qualitative terms
- Where they stand and how well they are doing (through periodic progress reviews)
- How to improve their performance and increase their contribution to the organization
- How to develop themselves in their jobs and in the organization (through specific coaching)

The second aspect of the internal communication processes has to do with the types of messages passed through the organization from top management and how employees translate these messages into their relations with customers. This is, as you might gather, intricately related to the mission statement.

Management to Employee	*Employee to Customer*
1. What are your problems, and how can I help solve them?	1. How may I be of assistance to you?
2. We want you to know what is happening in our organization. This is what is going on.	2. I am capable of helping you because I am in the know.

3. Each of us is the company, so we all share accountability for what happens around here.

3. I am empowered to help you and take pride in my ability to do so.

4. We treat each other with professional respect.

4. I have respect for you as the individual you are.

5. We stand behind each other's decisions and support each other.

5. You can count on me and my company to deliver on our promises.

Because this area is so vital to the establishment of a customer-oriented work force, we will examine each of these five messages in detail.

1. *What are your problems and how can I help solve them?*

1. *How may I be of assistance to you?*

To be successful, a service-oriented company must exhibit an acute awareness that if management solves employee problems, employees solve customers' problems. It is as simple as that. Simple, but not easy!

In the best of circumstances, communication channels between employees and management are always kept open. For example, as we noted earlier, no McDonald's offices have doors. People are thus encouraged to go directly to the person anywhere in the organization who can help solve job-related problems.

In addition, McDonald's puts its concern for the employees and their problems into action through a series of regular employee-input sessions. A cross section of nonexempt employees from the offices and the restaurants are asked by their supervisors and managers if they want to sit in on an "Operation Input" session with senior management. These sessions are designed specifically to encourage employees to tell how they perceive the company. Management says, "Tell us about your concerns, your problems, and what can we do to help make McDonald's a better place to work." The employees answer, and management listens and adopts as many of their suggestions as possible.

In the most enlightened companies, management's interest in solving employee problems extends beyond the workplace. There has been a significant increase in recent years in employee assistance programs that provide confidential help in a variety of situations — psychological, marital, or health problems, alcohol or drug dependency, financial or legal difficulties — and for which management pays the bill. Programs like this clearly say to the employee, "We care about you." On-site day-care centers and employee credit unions give similar messages.

A problem-solving focus implies an understanding boss with a sensitivity to employees' needs and the empathy to walk in their shoes. But while bosses should be understanding, they should not be weak. Most people want to work in a well-run, disciplined organization where the rules, policies, and procedures are clear, uniform, and consistently applied. Consistency and predictability are premiere characteristics of effective supervisors.

2. *We want you to know what is happening in our organization. This is what is going on.*

2. *I am capable of helping you because I am in the know.*

Successful service-oriented companies hold weekly staff meetings with all employees in small groups at all levels of the organization. At these meetings, the agenda tends to be flexible. The manager or supervisor shares with employees information about what is happening in various areas:

- The company — sales, profits, products, services, competition
- Other areas and departments within the company
- The departments that affect particular employees and their work and those departments that they affect

In addition, the manager or supervisor asks the following questions:

- Are we on target in what we said we would do in budgets, costs, goals, objectives, and implementation of service policies?
- What is on your mind? What are your concerns?

The latter questions initiate an open free-for-all so that all share in what is happening among the several functions within a given department.

Every year, Delta Airlines and General Electric—both known for their achievements in service superiority—bring together the entire employee population in small groups. They discuss the state of the business, competition, operating trends and results, market share, new products and services, and the effectiveness of present customer service policies and practices.

At General Electric's Hotpoint Division, the general manager and those who report directly to that person hold informative meetings for employees. At these meetings, each functional head discusses what is happening and outlines his or her goals, objectives, contributions to business results, job security, and so on. After the presentation, the floor is open for discussion. Employees ask direct questions and are given straight answers.

Weekly staff meetings and informal employee meetings serve to ensure that employees in the organization know what is going on. The thesis is that if everyone knows what is happening throughout the organization, any chance encounter with a customer, even by an employee not explicitly assigned to customer service, turns out to be a benefit. The well-informed employee never says (and is never permitted to say), "I don't know" or "It's not my job." If in fact the employee does not know, that person quickly finds out or immediately puts the customer in touch with someone who can help.

As a negative example, picture your own business dealings. Have you ever been put on hold, transferred several times, and then cut off? Why was it that your call to inquire about a delivery never got through? And how often have you had a message inaccurately relayed to the intended department, related to the wrong department, or not relayed at all?

In a more positive vein, companies that combine effective staff and employee information meetings with a sharing of all the things employees want and need to know are ensuring that their customers will get the proper service, whatever the circumstances. If is far better to err on the side of giving too much information than too little.

3. *Each of us is the company,*
   so we all share accountability
   for what happens around here.

3. *I am empowered to help you*
   and take pride in my ability
   to do so.

To build personal accountability in all employees so that they really believe that "each of us is the company," successful companies incorporate several elements into their "people management." First, as part of each employee's formal indoctrination, accountability is explained in detail, including answers to such questions as, What is it? Why is it important? How does it work around here? What is my specific role in accountability to other employees and the customer?

Customer-related actions beyond the call of duty are rewarded; those who set examples of personal accountability are publicly praised. There may also be a policy of commending employees for formal customer compliments, in addition to instantly routing customer feedback to the appropriate employee.

Not only are the compliments passed on; so are the less favorable comments. Any errors or customer dissatisfactions are instantly routed back to the specific employees who caused them. Accountability for one's actions cannot be left to chance; it must be constantly refined and reinforced.

Service leaders also back up decisions that employees make when interacting with customers. Enlightened managers will do their utmost to please the customer, but not at the expense of the employee. Both have needs that must be satisfied.

There is a wonderful restaurant in New York City. When asked how he deals with customer complaints, the owner said that he first apologizes directly to the customer for any inconvenience. Then he talks to the waiter or waitress involved, to get the other side of the story. He does not condemn the employee; instead, he requests an explanation, helps find a way to avoid repeating the problem, and finally says something like, "I'm sure it was a misunderstanding, because you're one of my best employees and that's not the kind of behavior you normally demonstrate." Then he dismisses the incident, with the caution that everyone must take special pains to please the customer, because "that's why we're in existence."

Service leaders also have policies for evaluating individual performance. They believe that all employees have a right to periodic progress reviews so that they know how well they are doing. Employees who do not fully accept accountability for their actions are dealt with within the context of a responsible grievance system that incorporates positive discipline.

As a result of these actions, companies that are truly oriented toward customer service achieve a full understanding of the scope of the individual's personal responsibility and the importance of every service transaction, and they manage to have employees who take pride in their jobs and the organizations for which they work.

4. *We treat each other with professional respect.*

4. *I have respect for you as the individual that you are.*

The law of psychological reciprocity states that if I treat you with dignity and respect, you will treat me likewise. In our many decades of combined experience in industry, we have seen companies develop profound problems in employee morale through the overt lack of respect for individual employees demonstrated by thoughtless supervisors and managers. Too often, such thoughtlessness occurs in organizations with masses of low-paid employees. The ultimate effect on customer service, and thus on the company, can be disastrous.

This lack of respect for the individual manifests itself in several ways: failing to recognize and acknowledge a job well done, calling people by numbers instead of names, shouting and using abusive language, providing unclean or inadequate facilities, never saying please or thank you, never making any attempt to understand the individual's point of view.

How do you suppose the employee who is not given respect is going to treat the customer? With a lack of respect, of course. If a customer is feeling belligerent or grouchy, that attitude will not be overlooked by the employee who feels "beaten on" most of the time. But the employee who is given respect shows respect and is more tolerant of customers who complain — whether rightfully or wrongfully.

In the description of a good boss listed earlier, more than half the 150 participants said that being treated with respect was one of the most important characteristics in an ideal boss and that one of the major reasons they would leave a firm was a lack of respect.

5. *We stand behind each other's decisions and support each other.*

5. *You can count on me and my company to deliver on our promises.*

All of us can think of times in our careers when we have had a nonsupportive boss—someone who inevitably passed the buck on to us for whatever went wrong and, worse still, took personal credit for our contributions. That same boss never protected us, never accepted partial responsibility for a mistake, and made promises and never kept them. Perhaps that same boss could have paid us what we really deserved but decided to chisel to make himself look good, or could have put us in for stock options but did not.

Unfortunately, there are all too many negative examples and all too few sterling role models. Yet support is essential from the employee point of view. The supportive boss fights to get the staffing and resources that we need to do our jobs. The supportive boss gets us the maximum pay increases and shares responsibility for anything that might go wrong. The supportive boss will not permit others to criticize us but personally accepts the criticism for something that went wrong (and then diplomatically and conscientiously listens to our side of the story before doing anything). The supportive boss does not overreact. And if this boss makes a promise to us, that promise is kept.

The ideal boss has ideal employees who can be counted on to fulfill their promises to the customer because the boss fulfills his or her promises to them.

Policy and Administration

The best-managed companies have simple, clear personnel policies and administer them consistently. Our philosophy is that policies should be relatively few, thoroughly communicated, and rigidly enforced. An exception all too soon becomes a rule, and employees are quick to pick up on a manager's inconsistencies. Solid, well-thought-through, basic, understandable personnel policies, applied with consistency and objectivity, serve to ensure fair and consistent treatment throughout the organization.

If one supervisor ignores or excuses employee absences or tardiness while another holds to the letter of the policy, this inconsistency in administration will penalize some while letting others off the hook. This will translate directly into inconsistency in customer service. Policies serve to protect both employees and the customer. They help to provide a clearly defined employment contract.

Typical policies, often formalized in a supervisor's manual, will cover time off, vacations and holidays, shift differentials, pay and incentives, progressive discipline, and work assignments. Less typical but equally essential are policies outlining requirements and rewards for exemplary service behavior.

Job Security

One need only look at what happens to productivity and customer service after a layoff to recognize fully the consequences of insecurity. To gain loyalty from their work force, companies must first demonstrate loyalty *to* that work force.

Loyalty on the part of the organization means that the work force is kept intact in bad times as well as good. The lifetime job security provided by Japanese companies is well known. While we strongly believe that it would be unwise to try to closely emulate the Japanese culture, we can certainly learn a thing or two from it.

In this country, the top companies within their respective industries generally try to have a no-layoff policy. They also happen to be tops in customer service, and this is not by accident. Loyalty begets loyalty.

Mind you, these firms are not soft. They are tough, and they are demanding. They have high expectations and stringent performance standards, but they get in return what they give.

To provide job security, McDonald's, for example, uses a variety of outside suppliers and a mostly temporary work force in its restaurants. Natural attrition is thus built in. For those who choose to stay and build a career with McDonald's, many of whom started out as part-time crew members, the future is secure and the growth opportunity is phenomenal. Promotion from within is a way of life. And this sense that McDonald's cares about its employees is then passed on to its customers.

Working Conditions

Within the context of the work environment, employers should show that they care for their employees by providing the best working conditions possible, given the limitations of the offices, factories, and facilities. They should treat the lowest-paid employee exactly as they themselves would like to be treated. It is as simple as that. A clean environment, a water cooler that works, accessible climate controls, a place for privacy, a sparkling clean washroom, an inviting dining room — these are minimum standards.

Sometimes it is necessary to work in relatively few square feet of floor space. But that space should be clean, neat, tidy, and orderly. It should be as safe and as comfortable as possible. This space should give what little privacy can be afforded, even to the extent of individual partitions.

Good working conditions should go well beyond merely satisfying the legal requirements. All walls, fixtures, floors, ceilings, and furniture should be well maintained, not allowed to drift into a state of disrepair. There is no reason that people should feel uncomfortable with their work surroundings. Never forget that if employers show respect for employees, employees will show respect for customers.

Involvement

The basic principle behind quality circles, performance teams, and participative management is involvement. People feel good about themselves when they become totally immersed and involved in the business, and everyone connected with that business receives added value and satisfaction. If the workplace and the management style are such that all employees are involved in as many aspects of the business as possible, a sense of ownership and stewardship is fostered. The customer ultimately benefits.

As an example, a high-tech manufacturing plant gave employees total responsibility for producing a quality product. The company's nontraditional floor plan helped employees to learn all aspects of the manufacturing process. They built the complete product from start to finish.

This system is similar to McDonald's, where the hourly employees literally run the operation, from opening the store, to mastering each work station, to closing at night. That involvement significantly increases the sense of ownership.

At the high-tech manufacturing plant, the system of product ownership has increased employee motivation, decreased throughput time by 40 percent, and doubled the number of flawless modules produced. In the staff performance teams, each individual was expected to perform all functions required to manufacture a component. Each employee gathered raw materials, then built, tested and shipped the components. There were no time clocks, no assembly lines, no supervisors, no quality-control inspectors, and no guards. Employees chose their own hours and planned their own schedules. Team members interfaced directly with customers.

This concept was successful because of employee ownership and responsibility. All employees put their initials on the product to say, "I did that." In similar fashion, employees at Weyco Group put their names on products they make. That act signifies a sense of pride, a sense of ownership.

Participation

People make the best decisions when they use the collective wisdom of the group. It is only natural for people to want to participate in decisions that affect them. Participation reduces resistance to change and gives employees a sense of ownership.

Part of the psychological contract that should be made with every employee is this: "We will first discuss with you any decisions that affect you directly in your work. We both need and want your ideas." When this input is sought and given, it should also be used; otherwise, a large part of the potential benefit is lost. Employees feel that managers are not serious if they do not adopt at least some of their suggestions. And when employee suggestions are adopted, management's expectations are often surpassed. Capital projects inevitably achieve their intended results earlier than anticipated.

One of the dairies we work with on a regular basis was extremely pressed for space. They needed a new separator, but they were not sure where to place it or what it would do to the work flow and the individuals involved. So they asked all the employees affected by the separator to come up with a solution on its location and the impact on work flow. The employees enthusiastically tackled the project and came up with a solution. No production was lost in the process. More important, the customers continued to receive the excellent service they had been accustomed to.

Advancement

Most people want to get ahead. Life becomes more meaningful when we have something to look forward to each day at work. Each job advancement becomes a new thrill, a new opportunity. When we no longer perceive opportunities personally and professionally, we quit. And when we quit, who is it that suffers? The customer, through poor service.

In our focus groups, 75 percent of the participants said that they would leave the company if they felt there was no opportunity to advance. Advancement does not necessarily imply frequent promotion, but it *does* imply the development of new skills and abilities. Even in a period of relatively flat growth, people can be given special assignments, such as participation in a task force or training for specialization or job enlargement.

Achievement

The overwhelming majority of people who come to work want very much to do the best job humanly possible. When people feel underutilized, they become restless and dissatisfied. When their suggestions are ignored, they retire on the job and stop using their minds. They virtually disappear into their job descriptions.

Each of us has a built-in mechanism called the "need to achieve." If we are deprived of achievement by bosses who fail to delegate, showing evidence of mistrust, we adopt an "I don't care" attitude and permit our bosses to hang themselves.

We often hear that most work forces can increase their productivity by 40 percent or more, that both white- and blue-collar workers are idle somewhere between 40 and 50 percent of their time. I believe that a major cause of this lost productivity is that the typical employee is underutilized, improperly trained, or both. The fact is that most people want to achieve, but the way that they are managed either turns them off or prevents them from doing so.

Organizations that set high levels of expectation for the work force consistently turn in better results in all areas, including customer service. David Cherrington, who teaches organizational behavior at Brigham Young University, surveyed hundreds of workers in more than fifty companies. He found that managers who established high levels of expectation got high levels of productivity. In one particular study, supervisors were told to communicate either high, low, or no performance standards. The highest performance rates were achieved by the groups whose superiors expected and communicated high standards of performance.

American workers, we firmly believe, have not lost their basic work ethic. The problem is that the environment that management creates makes it difficult for the individual to achieve. Too often, conformity, not creativity, is rewarded. And it is creativity that leads to achievement.

Recognition for Achievement

If supervisors and managers could do just one thing to achieve customer service superiority, it would be to learn to give recognition. Public recognition for exceptional performance in customer service sets the tone for the entire organization. It makes the individual who is recognized grow ten feet tall. It stimulates others in a healthy, competitive way to want to do likewise.

In the focus groups mentioned earlier, more than 80 percent of the participants felt that they were not sufficiently recognized for their achievements. The same percentage said that if more recognition were not forthcoming, they would seriously consider leaving the company.

It is said that the best reward for high achievement is to give the individual the opportunity to achieve more. That opportunity translates into broader job responsibilities and possibly promotion (which is one form of recognition). High achievement should certainly be accompanied by promotional recognition whenever possible, but do not stop there. Put it in the individual's paycheck as well. Reward achievement with money as well as praise and more opportunity to achieve.

Even if your system does not provide for differential rewards, there are ways to reward your best service employees. You can give them time off with full pay, extra carfare, free lunches, and lots of recognition. Otherwise, how can you possibly continue to maintain their loyalty, support, and motivation as a service team?

Compensation

Recognition for achievement is necessary, but it is not sufficient reward for a job well done. We have all heard the old expression, If you pay peanuts, you get monkeys. It is not surprising that the most gifted people in this country usually go to work for those organizations that pay the most money. Money has often been cited as only the third or fourth reason people quit their jobs. It is nevertheless a powerful motivator if applied properly. As organizations learn to link their reward systems to performance more effectively, money can become a super-motivator.

To use compensation as a motivator, it must be both externally competitive and internally equitable. This is important, because employees measure their self-worth in terms of what they earn versus what the market pays.

A Public Affairs Foundation poll showed that only 22 percent of hourly workers see any connection between how hard they work and how much they are paid. As a consequence, 73 percent of those workers exert less than full effort. In a real pay-for-performance system, workers should participate in identifying the measures on which their pay will be based.

An employee who feels improperly compensated will feel cheated, and cheated employees will not fully support the organization's goals. The commitment to service superiority that organizations seek will not occur when employees feel that management is exploiting them or holding back. Exploitation produces a negative attitude, which in turn influences how well employees meet one another's needs (as well as the needs of customers).

A similar negative effect can be produced if employees feel that they are improperly compensated in relation to one another or to comparable jobs within the organization. If person A produces more than person B working in a comparable job, A logically expects to get paid more than B.

We marvel at the naiveté of organizations that fail to perceive what happens when all employees get the same annual birthday increase of 5 percent. The best performers are driven out and the worst performers are encouraged to stay. In these organizations, morale is usually quite poor. It is the customers who suffer, but when they subsequently take their business elsewhere — as they will — the company suffers more. So it is important to link all of these factors to achieve service superiority.

Creative management of human resources in today's turbulent time means paying more attention to the needs of the work force so that the work force in turn will pay more attention to the needs of the customer. This will create that perceptible difference between you and your competition.

PART TWO

FIVE KEYS TO SERVICE SUPERIORITY

We have singled out five keys to service superiority, from establishing it within a company to ensuring that it is maintained. In this part, we discuss each of these five keys in some depth, one per chapter. Briefly put, these are the keys:

1. Create a customer focus throughout the organization.
2. Establish employee-based service performance standards.
3. Measure service performance against superior benchmarks.
4. Recognize and reward exemplary service behavior.
5. Maintain enthusiasm, consistency, and predictability for the customer.

Each of the keys contributes to the next. Each contributes, individually and as part of the whole, to increased sales and

63

market share. The keys, and how they relate to one another, are illustrated in the following figure.

Service Quality Model: Five Keys to Service Superiority

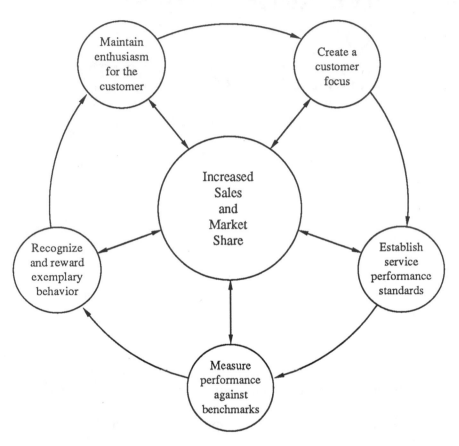

Our emphasis on these keys recognizes the importance of a company's present customer base. Cultivation of an established customer base through extraordinary service presents management's best opportunity to increase sales and market share.

Chapter 4

CREATE A CUSTOMER FOCUS THROUGHOUT THE ORGANIZATION

The only way to provide consistent customer service is to have each employee focus attention on how he/she impacts the ultimate customer — and identify ways to consistently exceed customer expectations.
— Robert J. Rauscher
Vice President of Marketing
Amoco Oil

Many otherwise brilliant senior managers fall victim to the assumption that everyone in the organization understands the importance of quality and customer service. After all, the corporate mission statement focuses on quality service. The importance of customer service is communicated in recruiting, hiring, and orienting — and in every newsletter. Employees are recognized for providing quality service. There is even a quality department, complete with a chief quality officer. Yet all of these excellent initiatives may or may not serve to create a real awareness of the customer service value among those employees who can most affect service delivery.

Consider the case of a regional life insurance company that had implemented all of the important steps mentioned above.

Through an employee survey, senior management learned that 62 percent of the company's secretarial and clerical personnel had at least 2 direct contacts with policyholders or agents each day — a total of at least 400 direct customer contacts daily. Yet when asked if they were generally familiar with the company's products and services, 82 percent of this group said that they were not. When asked if they felt that their job provided an opportunity to impact customer service, 64 percent said that it did not.

In a survey of its agents, this same company discovered that the agents perceived the company's greatest barriers to effective service to be (1) difficulties in locating someone who could provide basic information regarding the company's products and services, (2) extensive delays in handling telephone inquiries, and (3) the inability to track where within the company's administrative process a particular policy was lodged. All of these dysfunctions and lost opportunities for positive interaction with policyholders could have been readily addressed by an informed, empowered, and motivated group of secretarial and clerical employees.

To excel in customer service, an organization must have employees — from top to bottom — who share a commitment to providing superior service. A company can ensure this commitment by helping employees see that service superiority is in their own best interests. Not surprisingly, then, one of the things that highly successful service-oriented companies have in common is that they take every conceivable step to make sure employees understand that their personal job security is totally dependent on the firm's ability to satisfy the customers and make them want to come back.

Building a work force with this kind of understanding of and commitment to customer service starts with clarification of the company's image and mission. It then proceeds with establishment of clear corporate values of service superiority and the recruiting and hiring of people who share those values. It includes reorienting the existing work force to the same values and continually reinforcing those values throughout the organization, from the first day of orientation all the way to the retirement party.

Transferring Service Awareness to Employees

In organizations striving for service superiority, the importance of the individual is constantly stressed. The need for service superiority is sold to the individual employee in terms of what it can do for that employee. McDonald's, for instance, effectively emphasizes the tremendous benefits and personal satisfaction that come from serving the customer. Each potential employee is told about the following benefits of serving the customer:

- You will learn important skills, and they will help you succeed in life regardless of what you choose to do after McDonald's.
- You are special, and you want the satisfaction of knowing that your work helps others — other employees and customers as well as yourself.
- Whatever you want from life you can get, because you will learn how to motivate others — employees and customers.
- You will learn how to serve customers so that they will want to come back. You will discover things about yourself, including capabilities you did not know you possessed.
- You will get a clear idea of how a system runs and of all the little things that add up to the satisfaction of the customer and the crew — primarily yourself.

McDonald's gives its individual crew people the following message: "You can take charge of your life. McDonald's can help you do it." The organization provides a lesson in basic economics: "Your job, your pay, and your advancement will depend on how well the customers are served, because the company's overall profitability is tied to that."

What if the importance of the customer is *not* emphasized throughout the organization? In Chapter One we saw examples of differences between what the customer expects and what the customer receives in organizations that are not customer-oriented. You have no doubt experienced similar grating contrasts, from waiting interminably in a store that advertises instant checkout to receiving faulty information from an "expert" salesperson who knows considerably less about the product than your four-year-old.

Unless the customer is — *and is made to feel* — important, unpleasant consequences can pervade the organization. Customers may have long waits for service. What service is then given may be inattentive, unfriendly, and cold; worse, it may be downright rude. If customers feel unwelcome, ignored, or patronized, they may take their business elsewhere, never to return. Further, disgruntled former customers will, in all likelihood, repeat tales of incompetence and rude service to other potential customers. In addition, in part due to unsatisfactory contacts with customers, employees may quit. The organization may then be left with product, but no one to sell or buy it. So how do we break out of this negative spiral?

The secret of success for America's service superstars is employees and how they are hired, trained, motivated, and empowered. A survey conducted for the Cincinnati Institute for Small Enterprise in 1988 underscores the importance of selection. Five hundred CEOs of smaller companies were asked the following question: "In planning for near-term growth, which of the following are most important?"

- Increased sales
- More efficient production
- Reduction of overhead costs
- Balanced budget
- Reduced taxes
- Retention of competent employees
- Recruitment of competent employees

What were the results? Of the respondents, 39 percent said that retaining competent employees was most important; an additional 28 percent said that hiring competent employees was most important. Thus 67 percent of the CEOs were focused primarily on recruitment and retention.

Hiring the Right People

Customer service superiority begins with the people we hire, how we hire them, and how we bring them into our organization.

A training consultant recently told me, "If you hire bums and give them to me, I'll give you back trained bums." The idea, of course, is not to hire bums but to hire the kind of people who will want to give good service.

During the interview process itself, the organization's values need to be emphasized. This initial impression of the company is very important. Managers with Marriott Corporation do a tremendous job in this area. They make the job candidate feel important from the moment that person comes in for a personal interview. They provide comfortable furniture, thickly carpeted floors, fruit, cookies, coffee (regular and decaffeinated), and tea. The idea is that if the employee is made to feel important in that very first encounter, the customer will also feel important afterward.

Beyond making the candidate physically comfortable and at ease, the interviewer should set the stage for educating the candidate about the importance of customer service. After a series of open-ended questions are asked by the interviewer, the candidate is told what behaviors are rewarded and what behaviors are unacceptable. This is where the teaching process begins.

The best way to "select in" those with a predisposition toward customer service (and to screen out those who are likely to be deficient in this area) is through what is called a *behaviorally oriented interview*. The interviewer elicits information about a candidate's past job-related behavior and life experiences and uses that to predict how a candidate will behave in any given job and organization. In other words, the interviewer selects candidates who have already, in their life and work experiences, demonstrated a service orientation.

Some of the behavioral characteristics that indicate a service orientation include oral communication skills, cooperation and teamwork, problem-solving and decision-making skills, sensitivity and concern for others, dependability, good judgment, enthusiasm, a high energy level, flexibility, and adaptability. A behaviorally oriented interview will reveal these characteristics.

This type of interview uses a highly structured format in which candidates talk more than 70 percent of the time, describing their previous work experiences in response to open-ended questions. It is based on two fundamental premises: first, most newly hired employees want to succeed and, from a technical perspective, are able to do the job; second, most employment failures spring not from a lack of technical competence but from an individual's inability to adjust his or her behavior to conform to the organization's norms.

To prepare for a behaviorally oriented interview, the employer must first identify eight to ten specific job-related behavioral characteristics that successful employees exhibit in this particular position within this particular organization — in other words, those characteristics deemed necessary for a person to succeed.

Once the job-related behavioral characteristics have been identified, three to five questions are developed for each, to determine whether a candidate possesses the identified characteristics, and to what degree.

Suppose, for example, that you are hiring a vice president of sales and one of the major responsibilities that employee will assume is to train, develop, and motivate the sales force. The most important job-related behavioral characteristic here is people development. The following four representative questions are designed to get at an individual's skills in that area.

- How do you identify people with potential for promotion? Specify your criteria.
- What are some of the things you do to develop your people?
- What do you get out of a performance appraisal review and feedback session with an employee? How does it help you as a manager?
- What do you do with the subordinate who does things contrary to your direction? How do you measure the effectiveness of your approach?

Other job-related behavioral characteristics for a successful sales manager could include skills in problem analysis and problem solving, oral communication, organization and planning, decision making, delegation, administration, interviewing, and counseling, as well as quality of work standards. Specific questions could be developed that would bring these characteristics to light.

Imagine that three individuals from the company — typically, the personnel manager, the immediate supervisor to whom the position will report, and someone at the next higher level of management — are involved in the selection process. They ask these questions in turn, and then they compare notes on their evaluation of each candidate's responses. A great deal of interview subjectivity is removed with this approach, because all candidates can be compared on the same criteria.

Additional behavioral characteristics, followed by an open-ended question relevant to each, are listed below. (See Appendix C for suggested performance standards for these and other behavioral characteristics.)

- *Cooperation.* Give me an example or two of when you've done some things on your own for others on the job. What was the reaction?
- *Dependability.* Tell me about those times when you were unable to get your work done. What were the causes? How did you respond?
- *Motivation and initiative.* What have you done lately to make your job more interesting? More efficient? More enjoyable? Tell me about some of the things you've started on your own.
- *Ability to work under pressure.* Tell me about a recent experience where you had to do several jobs at the same time. What was your reaction? How did you cope with the situation?

While many of the job-related behavioral characteristics necessary for success are similar from one business to another, each company should customize its own list of requirements. For example, one company might place a premium on a high level of tolerance for frustration and stress, whereas another company in the same industry might put an equally high premium on decisiveness and action.

This brings us to a caveat to be observed in custom-designing a selection system for your organization: be sure that you (and others) share the values you want to instill in new-comers. If the same values emphasized in hiring are not trans-mitted to and shared by the existing work force, the result could be the creation of an undesirable subculture within the organi-zation. This in turn could seriously hamper interdepartmental cooperation.

One of the best ways to safeguard against this division is to involve the existing employees in determining behavioral performance standards for their peer groups. In our work with a variety of clients, we have done this by facilitating a series of focus groups, then putting together a composite of the re-sponses received.

As long as this safeguard is in place, the behaviorally oriented interview works. It succeeds because everyone involved in the selection process is comparing apples and apples. It is much more objective (and realistic) than relying on interviewers' subjective opinions and impressions and is a preferred method of selection interviewing for the following reasons:

- It reduces the risk of poor selection decisions.
- It "selects in" those who will share organizational values.
- It saves training time and money.
- It minimizes the risk of failure and performance problems.
- It is judged to be legally defensible.
- It saves the manager's time.

Using the behaviorally oriented interview can help employers make the best hiring decisions — and can help candidates for em-ployment make their best decisions. It is clearly key to hiring quality people attuned to the company's needs. The next phase — orienting those people in the organization — is also critical.

Providing Effective Orientation

If you are fortunate enough to lure potentially good employees to join your organization, do not turn them off on the first day or in the first week or in the first month. Hiring and orienta-tion must complement each other and work hand in hand, as they do in many of the best organizations. Joseph J. Melone, president of Prudential Insurance, recognizes this: in our interview, he noted that, in addition to the fact that Prudential's recruitment standards are getting tougher (the company now tests a candidate's "trainability quotient" at the outset), its orientation and subsequent training are both extensive and intensive.

Many experts believe that an effective orientation may well mean the difference between success and failure for the new employee. For better or for worse, the orientation leaves an immediate and lasting impression. The successful orientation process results in fewer mistakes, improved customer service, higher levels of productivity, and more harmonious employee relations. Ideally, the orientation process serves to welcome the employee to a warm, friendly, caring environment. The employee who feels welcome and important will make the customer feel welcome and important.

Most leading service corporations treat the employee's first day on the job as a cause for a two-way celebration. It is in those early stages that the individual should be made to feel comfortable, as well as familiar with whatever is necessary to understand and perform the job efficiently. This is the vital first step in integrating the employee's needs with those of the organization (and consequently those of the customer).

A successful orientation process should be customized to fit the particular needs of a given organization. However, there are certain characteristics that most successful orientation processes have in common.

- Responsibilities and accountabilities are fixed and clearly understood by all those involved in the organization process, from the personnel manager, to the immediate supervisor, to the "buddy" assigned to teach the new employee.
- The new employee is made to feel secure and welcome in the new and unfamiliar environment.
- The new employee learns all that is needed to perform the job well.
- There is ample, planned opportunity to meet the supervisory staff and other employees.

- The employee is given a basic understanding of the company, its history, its values, its traditions, its business, its customers, and its reward system.
- The new person is told of the performance expectations and specific duties in precise detail, as well as where and how to get help and how this particular job relates to other jobs in the organization.
- The process is spread out over a period of time—perhaps three sessions over two or three weeks—to avoid information overload. Then, after another week or two on the job, the employee may be invited to a follow-up session to discuss how things are going.
- Full information on pay, benefits, hours, working conditions, terms, and conditions of employment is provided.
- Opportunities for training, learning, and potential advancement are explained early on.
- Policies, rules, and regulations are described in detail; "how we do things around here" is made clear. Clear values of service superiority are also established.
- Written materials are provided for subsequent review and reference.
- Checklists are used to ensure that all topics in the orientation process are covered.
- Feedback is solicited from the employees, by an independent third party, on the effectiveness and thoroughness of the entire process.

The service superstars take orientation very seriously. John A. Young of Hewlett-Packard, for example, said in our interview, "I am a firm believer in very early training for every employee, including a thorough orientation, wherein you share your value system and your expectations. It all begins with a total quality orientation."

Across the board, the service leaders spend a lot of money to recruit the right people, so they invest more than others in assimilating the individual to the organization. Service role models spend approximately 2 percent of gross revenues on training. This is a realistic target—and one for which the organization is likely to see a two-to-one return on investment for training in the first year.

The sample orientation format shown below could be adapted for use in a variety of organizations. As was noted earlier, the three sessions would generally be spread over two or three weeks.

I. First Session
   A. Traditions program: who we are, what we represent, how we do business, our company values, our common language; explanation and discussion of why we are in business, who our competitors are, who our customers are, and how we treat them.
   B. A complete tour of the office facilities and plant operations.
II. Second Session
   A. Orientation to the employee's particular division, department, and function, including how decisions are made, how problems are solved, and what behaviors are rewarded. Training emphasizes the close teamwork needed to produce a product or deliver a quality service.
   B. Orientation to the nature of the work, the job itself, the challenges, and the opportunities. Training again emphasizes the need for interdependence and teamwork.
III. Third Session
   A. Orientation to the employee's specific job.
   B. A review of the job description, performance standards, expectations, and mutual responsibilities.
   C. How the person's work and mistakes affect others in the work unit and beyond.
   D. Why this particular job is important and exactly how it contributes to business results.

Fostering Ongoing Communication

After the orientation, ongoing communication is critical as a way to reinforce the company's goals and values among its employees. Ongoing communication is important for all employees; in fact, as we have seen earlier, communication ranks high in employees' listings of qualities of a good place to work. In organizations newly striving for customer service superiority, communication is especially crucial. New employees will get an initial sense of the importance of the customer through the recruitment, interview, and orientation process; employees hired before the commitment to the customer was emphasized must develop this sense through the communication of management attitudes. (Communication should flow in both directions, of course — from top management down to the floor and from the floor up to the executive suites.) And, as we have seen, the service message must be more than just lip service; it must have teeth.

By way of example, let us look at how two companies create awareness of the importance of the customer through their corporate communications.

"Operation Customer"

A midsize midwestern machine tool manufacturer creates awareness of customer importance through a customer service program entitled "Operation Customer," described in Dartnell Publication's *Customers: How to Find Them and How to Keep Them.* The goal of this intensive communication program is to raise employee awareness of the fact that the plant doors open every day solely because of the customer.

Ex-Cell-O's approach involves getting customer reactions back to the employees by a variety of methods. Bulletin boards and house organs do more than just feature new employees, promotions, and retirements. They talk about customer compliments and complaints on a regular basis. They describe contracts won and lost. In them, the company tells its employees exactly what it tells its customers.

In addition, customer reactions are bounced back to employees immediately via a traffic-signal system that works as follows: a green light is for orders received; an amber light is for customer grievances; a red light is for orders lost. Other news regarding customer satisfaction follows a color system similar to the traffic-signal system: green paper is for good news, amber paper is for customer gripes, and red paper is for failures with the customer.

Additionally, back-room employees are selected to interface directly with the customer on some occasions. For example, plant personnel join sales people on sales calls. Teaming up in this way helps to eliminate some of the problems previously faced—for example, sales people making commitments that plant operations people could not deliver. It also makes those in plant operations more aware of what the ultimate customer needs and what the sales staff can successfully sell. The teams are thus a plus equally for employees (from two areas) and customers, because expectations become more realistic on all three sides.

Interdepartmental meetings are held regularly to develop new strategies for meeting changing customer requirements. Customer complaints get top priority. As a consequence of these efforts, there has been a significant reduction in scrap and rework, customer orders are booming, employee awareness has been sustained, and the program has paid for itself many times over.

Many CEO members of The Executive Committee (cited in Chapter Two) whose companies have taken measures similar to these report major improvements in integrating the work of their various departments, in overall productivity, and in customer retention.

CEO Involvement

We have talked in earlier chapters about how important the CEO's involvement is in increasing customer satisfaction. That importance cannot be overstressed. Steve Watson, chair and CEO of Dayton Hudson, practices this involvement.

Once a month Watson holds a ten-minute question-and-answer session with employees in one of his department stores. He answers even tough questions quite specifically and responds to follow-up questions in two-way conversation. In the process, he talks about what Dayton Hudson is doing as a company and what the company's expectations and concerns are.

One goal of these sessions is to bring management closer to the people. Through these sessions and in other ways, there is a lot of interaction between top management and the first line. Everybody in the company is on a first-name basis, demonstrating that all employees are equally important. In addition, the company house magazine, *Headlines,* sends messages consistent with this philosophy.

Customer Service Teams: What Are They?

Beyond stressing the importance of the customer to the individual employee through recruiting, hiring, and orientation processes and various corporate communication channels, how does an organization create a more comprehensive attitude of service excellence? How does it create a number-one club that says to the world that this company is the best in terms of customer satisfaction? Customer service teams at all levels of the organization — from management down to the floor (the customer's first contact with the organization) — are being used in the organizations most successful as customer service leaders.

Management Teams

Project-oriented, cross-functional teams of managers and professionals are now often examining issues and making decisions that were formerly reserved for top management or functional (departmental) unit heads. The reasons for this trend include providing improved cross-functional communications (and so improving flexibility and business responsiveness); providing opportunities for new job challenges in the face of reduced promotional opportunities; providing an instant network for new employees; and reducing the need for additional levels of management.

As examples of this trend, we have seen and worked with the following:

- A midwestern utility where the CEO and those who report directly to him delegate many (perhaps most) decisions in areas such as purchasing, human resource policy and practice, uniforms, and construction to one of the more than forty-one cross-functional teams of managers and employees
- A regional insurance company reorganizing to divert operating decisions to a cross-functional team of officers and managers
- An international hotel corporation where all decisions within its operating units are made by local, on-site executive teams
- Companies embracing the concept of "*office* of the chief operating officer" staffed by a team of cross-functional unit heads

The art of "job design" within these organizations has changed radically: instead of forging the traditional restrictive covenant, which walls each individual into a set of approved and directed behaviors within a functional unit, managers issue the charge to "do whatever you see that it takes to achieve our corporate objectives." This shift requires that all potentially contributing individuals be thoroughly informed regarding corporate direction, oriented to the approved value framework of the organization, and systematically trained to understand the corporate consequences of their individual and group decisions. Like the CEO, they must be reasonably able to act for the good of the whole rather than solely for the good of their part.

These changes in upper management and in empowering individuals to take direct actions for customer satisfaction give rise to customer service teams at lower levels of the company as well.

Floor-Level Teams

Hourly employees "on the floor" are now being organized to work as units or teams. This trend at the floor level of the organization is being driven by a number of factors of the current marketplace and work force. The new, more complex, and increasingly interrelated technologies and organization designs demand a higher level of skill and general awareness on the part of the hourly worker. There is thus a relatively new need to provide disciplined, ongoing, cost-effective, and closely monitored on-the-job training for present and new hourly employees as new technologies are introduced into the work setting. Access to new skills and knowledge, as well as to upward mobility and rewards for hourly workers, must be fair and equitable.

To address these changes, companies are forming smaller, and frequently more autonomous, teams at the floor level. Let us look at several examples of this trend.

Until three years ago, all twenty-three of an international food processor's U.S. plants operated with the segmented hourly job classification system that had existed in most of its plants since the mid 1950s. During the past three years, sixteen hourly job classifications on the plant floor have been reduced to three, and the company recently opened a model plant in which there is only one plant-floor hourly job classification. There are three progressive levels within this classification. Each employee must accumulate skills, experience, and problem-solving capabilities to move from one level to the next. Most supervisory responsibilities have been delegated to organized shift teams or to the "shift council" that reports directly to the plant manager. Shift supervisors have been replaced by shift trainers, whose primary responsibility is to manage the systematic growth of team members in knowledge and skill acquisition. The trainer reports to the teams.

Another international organization, a fiberglass insulation manufacturer, uses a team and team council approach in its new plant organization. It has replaced plant staff functions in the areas of shipping, purchasing, employee relations, quality control, and scheduling with rotating employee groups, each of which reports to the plant manager and to staff personnel at headquarters.

An international restaurant company is testing the concept of distributing management paperwork functions to its hourly employees in an attempt to reduce the need for two levels of management. An added benefit and goal is that the organization will be able to expand the pool of trained and experienced personnel who might readily move into the company's management ranks.

There are common factors within these organizations and their approaches to customer service teams.

- Organization changes are beginning in *new* facilities with new sophisticated technologies.
- New floor personnel are carefully screened for the desire and capability to acquire multiple skills.
- The new facilities contain tried and proven financial and statistical methods to monitor performance, quality, and customer service.
- Management has a history and tradition of egalitarianism and a firm belief in the power of the "common worker."
- There is a progressive record of equal employment opportunity.
- Performance is valued more than artificial barriers to mobility.

Results within a variety of organizations indicate clear economic benefits to enlisting teams in the goal of attaining satisfactory, if not exemplary, customer service. Imagine, for example, the service that one might receive in a fine restaurant if the employees have been imbued with a sense of the importance of the customer and work as part of a team. If the employees are all linked and committed to customer service, every contact, from taking dinner reservations to retrieving someone's coat, can smooth the way for the customer and encourage the customer to return. If, on the other hand, the individual employees face their tasks without particular regard for the customer, and if they work independently of one another, the likelihood that the customer will have an impersonal, dissatisfying experience is increased.

Each employee — even those who do not meet the customer face to face — must have the customer's satisfaction in mind. This mind-set is obviously critical for the chef; it is less obviously so for other members of the kitchen staff. But a lipstick-stained wineglass or a table that is cleared noisily can result in unhappy customers — and have negative effects on the restaurant's bottom line.

Though the details of execution vary, customer-focused teamwork benefits any organization. Given that effective, well-planned teams help the bottom line, it is time to enlist their help.

Establishing Customer Service Teams

Colin Marshall, CEO of British Airways, recognized that managers have to model the behavior that they want from their staff. He instituted Customer First Teams to bring the work force into the challenge of improving service. Groups of volunteers were formed into teams and given the training and the opportunity to tell their managers how things might be done better.

Michael Bruce, senior development projects manager for British Airways, reports that the teams discovered several critical behaviors that served to point the way forward. These included management styles offering support, coaching, encouragement of trust, and delegation of responsibility. They also included establishing and communicating clear objectives, instituting performance appraisals, and providing feedback. Parochialism and local rivalries were addressed, and people were encouraged to think like *business*people — that is, to be less averse to risks. And these efforts bore fruit for both employees and the bottom line.

Managers in any organization attempting to establish customer service teams must be aware that each team leader's behaviors and performance are critical to success. To properly motivate a service performance team, a team leader must

- Provide clear objectives to team members so that there is little or no confusion about who is supposed to do what
- Define goals so that everyone has a common understanding of why the team was established
- Encourage communication among team members about the *whole* job and each member's part of it
- Handle personality conflicts
- Maintain focus so that team members do not get off the track
- Provide for (or be) a substitute when necessary
- Monitor the progress of individual members

- Take corrective action if schedules are not met
- Consolidate the resulting information for presentation

In effective customer service teams, team leadership often rotates rather than remaining as one member's permanent assignment. This shifting of the leadership role is reflective of a more egalitarian attitude within the organization and seems to contribute to a team's success. It is not clear, however, whether rotating leadership succeeds because each member pays attention (since each knows that he or she will someday have that role), because it taps the various resources of a diverse team, or because of some other factor.

And what of the teams themselves? Customer service teams that are effective in their company's quest to increase customer satisfaction, repeat business, and referral business share the following characteristics. Team members have positive attitudes and respect for each other. They all speak clearly, listen carefully, and encourage suggestions. They share responsibility and accountability, as well as any credit and recognition. The team itself is charged with a serious purpose and has the inclination and authority to deal with rather than ignore upsetting or potentially dangerous situations.

In contrast, in ineffective teams, hostile camps exist; various people will not speak to each other. Individuals are inflexible; for example, technicians resist tasks outside their traditional responsibilities. Assignments—who does what or gets what—are a matter of who is friendly with whom. Key information is held closely by small subgroups. Cooperation is not encouraged among members, instructions are hazy, and messages are not clear. As a result of these factors, there is little, if any, common cause or esprit de corps.

Teamwork: A Success Story

Throughout this chapter, we have said that a sense of the importance of the customer must be instilled in employees from the very start. We have also emphasized that customer service teams in management and on the floor can help reinforce this sense and help in meeting the organization's goals. To under-

score these points, let us look at the experience of a cable television company in San Diego.

When we were called in, the firm's disconnect rate was
high, and customers were waiting too long for service. The company had sixty employees divided among four main groups:
sales, installation and repair, customer service, and finance. Each
group's work affected each other group, and each individual employee's work affected other employees; but there was no company-wide recognition of this or of the interplay necessary for
a successful customer orientation. As a result, sales made commitments that installation and repair could not possibly honor.
Installation and repair then worked long hours and overtime
to meet the commitments. Problems developed in both the timeliness and the quality of the work. Those who answered the
phone were barraged with complaints from unhappy customers.

One of our main tasks in establishing customer service
performance teams at this site was to help the four main groups
understand how they impacted each other (and consequently
the customer). In a service organization such as this one, wide
circles of employees directly affect and have contact with the
customer. As a consequence, the functions and people who must
be included as part of the customer service team are very broad.
They include those who prepare and place the advertising, those
who receive orders for installation, and those who actually hook
up the cable. They also include those who handle inquiries, problems, complaints, and bills. In short, everyone in the organization must be involved.

The company soon realized this and empowered its people to meet customer needs. It enabled installation and repair
people, customer service representatives, and customer service
phone people to coordinate their efforts. It also authorized them
to adjust customers' bills without prior management approval.

Because the employees now feel important, responsible,
responsive, and accountable, the company's cable customers now
receive better service. The continuing goal is consistency and
predictability, both of which are necessary to retain customers,
obtain customer referrals, and avoid disconnects. These were
our service performance standards for the company, a subject
we discuss thoroughly in the next chapter.

Chapter 5

ESTABLISH EMPLOYEE-BASED SERVICE PERFORMANCE STANDARDS

All systems are designed to draw on the ideas and enthusiasm of every individual in the entire company. This means involvement at all levels. Our employees own the process. We empower our people because most people generally want to do a good job.

—John A. Young
President and CEO
Hewlett-Packard

When companies strive for a high level of customer service, it soon becomes clear that it is not enough to say, "Be nice to the customer." Eventually you have to define just what *nice* means. Simply put, good intentions are no guarantee of quality service.

Employees need to understand what they will be held accountable for and what standards their performance will be measured against. Two things are involved; they work in concert, and both are needed: a precise, written job description, delineating the exact areas for which each employee is responsible, and a detailed set of employee-based behavioral performance standards for each job, setting out as specifically as possible the behavior expected in all elements of the job. As we will see, these

85

requirements are needed for all employees, from those in immediate contact with the customer, to the supervisors, to upper-level managers.

Job Descriptions

All too often, employees waste time and effort simply because they do not fully understand what they are responsible and accountable for. Instead of working, they spend a great deal of time in defensive maneuvering.

The boss often assumes — incorrectly — that the employee knows exactly what to do and how (and in what priority) to do it. Quite the opposite is true. In fact, an astonishing number of employees — in some groups we have worked with, as high as 70 percent — are unclear what their own performance is measured against. Even many middle and senior managers are not aware of the standards for their jobs, the impact they are expected to make, or the basis on which they will be measured. What these employees need are clear, well-defined job descriptions with meaningful, precise, well-communicated performance standards.

In a medium-sized midwestern company where Desatnick served as personnel director, we initiated a job description process. As a first step, we asked people to provide their own job descriptions. We found that anywhere from one to three people each claimed responsibility and accountability for the exact same job factors, a few people noted two or more direct reporting relationships, and a number of jobs were nonjobs — crutches for those who could not perform.

At McDonald's, everybody — all restaurant employees and all managers — has a written job description. The job descriptions for restaurant employees incorporate customer service standards to ensure the achievement of the organization's objectives in quality, service, cleanliness, and value to the customer. Job descriptions for management incorporate additional areas of responsibility and reflect the same behavioral characteristics that are explored in the interviewing process. Ultimately, managers are expected to help establish and reinforce service performance standards for all customer-contact employees.

A good job description benefits employees and the company; it can also become the basis for many critical human resource functions. Specifically, a good job description provides a foundation for the selection, induction, orientation, and training of employees; for the determination of compensation, standards of performance, and new goals and objectives; and for the development of employees, from performance coaching, progress reviews, and performance appraisal and review to employee development, planned advancement, and career-path planning.

To put together job descriptions and begin the process of establishing service performance standards, consider the following steps:

1. Ask all who report to you to list the six to eight major responsibilities of their position, by priority of importance.
2. You do the same, for each employee.
3. Exchange papers. Now you have begun to provide the basis for a clear understanding of the job responsibilities, accountability for business results, and priorities. Normally, there are two or three items on one person's list that do not appear on the other's. Small wonder that there is so much misunderstanding about standards!
4. Next, have the individual describe briefly for each of those six to eight major job responsibilities the exact condition that should exist (quantitatively or qualitatively) if that particular job responsibility is being performed to standard, above-standard, and below-standard levels. Get your employees to put themselves in the position of the customer and imagine how they would like to be treated. You have now started the second step: using the job description to establish performance standards.

Performance Standards

Mary Kay Ash, chair of Mary Kay Cosmetics, recently noted that many companies talked about excellence, but unless they establish measurable and obtainable performance standards, employees do not have a target at which to aim.

Performance standards describe in detail for each position and each individual responsibility within that position exactly what conditions will exist if service superiority is to become a reality. (And that includes accidental, happenstance encounters with customers by employees not generally in contact with the public. Nothing should be left to chance.) Performance standards are statements of the conditions that should exist if the job is being performed properly. Standards should be quantitative, if at all possible. At minimum, qualitative standards are a must.

The creation of standards of performance excellence is critical to the achievement of excellence. The absence of these standards explains, for the most part, what Lawrence Miller has described as our passion for mediocrity. Most organizations do a reasonably adequate job establishing performance standards in such areas as financial results, operating results, budgets and expenses, productivity, and quality of output. But they neglect the so-called soft areas, which actually drive the financial results. Six areas of benign neglect, listed below (and discussed in greater detail later in the chapter), must be addressed if an organization hopes to excel in service:

- Standards for individual job-related behaviors
- Standards for managerial and supervisory job-related behaviors
- Standards targeting job satisfaction
- Standards targeting internal customer satisfaction
- Standards targeting external customer satisfaction
- Standards targeting telephone usage

Before looking at each of these areas in turn, let us look at four companies that distinguish themselves from their competition by their performance standards. The standards themselves vary, from detailed, step-by-step instructions to more generic standards premised on the main thrust of the mission statement, but all have measurable effects on internal and external customers.

McDonald's Standards

As our first illustration, let us look at the training and service standards of an hourly employee at McDonald's. The cashier at the counter is taught six very exact steps for taking a customer's order, from greeting the customer to counting the change and thanking the customer. For each of those six steps, there are precise behavioral service standards. Take a look at the second step for breakfast:

Step 2. Take the Order
Standards

1. Register the order into the cash register as the customer is giving it.
2. Be thoroughly familiar with all items on the menu.
3. Answer each question the customer may ask about ingredients, food freshness, content, and handling times.
4. If you receive orders for items we do not carry, suggest a similar or related menu item. Do not say, "We don't carry that particular product."
5. Be particularly helpful with detailed explanations to new customers and they will become repeat customers.
6. If a customer orders an item after the breakfast period has ended, explain politely that the cutoff time is necessary to provide quality service and fresh food.
7. Suggest only one additional item to your customer. That person will appreciate it. For example, "How about a nice hot Danish to go with that steaming hot cup of coffee?"
8. Accept special orders graciously.
9. It is okay to substitute or ask for additional portions, but make the appropriate price adjustment.

One of the real benefits of precise and exact behavioral performance standards is that they create in the employee's mind an acute sense of customer awareness. Thus the importance of the customer is emphasized (and reemphasized) with each and every transaction.

As an hourly crew chief advances into a management trainee role at McDonald's, customer awareness takes on new dimensions of meaning. As a crew person, that individual was trained in aspects of customer awareness having to do with quality, service, cleanliness, and value. As a manager, that individual is now taught how to make additional decisions that directly relate to customer satisfaction in such areas as handling customer complaints, dealing with injuries to customers, and managing unruly individuals or groups. For all these areas, too, there are very precise performance standards. Here is an example:

A Customer Complains About an Order
Standards

1. Apologize for any possible mistake.
2. Use your judgment in replacing the order. Err on the side of the customer.
3. Do not ask for more money.
4. Show concern in your remarks and in your approach.
5. Make sure the customer is satisfied before you walk away.

This same meticulous attention to detail, to precise standards of behavior, is also applied to such management concerns as customer injury on the premises, damage to store property, disturbances by individuals or groups, and complaints regarding short change.

To ensure that the standards are truly understood and internalized, management trainees are thoroughly examined and evaluated. After they read the appropriate module's instruction form, they discuss it with the manager. Then they take a test covering all the material for that particular module. They might, for example, have to answer a series of open-ended questions to measure understanding and application of the correct behavioral performance standards for helping a customer file an insurance claim. The test of knowledge, ability, and understanding continues with observation by the manager and discussion with the trainee. Observations include the actual handling of, for example, three customer complaints.

Finally, the management trainee, as part of the normal job routine, is asked to convey to the crew, by word and deed, the total importance of customer satisfaction.

World-Class Hotel Standards

What do McDonald's and world-class hotels have in common? An emphasis on service. Consider the following list of performance standards for all managers in a hotel chain.

1. *Communication with guests.* Accepts feedback on performance, solicits suggestions for improvement; exercises aggressive hospitality; acknowledges and takes initiative to solve guest problems; delivers service in a friendly, professional manner.
2. *Communication with subordinates.* Provides effective, timely information to subordinates; solicits input on problems and suggestions for improvement; accepts feedback on performance.
3. *Communication with superiors.* Provides effective, timely information and feedback to superiors; solicits input on problems and suggestions for improvement; accepts feedback on performance.
4. *Communication with other departments.* Provides effective, timely information and feedback to other departments; solicits input on problems and suggestions for improvement; accepts feedback on performance.
5. *Conducting meetings.* Prepares agenda prior to meetings; adheres to and completes agenda; holds meetings when needed and as required; encourages participation and facilitates discussion appropriately.
6. *Self-development.* Identifies own developmental needs with superior; establishes, actively pursues, and reaches specific self-development goals; updates goals on an ongoing basis.
7. *Subordinate training and development.* Identifies subordinates' specific training needs with subordinates' input; develops skills and knowledge of subordinates on a timely and ongoing basis; follows up to ensure desired growth is being achieved.

8. *Ongoing critique.* Gives ongoing, timely feedback (including praise) to subordinates about their performance; creates an environment conducive to hearing and responding to subordinates' problems.

9. *Counseling.* Addresses specific problems with subordinates as soon after the fact as possible; seeks their input; develops plan with them to solve problems; follows up with feedback and encouragement to ensure resolution of problems.

10. *Discipline.* Acts fairly on discipline matters; adheres to disciplinary policies; follows and encourages use of the Guarantee of Fair Treatment.

11. *Subordinate evaluation.* Objectively evaluates subordinates' performance against standards and goals; discusses performance in a manner that effectively fosters improvement; evaluates subordinates on time; obtains necessary approvals and processes paperwork in a timely manner.

12. *Following directions.* Effectively carries out instructions of superiors; acts on suggestions and feedback from superiors; meets deadlines.

13. *Delegation.* Delegates appropriate responsibility and authority to subordinates for specific tasks, decisions, and follow-up; provides clear and complete instructions; states expectations precisely; uses subordinates' capabilities most effectively.

14. *Motivation.* Encourages and inspires subordinates to accomplish tasks; creates enthusiasm and positive work environments for subordinates; rewards superior performance; sets good example.

15. *Teamwork.* Coordinates work of subordinates to ensure that appropriate attention is paid to highest-priority tasks; encourages and generates collective effort within department and with other departments to work for common goals.

16. *Goal-setting.* Sets precise, measurable, achievable goals for department and with subordinates, goals that are realistic and challenging and that meet the most critical business needs; sets specific intermediate action steps, with due dates, to accomplish goals; prioritizes goals appropriately.

17. *Identifying problems.* Recognizes early signs of changing con-

ditions and potential problems; analyzes causes for problems using all available and appropriate resources (including subordinates).

18. *Solving problems.* Calls on appropriate people to help identify and creatively explore alternative solutions, select best solutions, and implement solutions in a timely manner; assists others in solving problems; follows up to ensure problems are resolved; takes corrective actions when necessary.

19. *Productivity.* Achieves quantity and quality standards while maintaining minimum labor costs; understands and effectively uses forecasting and labor management policies, systems, and procedures.

More Exemplary Standards

An excellent example of service performance standards is cited in *The Service Edge* by Ron Zemke with Dick Schaaf—Deluxe Check Printers in St. Paul, Minnesota.

Deluxe Check Printers has dual performance standards: error-free printing and a two-day turnaround. It meets these standards in its sixty regional plants about 98 percent of the time.

A music retailer set a new standard for movers. It recognizes that on occasion a piano mover may cause damage. If a carpet is stained during a move, the company guarantees cleanup within twenty-four hours. If a wall is damaged during installation, the company has an independent repair company fix the problems at the convenience of the customer.

Having seen the positive impact that performance standards can have, we return to the six areas of benign neglect: standards for individual job-related behaviors, standards for managerial and supervisory job-related behaviors, standards targeting job satisfaction, standards targeting internal customer satisfaction, standards targeting external customer satisfaction, and standards targeting telephone usage.

Standards for Individual Job-Related Behaviors

How does a company develop performance standards that will be effective and make the company's service exemplary? Establishing such standards may well be the most difficult part of a manager's job. Yet they are necessary in all areas — for technical, professional, and clerical jobs as well as for jobs in the manufacturing sector — if managers are to control results and to achieve the goals set by the organization. Without standards, goals are difficult to establish, measurements are fuzzy, and formal performance appraisals and reviews are unsatisfactory.

Standards of performance must resonate with the company's mission statement. Once articulated, they must be constantly reinforced, especially during orientation of new and newly promoted employees and reorientation of the existing work force.

The Standards Process for Newly Hired Employees

Advising the newly hired of what is expected of them starts with a one-page job description. This should explain why the position exists, what it contributes to the organization's goals, what the six to eight principle responsibilities are, where and how the position fits into the total picture, and how performance will be measured (that is, the standards against which the employee will be judged). Performance standards should include behavioral as well as technical, financial, and operating results.

The Standards Process for Existing Employees

Earlier, we recommended involving existing employees in the development of job descriptions. This process has benefits beyond getting accurate and functional descriptions. The involvement alone can foster employee support for the process. Further, the mutually achieved revelations of differences in perceptions between employees and management (and their resolution) can encourage a sense of ownership and responsibility throughout the organization.

Once a clear mutual understanding on all aspects of the job description is established, the next step is to actually set the standards. This step should also involve existing employees, either individually or in focus groups. Companies that involve their employees empower them to do the job; in so doing, they positively impact customer relations as well.

Setting Standards with Individuals. For one-of-a-kind positions, the manager asks the employee to describe, quantitatively and/or qualitatively, what conditions should exist if all aspects of the position (technical, operating, financial, and behavioral) are being performed in an above-standard manner, a standard (or satisfactory) manner, and a below-standard manner.

The end result is a psychological contract between manager and employee to strive for above-standard behavior and performance in all aspects of the position. The manager also contracts to provide the skills training necessary for above-standard achievement, along with tools, materials, supplies, information, support, and assistance that enable the employee to perform consistently above standard.

Setting Standards in Focus Groups. The best method we know of for establishing behavioral performance standards that will apply to a large group of people is to involve a representative sample of the total work force (say 10 to 20 percent) in focus groups. (This can also be done as a paper-and-pencil survey.)

In the focus-group approach, a trained facilitator assembles seven to ten people who hold similar job classifications but have varied job descriptions. (For example, one group of nonexempt salaried employees would consist of typists, word processors, secretaries, accountants, and bookkeepers.) The facilitator asks each person in the group to think of a person with whom he or she really enjoys working. Each employee is then asked what that person does differently from someone who is just okay and what that person does differently from someone who is not working out. The responses highlight behavioral characteristics (dependability, for example). Each person in the focus group is then asked to voluntarily give additional examples to illustrate the behavior being discussed. The next step is to get the group to describe — not by example, as before, but explicitly — what is above-standard, standard, and below-standard behavior.

This process is then repeated through all levels of the organization, up to and including the executive committee. Each focus group should be composed exclusively of peers, however; in no case should an employee and his or her manager attend the same session, because of the intimidation factor.

After each session, all the information elicited should be pooled and edited into a composite of above-standard, standard, and below-standard behavior for each characteristic included. This composite should then be distributed to all employees for review. The behavioral performance standards presented in Appendix C were developed using this process for numerous organizations interested in achieving service superiority. In all cases, the intention was to achieve consistency and to disseminate common values throughout the organization.

The Standards Process for Employee Groups

Once a set of consistent behaviors, along with their accompanying performance standards, has been established for individuals, the next logical step is to examine each department, function, and unit within the organization and establish performance standards for the entire work unit. By way of example, see the circle diagram of the interrelated departments of a hospital shown in Figure 5.1. Performance standards are required for each department. For example, representative standards that have been developed for radiology include the following:

- No waiting time when the patient arrives for an X-ray
- Immediate feedback to the physician and the patient
- No lost or misplaced X-rays
- Immediate physician access to the right X-ray on weekends

The goal is to determine a set of standards for each specific work unit that will result in exemplary service performance from a customer's perspective (whether internal or external).

The Alternative to Performance Standards

Readers who remain unconvinced of the need for formal performance standards should be reminded that corporate life without them is characterized by the following:

- *Defensive maneuvering.* Because it is unclear how performance will be measured, employees eventually virtually disappear into their job descriptions.

Figure 5.1. Service Delivery System.

- *Low productivity.* Employees tend to do as little as is necessary to get by, because the basis for judging performance has not been defined by the manager.
- *Unclear instructions.* Communication tends to take the nature of continuous crisis orientation. Everything is ad hoc. Priorities change from week to week (or even more often).
- *Slippage through the cracks.* Not everything gets done: some things are overemphasized, others are underemphasized, and

some do not get done at all. Everything eventually becomes
a top priority.

- *Excessive mistakes.* Having let things slide, employees rush
  to get now-urgent things done; their behavior and effort are
  unfocused. Workload distribution is uneven, and a crisis
  orientation prevails. The end result is frequent errors.

- *Poor appraisal review sessions.* In the absence of specific performance standards, the annual appraisal lacks objectivity
  and is therefore highly unsatisfactory. In our experience,
  service employees complain about appraisals for two reasons, both of which suggest faulty implementation: one group
  complains because of excessive delays (up to two years between appraisals); another group, having received timely
  reviews, regrets having been appraised.

- *Employee and customer alienation.* As the frustration continues
  to build up, employees practice avoidance behavior with the
  boss, uncertain what to do next. When mistakes begin to
  multiply — as they surely will — the ultimate customer is negatively impacted, because employees treat customers (both
  internal and external) the same way they are treated. Ultimately, finger pointing and charges of favoritism take over.
  Managers with no objective basis to measure performance
  against rate the employees they favor more highly than those
  they favor less.

Standards for Managerial and
Supervisory Job-Related Behaviors

Traditionally, we have appraised managers almost exclusively
on financial and operating results and have not measured them
as managers of employees. In many organizations, it matters
not if a manager has 50 percent employee turnover, poor unit
morale, and a lack of promotions from and within the unit over
long periods of time. If there are no managerial standards in
these areas, there is no accountability, yet such behaviors will
produce a negative impact on the bottom line.

Our research in our consulting practices has indicated a
need for managerial performance standards in the following

areas: planning, organizing, staffing, integrating, leading and directing, measuring and controlling, contributing to organization goals, showing creativity and innovation, achieving internal customer satisfaction, and achieving external customer satisfaction. We have noted that if a person in a management position performs consistently above standard in these areas, the financial operating results and the technical aspects of the work itself will also be above standard.

In our opinion, an organization's success can be asssured only through the quality of its management. Good management begets good people. Each manager should contribute "added value" to the job, doing more and better work than his or her predecessor. Each manager should strive for perfection and contribute to the overall well-being of the organization by suggesting and implementing new methods, procedures, and processes and by bringing about improved work flow and customer satisfaction, both internal and external. If standards are not set in these areas, however, and if managers are not held accountable for the achievement of those standards, perfection — or even improvement — will not happen. The behavior you reward is the behavior you get.

Standards Targeting Job Satisfaction

Most organizations are familiar with employee attitude, opinion, and morale surveys. Too often, however, they wait until a union is knocking at the door before surveying their employees. If in advance of a union organizing drive the organization were to establish standards for employee job satisfaction, labor problems would be minimized. If standards for levels of job satisfaction are not set *before* instead of after survey results, by the time the results come back it may be too late. In short, managers must be held accountable for employee morale, motivation, and retention through specific measurable standards, or they will not succeed in these areas.

First, the organization must determine what level of employee job satisfaction it seeks. Then it needs to establish standards of performance to identify the degree of satisfaction experienced by employees in such areas as these:

- Pay
- Benefits
- Working conditions
- Promotion opportunities
- Quality of supervision
- Work pressures
- Overall satisfaction with top management
- Objectivity of decision-making process
- Fairness
- Quality of life

Standards Targeting Internal Customer Satisfaction

There is a rapidly growing awareness of the importance of the internal customer or client as the key factor in external customer satisfaction, as we have noted. But assessing and maintaining internal customer satisfaction is not easy, especially in large firms. When an organization reaches more than fifty employees, it must pay serious attention to performance standards targeting internal customer satisfaction.

According to William F. Blount, past president of the Network Operations Group of AT&T, "Successful service delivery in the 1990's will be driven by relationships. The quality of the relationships with and among customers, technology, and people—employees, peers, union officials, and suppliers included—will be the critical success factor. We cannot achieve real customer satisfaction if we do not satisfy the tiers of internal customers whose performance ultimately affects the outside customer."

The method we recommend for senior management pursuing a focus on internal customer satisfaction involves the following steps:

1. Management identifies critical internal service encounters and establishes service performance standards for each factor within these encounters.
2. Management identifies the most critical department and selects the three or four other departments that most significantly impact the quality of work and the output of the critical department.

3. The critical department meets with the three or four iden-
    tified departments to jointly establish standards of excel-
    lence for internal customer satisfaction for each of the fac-
    tors identified in the first step.

By going through this process, managers leave little to chance;
no real surprises should occur. If a problem does crop up, an
immediate joint effort can be launched to resolve it and avoid
any kind of recurrence.

In the next chapter, we present a worksheet for this method
of analyzing and improving internal customer satisfaction (see
Table 6.2). For each standard shown to be in need of improvement, managers must be prepared to discuss possible obstacles
to bringing the standard up to an outstanding rating.

We have developed a set of standards for critical service
encounters and have used them in measuring internal customer
satisfaction with more than 250 CEOs of small and medium-
sized companies dealing in sales, manufacturing, distribution,
and service. We are therefore confident of the usefulness and
wide applicability of these standards, defined as follows:

- *Quality:* how frequently the quality of the work, materials,
  supplies, and subassemblies meets an established measure
  (for example, 98 percent error-free)
- *Quantity:* how reliably the appropriate quantity of work is available to ensure an adequate supply to the operations department
- *Accuracy:* how accurately the paperwork flowing from one
  department to another is prepared
- *Timeliness:* how promptly the right amount of product, information, supplies, and materials is delivered
- *Responsiveness:* how readily the supplier departments respond
  to other departments' needs and to special requests from the
  operations group
- *Problem solving:* how quickly action is taken to resolve a problem once and for all (versus a stopgap approach)
- *Concern:* how fully the department genuinely understands the
  work of other departments and reflects that understanding
  through concern for internal customer satisfaction

- *Anticipation:* how effectively the departments anticipate the needs of other departments, determine what could go wrong, and then take preventive measures to minimize difficulties in production
- *Joint standards:* how often — and how successfully — departments meet to establish joint standards for critical service encounters
- *Planning effectiveness:* how far in advance and how effective planning processes are
- *Overall satisfaction:* how satisfied, overall, one department is with the services provided by another

Standards Targeting External Customer Satisfaction

Bear in mind that performance standards relate — in a very direct way — to customer expectations and satisfaction. This relationship is shown in the list below:

Customer Expectations (Internal and External)	*Necessary Job-Related Behaviors*
Help and assistance	Cooperation and teamwork
Respect	Integrity and honesty
Comfort	Ability to work under pressure
Empathy	Interpersonal skills
Timely service	Dependability
Orderly service	Ability to prioritize
Trouble-free service	Initiative and motivation
Understanding and information	Oral and written communication skills
Appreciation	Initiative and motivation
Recognition	Judgment and decision-making skills
Friendly service	Enthusiasm

For an example of an organization that has made standards such as these work, we look to Hewlett-Packard. The success of Hewlett-Packard's customer support can be traced in large measure to its cycle of an integrated set of services for customers over the life cycle of the product. This life cycle is broken down into three phases:

- *Planning.* Hewlett-Packard helps the customer understand the problem and recommends the appropriate solution.
- *Implementation.* Hewlett-Packard installs and implements the particular solution.
- *Operations.* Hewlett-Packard's support enhances the system's solution.

Not surprisingly, Hewlett-Packard has been rated highly among its competitors in support satisfaction (including maintenance, effectiveness, responsiveness, trouble shooting, education, software support, and documentation).

Determining your specific customers' expectations and levels of satisfaction is not a difficult task. It simply requires asking the customers (1) what they want (then tempering their expectations with the reality of what you can provide at a fair price in relation to what your competitors are providing) and (2) how pleased they are with what they got.

A client of ours, a medical supplies distributor with approximately 250 employees, decided to survey its customers. The surveyors discovered that in approximately 20 percent of the areas in which they felt they excelled, their customers noted a need for improvement. On the other hand, in 20 percent of the areas where they felt improvement was needed, the customers were highly satisfied. It pays to ask your customers!

Standards Targeting Telephone Usage

Every organization has at least one telephone, and many have thousands. In many instances, a client's first impression of the company is through the telephone. For these reasons (and others), every employee — whether a temporary receptionist or the CEO — should be trained in proper telephone usage. The telephone may, after all, be your most potent business tool. Unfortunately, it may also be the most misused.

There are some drawbacks to this wonder of technology. It requires speakers to be constantly alert, because only a minor part of communication is attributed to verbal expression. A greater part of communication is transmitted by our tone of voice, and the largest part of communication comes from our body language, including facial expression. Because body language cannot be relied on in telephone conversations, tone of voice and expression become even more important. Without the benefit of expressing ourselves visually, we have less than a minute to make a favorable first impression.

No matter how many calls managers and employees place and receive during the business day, the company's reputation is on line with every call. To the person on the other end of the line, the speaker *is* the company. Staff members who are less than professional in telephone conversations affect the caller's perception of the entire business. For material on improving professionalism in the use of the telephone, see Appendix D, which has been contributed to this book by Eileen Montgomery, a speaker and consultant to businesses.

Effective Employee Training

Performance standards cannot be considered *established* until they are absorbed into the corporate culture. The primary means by which this process occurs is employee training. Those organizations that aspire to superlative customer service must reinforce their standards — especially those targeting customer service — with effective training.

Superiority in customer service does not happen by chance. Employees will do the right things, and do things right, only if they are properly trained to do so. Employees who are well trained produce superior products, which in turn require a minimum of service. But training must be repeated regularly to reinforce the learning and maintain the desired behaviors.

Education within businesses has three phases: executive education, in which senior management learns its role; management education, in which those who must implement the process learn how to do it; and employee education, in which all the employees of the company learn their roles, including how to contribute to service superiority.

All of the service superstars endorse the philosophy of training. Each makes major investments—often as much as 2 percent of gross sales—in formal, ongoing training programs. It is an investment they cannot afford to pass up.

In a broad sense, all the service superstars' training programs focus on developing and maintaining skills in three general areas: job-related skills, positive attitudes toward customers and co-workers, and overall company knowledge. All three are closely interrelated, and all pertain directly to the achievement and maintenance of service superiority.

In line with the service performance standards, all employees are taught exactly what is meant by service superiority and exactly how to achieve it. The values of teamwork and interdependence are emphasized as vital links in the chain of service superiority. All employees are taught how their work and their mistakes affect others, and vice versa. They are taught that even though the customer picks up the tab, it is ultimately the employee who suffers and pays.

To emphasize the importance of training, consider the following two situations. The first concerns a large publishing and printing operation that built a very sophisticated and very expensive ($100 million plus) automated factory. Two years later, the plant was running at less than 70 percent efficiency.

On close inspection, it was discovered that only $50,000 had been allotted to training. Middle managers, supervisors, and employees, unable to cope with the multitude of changes in working relationships brought on by the new technology, were given little assistance. The end result was that many customers did not get their magazines and newspapers on time. The training budget was then increased to $250,000, and within six months 90 percent capacity had been achieved.

In Central Falls, Rhode Island, GTE Lighting Products had just two months to open a plant that had been purchased from Corning. Comprehensive training played a major role in this transition. The trainers were hourly employees who had expertise in the production of fluorescent tubes. They all had a stake in seeing that newly hired employees did well.

In close cooperation with the training administrator, the hourly trainers wrote the training manuals. They then acted out the step-by-step instructions for each operation and video-taped the correct way to do things. Afterward, each newly hired employee was assigned to one of the trainers for at least six to ten hours of classroom work and practice experience on the shop floor.

Each new employee studied the manual, watched the videotape, and then practiced steps on the shop floor. After that, the employee was videotaped on the job, and the trainer and the employee reviewed the tape and decided what changes were necessary. Then the employee practiced again (and again, as needed), until it was perfect. When the employee was ready, the trainer "signed off" to certify readiness.

GTE expanded its training program in every area after the success of this venture, because it brought an employee's productivity up to standard more quickly than just sending the new person out to the line operation, lowered employee turn-over, and elevated product quality. Because the skills were taught properly up front, quality was excellent from the start. This meant virtually no customer service problems.

Lifelong Career Training

As we have seen, the service leaders begin training during the selection process itself and continue right on to an individual's retirement. If service superiority is to be achieved and then main-tained, training must be a lifelong process, as shown in Figure 5.2.

In the role-model companies, just about everybody goes to school for at least a full week every year to reinforce and main-tain those desired behaviors once established. Every supervisor at General Electric and IBM, for example, goes to school regu-larly to make sure that slippage does not occur.

O'Toole identifies lifelong career training as one of the major features that characterize superiority in service and pro-

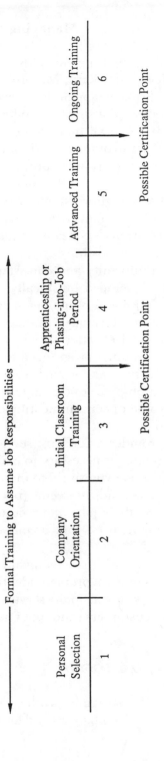

Figure 5.2. The Professionalization Path for Service Personnel.

→ Formal Training to Assume Job Responsibilities →

| Personal Selection | Company Orientation | Initial Classroom Training | Apprenticeship or Phasing-into-Job Period | Advanced Training | Ongoing Training |
| 1 | 2 | 3 | 4 | 5 | 6 |

Possible Certification Point

Possible Certification Point

ductivity. Among the firms he holds up as models are Johnson
& Johnson, Hewlett-Packard, Motorola, and John Deere. Coin-
cidentally, the firms he applauds for excellence in training also
lead their respective industries in productivity, cost-effectiveness,
profitability, and overall management effectiveness.

Here are some of the considerations that go into the service leaders' ongoing training programs:

- Employees are taught what questions to ask their supervisors.
- Supervisors are taught how to respond to those questions.
- Clear expectations — considered just as important as skills
  training — are set forth.
- To ensure uniformity and consistency, all formal training
  is centrally developed but locally implemented.
- There is a full menu of management training in such sub-
  ject areas as performance management, human resource
  motivation, and effective supervision.
- Supervisory training programs are mandatory — at least one
  full week every year for each supervisor.
- Training emphasizes to employees, supervisors, and man-
  agers the value of communicating openly and provides the
  skills to do so.
- Training provides a constant service focus for employees.
  Ongoing training is necessary to maintain service standards.
- Training is used extensively to motivate and sustain service
  attitudes in behind-the-scene (back-room) employees by
  stressing how their jobs affect customers indirectly.
- All heavy phone users take a course in "Putting a Smile in
  Your Voice."
- Training is used to create teamwork and team spirit, stressing that everyone is a problem identifier or fixer (not a problem creator), we are all in the service business, and all departments have customers (and all of us are customers of other
  departments).

The Example of One Industry

Industries today are struggling with decreasing productivity, intense competition for employees and for business, and increasing

turnover. Fast-food executives and restaurant experts, among others, are looking to employee training as a solution to these problems. In the highly competitive fast-food business, formal training programs are viewed as a matter of survival; even during tight economic times training budgets are being maintained in restaurants and hotels as well.

As organizations struggle to create a perceptible difference in service, they find that it is not necessary to reinvent the wheel. They need merely look to see what others have done, and follow their example. The best example we know of is McDonald's.

Training at McDonald's is intensive and progressive. For each work station, there is a precise series of steps. Each employee

1. Reads the specifics about the particular work station.
2. Watches a precise audiovisual on the assigned work station and takes notes.
3. Receives additional personal instruction in a private or semi-private setting from the training coordinator.
4. Is assigned a buddy (a star/mentor) to help out. The mentor actually works the station, explains it in detail, and watches the trainee go through it. Accuracy is stressed before speed, and the objectives of the station are spelled out in detail.
5. Takes a basic knowledge test, oral and written.
6. Works the station alone but under observation and with ongoing feedback and progress reviews.
7. Receives a performance evaluation against specific standards and station objectives.
8. Moves on to the next station and repeats the process. This gives flexibility and versatility to the work force.

The continuous repetition of this kind of training does not allow one to forget. Mistakes are corrected positively and diplomatically but immediately. Psychologically, the employees want to prove that they are up to the task. Each detailed step has a detailed standard of performance attached to it (as we saw earlier in the chapter).

For each of the steps at the counter, training is detailed in huge operating manuals with lesson plans, specific audio-visuals, basic and advanced tests (oral and written), and objectives for each station. After trainees learn the basic steps involved in delivering accuracy and quality, they practice getting up to speed.

At Hamburger University, McDonald's teaches the value of devoting time and personal attention to crew training and discusses how it affects employee enthusiasm and involvement in the business. And McDonald's is not alone. The same meticulous attention to detail through rigorous training is being applied by most fast-food and other restaurants, hotels, banks, airlines, auto rental agencies, hospitals, and retail organizations. The competition is tough out there, and all are attempting to create a competitive edge by establishing that perceptible difference in the customer's mind.

How Others Do It

Franchisees of International Dairy Queen have learned that the biggest reason hourly employees leave Dairy Queen is a lack of proper training. When employees do not know what is expected of them, they naturally get frustrated, and then they quit.

The core of training at Church's Chicken is the Master Merchant program, which trains hourly employees in all aspects of the operation. A Master Merchant display board, which lists the names of all employees, is divided into three sections — cooking, serving, and processing. When an individual becomes skilled in one area (which is determined by a performance test, a one-on-one verbal quiz, and a written exam), the job slot is checked off. When all three slots are checked off, that person becomes a "team leader," with responsibility for orientation and training for new employees. A modest pay increase is also awarded. There are other forms of recognition, including pins for achievement and a special badge for mastering all three stations.

The Trans/Pacific Restaurants in California selectively screen employment candidates and then give them intensive training. Each manager selects two employees with outstanding skills to be training servers. They receive a small pay increase and take over the responsibility of teaching the operation to new employees. Each new employee is tested by the training server and by the manager, first at the end of the orientation period and then again after thirty days to maintain the standards.

At Pizza Inn in Dallas, training programs are conducted for both servers and managers. The goal is to foster one-on-one communication between the manager and every member of his or her service team.

Kentucky Fried Chicken has made a multi-million-dollar commitment to training, viewing training not as an expense but as an investment. And that investment has paid off! Because of training, turnover has been satisfactorily reduced and standards of quality, service, and cleanliness, as evaluated by mystery shoppers, are highly favorable.

After their initial interview and orientation sessions, new employees at one hotel are thoroughly trained before they are put to work at their particular station. Once on the job, they are given periodic refresher training to maintain their high standards.

Room attendants, for example, take a ten-session workshop. Early-morning classes are held twice a week for five weeks, with sessions covering the following:

- Policies, benefits, and rules
- Facts about the hotel and the chain
- Information on cleaning products
- Housekeeping terminology
- Staff organization
- Checking in, picking up keys, picking up supplies, cleaning hallway, checking work cart (slide presentation)
- How to clean a bathroom, make a bed, put on a pillowcase, dust, place items in guest room
- Emptying linen and trash sacks, stocking cart, cleaning linen closet, making evening report, bringing down cleaning supplies, signing out
- The care of equipment and hotel security

Then, in the final session, employees are tested on what they have learned.

Effective Training for Managers

Employees who are being prepared for positions as managers or supervisors are usually given the same training as other employees — and then some. To ensure uniformity in the communication and maintenance of service values and to avoid any possible erosion in standards, the role-model companies provide their managers with intensive training sessions. Each individual can plan on going back to school at least one week a year for training in a variety of areas, including the following:

- Selection interviewing for job-related behaviors
- Employee orientation
- Group dynamics and how to run a successful meeting
- Teaching and counseling
- Progress reviews and feedback
- One-on-one encounters as developmental opportunities
- Rewards and recognition
- Performance planning
- Performance standards
- Performance appraisal and feedback
- Constructive discipline that motivates
- Negotiation skills
- Conflict management
- Stress management
- Time management

These workshops are generally mandatory. In order to achieve consistency in the treatment of employees and customers, managers and supervisors must be trained. They must be provided with the skills to enable them to manage before they can be held accountable for results. The idea is that management can be learned, but it must be taught.

The purpose of these workshops is to provide managers and supervisors with the skills to enable them to lead and motivate well-trained employees, who will in turn be motivated to please the customers. We strongly advocate having the chairperson and the president visibly involved in an organization's training sessions. Having these leaders serve as behavioral role models helps employees put their training into practice. This is where it all begins — with total support and commitment. If other managers, supervisors, and employees observe the CEO's participation, the behaviors will stick.

McDonald's has a four-day management training program called "Managing the McDonald's Team," which has become a vital part of the curriculum of Hamburger University. Some of the topics covered in the four days include:

- Learning the manager's function
- Learning to set priorities
- Improving communications
- Motivating people
- Improving listening awareness
- Conducting reviews
- Recruiting and selecting crew members
- Recognizing signs of trouble
- Developing a store plan

Most of the learning is accomplished by role playing, simulation scenarios, and other participatory exercises.

At McDonald's, the best store managers and supervisors are selected to be full-time faculty members at Hamburger University. Teaching and training are judged to be too important to be left in the hands of the personnel department.

Evaluating the Training Program

How does an organization know if its training efforts are effective? How does a company determine whether training produces the intended results — fully satisfied customers and repeat business? Firms should always ask themselves, After training, what will have changed and how will we know it has changed? When will the changes take place, and what new skills will people have to acquire to cope?

In auditing the effectiveness of service training for consistency, management should use this approach: if sales and productivity figures are inconsistent, the likelihood is that the quality of the product or service is also inconsistent. A good overall philosophy is to give people responsibility and help and not bounce them for mistakes. Companies like to protect their expensive investment. Effective evaluations of training programs should address these questions:

- Which parts of the training were most effective, and why?
- Which parts of the training were least effective, and why?
- What was actually learned and retained?
- What was not learned or retained?
- How did the training help individuals do their job more effectively?
- Did customer satisfaction improve, and to what degree?
- What are the major problems now being experienced in relating to customers?
- What difficulties or obstructions were encountered in applying what was learned? Why?
- What can be done to prevent these problems in the future?
- Which parts of the training should have been expanded or deleted?
- What else should be included?

Several broader questions must be asked and answered as well. What are the needs — real and imagined — of the participants and of the customers? How can we translate both sets of needs into measurable training objectives? What evaluation techniques will we use to measure our training objectives? How can we design the class to meet these objectives? After the training program, we must analyze the data, report it, and follow up. As with performance standards, the results of training should permit specific, quantitative measures. These measures should show constant movement toward the goal of customer satisfaction, as we discuss further in the next chapter.

Chapter 6

MEASURE SERVICE PERFORMANCE AGAINST SUPERIOR BENCHMARKS

There is little question that the business of service is service. It's really a profit-driven concept, not a cost- or expense-driven concept.
— Joseph J. Melone
President
Prudential Insurance

    The CEO of a major fast-food organization recently announced the company's 107th consecutive quarter of record revenues and profits. A bystander commented, "That's outstanding!" The CEO glared at the bystander and responded, "How do you know?" His point was that the announced records could be judged as excellent or poor only on the basis of what was perceived as possible.

    While traditional financial measures are still grossly underutilized in most organizations as measures of performance and means of accountability, these measures are normally not sufficient. At the very least, every organization also needs systematic feedback from its customers to effectively gauge the costs of present financial performance and to capitalize on available opportunities.

Effective management and performance measurement of the modern organization requires at least three information systems. The most important is financial, and its use in most organizations is extremely restricted. The second information system is linked to customers, and the third is linked to employees. These three information systems, together with the employee-based behavioral performance standards discussed in the previous chapter, form the basis for setting the quantitative standards against which organization management can effectively be judged.

One common denominator among companies with a reputation for high-quality service is a demanding set of service standards and the *prodigious measurement* of how well those standards are met. The systems these companies use, and the questions they ask, are designed to produce results that employees can act upon. They focus on performance standards for the details that make up every business transaction: speed, accuracy, cordiality, helpfulness, completeness of information, response to inquiries, cleanliness, or whatever other elements best define their business from a customer's perspective.

If we are to intelligently manage all of the experiences of the customer in the total service cycle, we must have a precisely honed and accurate service delivery system. At any point in time, we must know exactly the status of a customer's order and account so that we can ensure customer satisfaction. In this and other respects, Federal Express comes close to the ideal, in our opinion.

On a visit to the hub of Federal Express in Memphis, Tennessee, we spoke to Tom Oliver, executive vice president of worldwide customer operations. What he told us raised our already high confidence levels in Federal Express. Oliver said that there are sixty different things that can go wrong with a package entrusted to Federal Express. The company's Service Quality Indicator (SQI) monitors and measures each of them. Being good is just not good enough for Federal Express; its goal is 100 percent accuracy and on-time delivery.

Federal Express's commitment to service superiority demands a high ongoing investment in technology. With this technology and commitment, the company can determine the exact status of a customer's package — any of the more than 1.6 million packages Federal Express delivers around the world each business day — within half an hour. Its success in this area is evidenced by a stunning percentage of repeat business — and by the fact that in 1990 Federal Express was the first company awarded the prestigious Malcolm Baldrige National Quality Award in the service category.

Appraising Customer Service Performance

Achieving a superior level of customer service, producing the kind of repeat business on which business success depends, is not a one-shot event. It demands a day-by-day, minute-by-minute dedication to preserving high standards. And that calls for a *systems approach,* including the periodic measurement of the gap between what is and what ought to be and the correction of any slips that show up.

The systems approach to customer service superiority is, in brief: first train to the exacting standards as defined; then continually audit performance against those standards to identify any possible slippage. During the course of the audit, it is important to examine these issues:

- What caused the poor performance? Inadequate experience, inability, or unwillingness on the part of employees? Understaffing or ineffective supervision?
- How frequently does the problem occur? How much has it grown? How important is it to the customer?
- Has the problem been contained, or does it continue to grow in size? What can be done about it?
- Who is affected by the problem (in addition to the customers)?
- What will happen if the problem is not corrected?
- What will it cost to solve the problem? How soon may we correct it permanently?

The Performance Review Process

The next step is to take these evaluations down to the individual level. Frequent individual performance reviews (or *appraisals*) are vital to customer service superiority. If you have done your homework in establishing service standards and measurements, the individual employee should really know in advance of the review just exactly how closely his or her performance matches the standards.

The performance appraisal should measure and evaluate the individual's contribution to business results and put the individual on the path toward improvement. In recognition of and appreciation for good work (and to improve lackluster performance), the appraisal should be related to the reward system; it should be an integral part of a fair and equitable system of compensation that rewards excellent performance.

The appraisal should stress accomplishment as opposed to personality and should identify an individual's strengths, weaknesses, and potential. It should provide (or trigger) specific guidance for improvement and training opportunities for professional growth and development; in doing so, it should help identify the better people and make them available for promotion (thus addressing the company's need for managers). The appraisal should help a manager evaluate his or her performance as a manager and bridge any communication gap between the manager and subordinates. It should look to future priorities and performance standards and result in specific, mutually agreeable goals for the next business cycle.

The Problem-Solving Approach to Performance Review

Having discussed what the performance review should accomplish, we now turn to logistics. We recommend the problem-solving approach to performance review, illustrated in Figure 6.1, which is designed to ensure a constructive, rather than a destructive (or even punitive), review. The first phase involves setting up a positive climate for the upcoming meeting. To help ensure that the subordinate understands the purpose of the review session, he or she is asked to prepare for the interview, and the role that the subordinate is expected to play — that of active participant — is emphasized. Both manager and subordinate prepare individually for the meeting, following the same preparation steps. Then, when the interview is conducted, the manager starts the session by putting the subordinate at ease. The manager must also set a constructive tone for the interview and clearly state the objectives of the session. The first objective is to evaluate the employee's present performance. In so doing, the manager should first listen to the subordinate's self-appraisal. Then the manager should present a prepared evaluation of the subordinate's present job performance, discuss with the subordinate any areas of difference, and work toward agreement.

The manager and subordinate should then analyze the causes of inadequate present performance. These causes might include the following:

- The subordinate's confusion about what was expected
- The subordinate's unawareness of performance problems
- The subordinate's lack of certain skills necessary for effective job performance
- The subordinate's lack of motivation
- Uncontrollable factors that affect the subordinate's performance

After analyzing the causes of inadequate performance, the manager and subordinate should prepare for the future by developing plans to improve performance and identifying specific action steps. The manager should then conclude the session, after first confirming agreements, making his or her feelings known (and asking about the subordinate's feelings), and deciding whether another meeting is needed. As a final step, the manager should follow up on the performance review meeting by completing final documentation, arranging for future development activities, monitoring progress against objectives, and giving timely feedback.

Performance Review Guidelines and Assessment

Another way to think about the performance review process is presented graphically in Figure 6.2, which suggests some questions that will help a manager stay on target when planning and conducting the appraisal.

Figure 6.1. The Problem-Solving Approach to Performance Review.

Setting the Climate

```
┌──────────────────────┐
│     Manager's        │──────────────────────────────►
│    Preparation       │
└──────────────────────┘
```

• Review the key job responsibilities
  of the subordinate's position.

• Review current performance objectives.

• Review the personal qualities needed
  in the subordinate's position.

• Prepare a tentative evaluation of the
  subordinate's performance in the
  current job.

• Think about ways of improving
  inadequate performance.

• Secure second-level approval of
  the appraisal.

```
              ┌──────────────────────┐
              │    Subordinate's     │
              │     Preparation      │
              └──────────────────────┘
```

• Review the key job responsibilities
  of the position.

• Review current performance objectives.

• Review the personal qualities needed
  in the position.

• Make a tentative self-appraisal of
  job performance.

• Think about ways of improving
  inadequate performance.

Figure 6.1. The Problem-Solving Approach to Performance Review, Cont'd.

Conducting the Interview

Concluding the Process

Starting the Session

Following Up

• Put the subordinate at ease.

• Complete performance
appraisal documentation.

• Set a constructive tone.

• Arrange for future
developmental activities.

• State the objectives for the meeting.

Evaluating Present
Performance

• Monitor the subordinate's
progress against objectives.

• Give timely feedback to
the subordinate.

• Listen to the subordinate's
self-appraisal.

• Present the manager's evaluation.

• Discuss differences of opinion
and reach agreement.

• Analyze the causes of inadequate
performance.

Planning for the Future

• Develop plans to build on current
performance in the present job.

• Identify specific action steps.

Closing the Session

• Confirm agreements.

• Discuss feelings about meeting.

• Ask whether another meeting is desirable.

Figure 6.2. Performance Review Guidelines.

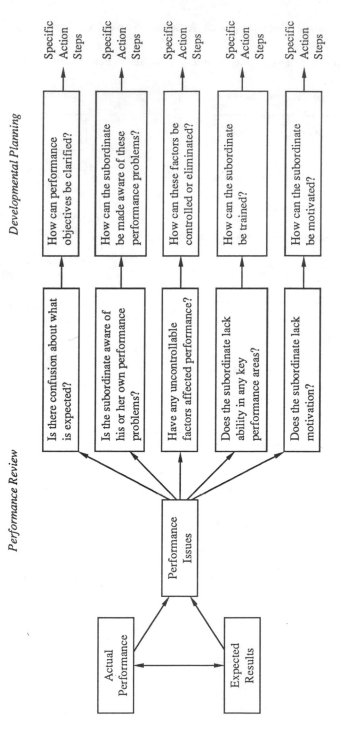

Performance Review

Developmental Planning

Actual Performance

Expected Results

Performance Issues

Is there confusion about what is expected?

Is the subordinate aware of his or her own performance problems?

Have any uncontrollable factors affected performance?

Does the subordinate lack ability in any key performance areas?

Does the subordinate lack motivation?

How can performance objectives be clarified?

How can the subordinate be made aware of these performance problems?

How can these factors be controlled or eliminated?

How can the subordinate be trained?

How can the subordinate be motivated?

Specific Action Steps

Specific Action Steps

Specific Action Steps

Specific Action Steps

Specific Action Steps

A good manager recognizes that the performance appraisal is a tense time and accepts responsibility for conducting the interview in a positive, constructive way. Sensitive managers may well want to appraise their own performance and ask themselves these questions in retrospect.

- Did I have clear objectives?
- Was the purpose of the interview made clear to the interviewee?
- Did I make the interviewee feel comfortable?
- Did I avoid doing other things while conducting the interview?
- Were my introductory remarks well prepared?
- Did I try to develop a good atmosphere for the interview?
- How well was rapport established with the interviewee?
- How well did I overcome any defensive attitude on the part of the interviewee?
- Did I talk on the interviewee's level, in familiar terms?
- Did I instill confidence?
- Did I listen carefully?
- Did I make an attempt to understand the interviewee's viewpoint?
- Did I avoid interrupting?
- Did I avoid snap judgments?
- Was I primarily nonjudgmental in my attitude?
- Did I look for hidden indications of how the interview was going?
- Did I give the interviewee the opportunity to express feelings and emotions?
- Was I objective?
- Was I interested in what the interviewee was telling me?
- Was I encouraging to the interviewee?
- Did I use the technique of reflecting the interviewee's views and feelings?
- Did I avoid asking closed and dead-end questions?
- Did I summarize what had been said and decided?
- Did I give the other person an opportunity to ask questions?
- Was I repetitious?

- Did I give the interviewee the opportunity to formulate his or her own plans?
- Did I give unwarranted assurances?
- Did I try to get the interviewee to recognize his or her own problems?

Performance Coaching

Closely allied to performance appraisal is the one-on-one technique we call *performance coaching*. It is an essential part of the total evaluation process and the systems approach to service superiority. It serves to maintain consistency in service over time.

Each of us views our job as advancing our own ends in the business world and helping us become as successful as possible. And rightly so. But our success depends very largely and directly on our ability to make the people we manage as productive and successful as possible.

One of the most effective tools in accomplishing this is performance coaching, a management tool that helps managers identify and correct the real causes of nonperformance. To improve an employee's behavior, it is necessary to first identify what the employee is doing that is unsatisfactory. In an extraordinary number of cases, employees either do not know that their performance is not satisfactory or do not know what is supposed to be done or how to do it. It is the task of the manager to clarify any of these points for the employee so that corrective action can be taken. Performance coaching can help in this task, as we show step by step.

Reach Agreement on the Problem

A one-on-one performance interview must be set up to review unsatisfactory performance with the employee (either as part of the formal performance appraisal or as problems arise). Hold the discussion in a private place where it will not be overheard; make sure that no one else is present and that no interruptions will occur. Get away from the office or work area, with all its distractions; avoid holding the discussion in a car when either of you is at the wheel. Allow plenty of time for the discussion.

Do your homework on the unsatisfactory performance in question, and make sure that you are not making vague, general accusations. For example, if the problem is the employee's failure to handle difficult customers, have information at hand on specific incidents: who did what and how each reacted—the employee and the customer. Decide three things in advance: (1) what minimum action is acceptable as the outcome of the discussion, (2) what possible alternative solutions there may be, and (3) what the timetable for performance improvement should be.

The first part of the performance discussion—getting the employee to agree that a problem exists—is the most critical and may take half the total time. Agreement may not be as simple as it sounds, because many employees feel that their performance in certain areas is no better or worse than people around them: "Everybody else is late too. Why are you picking on me?" Or they cannot comprehend that what they are doing constitutes a problem: "Oh, I didn't realize that I was being defensive or argumentative with the customers."

The best way to convince an employee that a problem exists is to make clear the consequences of unsatisfactory performance on several levels: to the customer, to the company, to fellow employees, and to the employee personally. For example, you could say, "By arguing with that customer, you aggravated the situation and upset others within earshot." Or, "When you're absent from your work station a number of times during the day, someone else has to double up to cover your absence." If employees do not see their actions as a problem, they can hardly appreciate the consequences to themselves of what they are doing or failing to do. "I can't advance your name for promotion unless you improve your attendance to a satisfactory level." Or, "How can I give you an outstanding rating at the front counter unless the customer is satisfied?" The key here is to have the employee say, in these or similar words, "Yes, I agree that that's a problem." Only then can you move ahead.

Discuss a Variety of Possible Solutions

Next comes a mutual discussion of solutions. Where there are alternatives available, it is important not to rank solutions or immediately choose the most desirable but simply to brainstorm all possible solutions that you and the employee can think of. Even the solutions that sound least likely may trigger an idea from the other person. Remember, too, that this is a mutual process; both of you should contribute. If the employee cannot contribute, then you must provide the necessary solutions. But as much as possible, allow the employee to suggest the remedies to be taken.

Obtain Agreement on Implementing Solutions

The next step is to arrive at mutual agreement on which step will be implemented. "Okay, I'll start by catching the earlier train and then walk from the station to work so I don't have to depend on the bus." Or, "I'll make personal calls only on my coffee break." The problem employee may want to settle for a general solution — "Okay, I'll do better." But you are after specific solutions, resulting in specific improvements that you can both agree on and measure. "I agree to be at work every day unless it's absolutely impossible for me to do so." Or, "I'll make sure no customer leaves without a satisfactory solution to the problem."

Follow Up to Prevent Slippage

The fourth step is yours. You must follow up to make sure that the solutions you and the employee agreed on are implemented. If you do not take this step, all your work will have been wasted. Do not assume that your employee will make the changes; instead, audit and measure them yourself. You may encounter some resistance on this point from the employee, but remember that your job as a manager is to make sure that your employees are performing their jobs successfully. Explain to them that if you did not do your job and follow up their performance, you would be remiss on your own behalf as well as on theirs.

In many cases, employees *do* change and implement positive solutions to performance problems — but only temporarily. If you as a manager do not reinforce employee actions, employees can easily slip back into their previous bad habits. If an employee fails to maintain improved performance, you must know about it and offer your continuing help. This may consist of going back to the list of alternatives and mutually choosing some new solutions if the previous ones did not work. Or it may mean clearing from the path some obstacles to the achievement of these solutions. "Why don't we role play, and you be the disgruntled customer?"

Perhaps you must offer the employee further clarification of what you expect him or her to do, when it must be done, and how you will both know when it is done; for example, if a customer apologizes for being rude, it is clear that the employee remained calm and helpful throughout the discussion. To make sure that you are both on the same wavelength, ask the employee to summarize his or her understanding of the discussion. This lets you end the coaching session on a note of mutual agreement.

Recognize and Compliment Achievement

The last step is one of the most important in performance coaching. You must recognize *any* achievement when it happens. Do not wait for perfection, or even for 75 percent improvement. When employees demonstrate a noticeable improvement, your recognition can let them know that they are on the right track toward solving the problem completely. Recognize any achievement and reinforce it as soon as possible after it happens. Thank employees in person for improvement and keep on providing recognition as long as improvement continues.

If you promised a certain reward for improvement, come through with it. And do not keep promising the same reward for improvement in different areas. Find a different incentive for different solutions.

Following these five performance-coaching steps — getting agreement that a problem exists, mutually discussing alternative solutions, mutually agreeing on remedies to be taken, following up and measuring results, and recognizing any achievement promptly — will ensure your own success as a manager by helping your employees be as successful as possible.

Evaluating the Manager

If there is one constant theme in the maintenance of service superiority, it is the importance of behind-the-scenes motivation to foster positive service attitudes. Managers help employees develop these attitudes by thorough training, constructive appraisals, and effective corrective coaching. Let us not forget that the managers themselves receive their share of training, evaluation, and retraining. In the service leaders, the very high standards of service superiority are never compromised to achieve short-term profits.

The performance appraisals of each restaurant's management team at McDonald's reflect this philosophy. They underlie all aspects of the manager's performance review, which includes service components ranging from product freshness, to crew development, to making time for the customer, to cleanliness.

On each of more than thirty service items — and many others — each member of the management team is rated as above standard, standard, or below standard. If the majority of the ratings are not above standard, it is time to retrain.

In addition, McDonald's has an informal review process for managers called Communication Days — a process that provides managers with the opportunity to meet with area supervisors for a time of idea sharing and performance improvement. It is a blend of evaluation and training, and thus it exemplifies the total systems approach that typifies the companies that lead their industries in service superiority.

In each restaurant, one day each month — a Communication Day — is reserved for the area supervisor to spend time individually with each of the four or five members of the restaurant management team. The managers and assistant managers have the opportunity to discuss with the area supervisor their progress, their personal and professional goals, their training and advancement opportunities, their overall future with the company, and anything else that is on their minds.

The single biggest advantage in our observation is the rapport built between the area supervisors and their management teams. Communication Days are opportunities to change behavior, to discuss and resolve special problems, to answer questions, to provide information and feedback, and to build on individual strengths while providing for development needs.

This systems approach to service dedication can be found in any area, any industry. To emphasize the link between performance standards and performance appraisal, here is an example of a review spectrum for managers. It would be used to evaluate a supervisor who is responsible for management of five or six other supervisors of functional departments. The review spectrum defines four skill areas and gives performance standards for each.

1. *Oral and written communication.* Defined as effectiveness in stand-up presentations, one-on-one encounters, conciseness and precision of words, accurate and timely reports, keeping senior management informed, and providing constructive input on policy issues and effective exchange of relevant information with other departments.

> *Above*
> *Standard*
> - Demonstrates ability and interest in the need for policy change by frequently initiating or contributing to discussion on policy issues.
> - Keeps senior updated on all major problems and actions taken, whether internally or externally generated.
>
> *Standard*
> - Passes information needed by other departments to those departments as requested; at times anticipates the need.
> - Forgets to inform management of major changes; does not work effectively with other departments on occasion because of misinformation.
>
> *Below*
> *Standard*
> - Provides reports that are often late, incomplete, and difficult to read.

2. *Communication with subordinate managers.* Defined as demonstrated recognition of the importance of keeping team management informed of goals, direction, plans, progress, and information generally needed to improve operating efficiency.

Above   • Regularly distributes pertinent information in
Standard   a timely manner to subordinate managers on
    all aspects that affect their operations.
        • Keeps managers informed of any changes in
    policy, procedure, or direction.
Standard • Ensures that managers pass on information
    from the supervisors' staff meeting.
        • Does not listen well to subordinates; monopo-
    lizes the conversation and is too casual about
    the manner in which information is passed down.
Below   • Does not provide unit managers with necessary
Standard   information concerning policies, procedures,
    and changes in direction.

3. *Training and development.* Defined as demonstrated interest
in and concern for the effectiveness of team training, including such issues as training requirements, priorities,
progress, recognition programs, and promotional opportunities for unit managers.

Above   • Delegates responsibility, accountability, and au-
Standard   thority commensurate with the manager's abil-
    ities to accept same.
        • Primarily supervises in a general sense, stress-
    ing operational effectiveness.
        • Provides for profit walk-throughs along with au-
    dits of service quality and housekeeping on a
    regular basis with unit managers.
Standard • Participates in unit manager meetings on a
    regular basis. Conducts oral and written exami-
    nations of trainee progress.
        • Seldom has training meetings for assistance.
        • Does not keep well informed of trainee progress.
Below   • Makes decisions for others and is not involved
Standard   in training assistants.

4. *Problem solving.* Defined as the ability to recognize the real
causes of problems as opposed to mere symptoms, to involve subordinates in problem-solving procedures, to implement creative solutions to problems so that they do not

recur, to involve unit managers in the problem-solving process, and to quickly identify potential problems and prevent them from arising.

Above • Offers timely solutions to problems when dis-
Standard   cussing them with upper management.
Standard • Is good at solving short-term problems but is
            not adept at attaining longer-term solutions. Is
            risk-adversive. Can usually identify problems
            but procrastinates in solving them. Looks to
            others for solutions.
Below • Allows small problems to become major prob-
Standard   lems because of inaction.

In a similar vein, evaluation standards are established for such areas as uniform and consistent application of company policies, relationships with managers in other departments, acceptance and fulfillment of administrative responsibilities, personnel relations with hourly employees, and personnel relations with subordinate unit managers.

The key point to be made here is that if standards are not used to measure the effectiveness of what happens within the organization or the individual function, systems will eventually break down. In the long run, the customer will suffer — and then the bottom line. A logical next step toward service superiority, then, is that of determining how the company's customers perceive the services provided.

Measuring Customer Service Results with Surveys

If service superiority is to be maintained, companies must have a clear, measurable picture of how their customers perceive them. One mistake can cost a major customer. Fortunately, the so-called soft areas, such as employee relations and customer service, can now be quantified and directly related to an organization's economic prosperity. The primary vehicle for accomplishing this is the survey.

At least once annually the service role models survey

everyone who has a relationship with the organization, to ask, "How well are we doing?" Survey data are gathered from customers, employees, supervisors, managers, community members, visitors, and internal clients. All survey participants are encouraged to "tell it like it is," and their individual anonymity and confidentiality are guaranteed, since the results are sent directly to an outside consultant and tabulated by a computer.

Surveys tell management what people at all levels of the organization perceive to be the real values of that organization. This is particularly important, because employees behave in accordance with their perceptions of what is rewarded and what is not. If, for example, more than 25 percent of survey respondents disagreed with a statement such as "The best performers get the highest rewards," management would have a serious problem.

Another excellent reason for periodically asking people their opinions is the underlying message that is conveyed. Management is in effect saying to those surveyed — employees and customers — "You are important to us and we respect you. We care about you, and we will use your input to make this a better place to work and do business."

A survey provides a quantitative snapshot of an organization's health at a given point in time. It is designed to elicit specific opinions on specific subjects from specific groups of people. A survey literally measures what people perceive to be the facts in a given situation. And because people act according to their perceptions, survey information is vital.

Surveys are highly important to management, because they measure levels of satisfaction and dissatisfaction with the organization's products and services. They measure how well or how poorly an organization is functioning internally, in terms of how the various departments and functions service each other. They measure employee satisfaction and dissatisfaction with management. For example, professionally prepared and customized survey data can predict with considerable accuracy whether or not there will be a union organizing drive and who will win it.

Survey data can also predict management and employee

turnover. Suppose a management climate survey reveals that 25 percent of the managers do not feel free to make decisions and take independent action necessary to perform their jobs. How long do you suppose those 25 percent are going to stay around?

Perhaps most important of all, surveys can tell a company what its customers think. When McDonald's conducted surveys of customer satisfaction, it learned exactly how many people would come back for repeat business and how many would choose to go elsewhere to eat.

Certainly, businesses can get a feel for the degree of customer dissatisfaction through a review of complaint logs, returns and allowances, letters of complaint, phone calls, employee and management turnover, grievances, strikes, slowdowns, theft, and sabotage. But it is impossible to quantify precisely the degree of dissatisfaction or pinpoint the real issues and concerns without survey data.

Our recommendation concerning which surveys to use, and the priority order in which to use them, follows.

- *The management climate survey.* This survey measures the degree to which supervisors and managers are satisfied with the way the organization is managed and, in particular, with how well *they* are managed. It makes sense for management to puts its own house in order first.
- *The employee opinion survey.* This survey tells supervisors and managers what employees think and how they feel about their bosses, pay, benefits, working conditions, security, and opportunity for advancement and elicits their perceptions of how well or how poorly they are managed. If employee dissatisfaction is high, customer dissatisfaction with service practices will be equally high. Employees simply do not respond with enthusiasm to customer demands if their basic job-related needs are not being fulfilled.
- *The customer satisfaction survey.* This survey feeds back to management how customers feel about service policies, practices, and procedures at the point of sale and the point of complaint. It gives management precise information on the degree of dissatisfaction with its products, services, and personnel.

- *The internal client survey.* This survey measures how well the different departments, functions, and people within an organization service each other's needs. The idea behind the internal client (or customer) survey is that the customer cannot be serviced properly if the individual who provides that service does not know what is needed. Each department is a customer of other departments, and each provides services to other departments. As you might imagine, the service role models pay a great deal of attention to the interdependence of service teams within their organizations. They measure the quality, timeliness, accuracy, courtesy, and responsiveness of the departments that service each other's needs for information, materials, supplies, or services.

The Survey Process

Businesses that have never conducted surveys may have some questions about how to proceed. The key issues to be decided are discussed below.

Using a Consultant

We recommend that an outside consultant always be used, if for no other reason than to guarantee the participants' complete anonymity and the survey's confidentiality. In many organizations, there is a high negative response rate to questions dealing with the degree of openness and trust in management. This lack of trust carries through to the survey data itself.

Doing everything in-house is certainly more economical, but it greatly increases the likelihood of data distortion. If there is any suspicion at all, people will not give honest answers. They will tell management what it wants to hear. For example, a hospital conducted an in-house survey of employee attitudes and received highly favorable results. To their surprise, two months later they experienced a union organizing drive.

Employees concerned about survey anonymity even with an outside consultant may be reassured by a "lock box." The consultant can explain the survey—the how and the why and what will happen afterward — and then step into the background. In such circumstances, employees are likely to complete the survey and drop it in the lock box with no reservations, knowing that the consultant will soon be off to the airport with the box. The impersonality of the process allows employees to feel more comfortable and encourages them to provide honest answers to some very touchy questions.

Determining Survey Frequency

Under normal circumstances, each of the surveys should be conducted once a year. Our preference is to do one of the four each quarter. This gives a company four quarterly snapshots, four different perspectives of an organization's health, at four separate times within a calendar year.

If survey results show high percentages of dissatisfaction and game plans to address survey findings are quickly set into motion, we recommend using that same instrument to survey that same population six months later. One year is too long to wait to find out what impact changing management practices had on important issues and concerns.

Suppose you had one or more of these four conditions in the first quarter of your fiscal year: a large layoff, a union organizing drive, a significant increase in the size of the work force, or an extremely unfavorable survey result. The rule of thumb for any of those conditions is to survey semiannually.

Dealing with the Results

A survey of any nature raises the expectations of the population surveyed. When employees, customers, supervisors, and managers give their input, it is with the clear expectation that management fully intends to respond positively, quickly, and thoroughly to the issues and concerns raised.

If management is unwilling to commit itself to feeding back survey results to all participants, and to actually addressing survey findings as quickly as possible, it is better not to do the survey at all. Conducting a survey but failing to take action says to the employees, "We're only trying to be nice; we never really intended to use your ideas anyway." The first showing should be in private with the chief executive officer and the chief operating officer, to whom the overall results should be explained in detail.

But sharing the results is only the first step. Turning the survey data into an action plan that will address the problems revealed by the survey is the linchpin for the entire process.

Table 6.1 displays an action plan developed by a training manager at Procter & Gamble.

A word of caution: attitude and climate survey results should not be used to hold a manager's feet to the fire, to bully a person into behavioral change, or as an excuse for discharging someone. A survey will lose all credibility with participants if the results are used to initiate personnel actions such as terminations.

Instead, first familiarize supervisors and managers with the implications of survey results and their potential impact on productivity, profitability, and service. Discuss the situation, not the individual. Seek ways to manage more effectively. Neither give nor withhold rewards for first-time survey results.

When commitments are made and action plans put together, the annual follow-up survey then becomes a basis for possible actions. At this stage, people may be held accountable for survey results because they will have made certain commitments, have been given certain management skills training, and have had a full year to initiate corrective actions based on survey findings.

When you seek a standard for evaluating attitude survey data, the most useful norms are your own data. Compare the different departments with each other and with the overall norms for the organization. Then compare both against themselves through the annual follow-up survey.

Choosing the Survey Instrument

Now let us look at the four types of surveys in some detail. Each contributes significant details to an organization profile.

The Management Climate Survey

A management climate survey measures what people perceive to be the real values of the corporation. It examines how people react to an organization's culture — its values, norms, traditions, social mores, and sacred cows.

People behave in accordance with what they believe to be true. It is these very standards of expected behavior that determine how decisions are made and how problems are solved within an organization. These perceptions of values affect the performance of the management team, the individual's motivation, and the total collective performance of the business unit.

A management climate survey may include from 25 to 100 questions or more and can be customized to focus on certain aspects of an organization. A sample survey is contained in Appendix B.

Most management climate surveys attempt to measure most of the following categories:

- Clarity of an organization's goals and overall direction, coupled with a clear, shared understanding by its managers and supervisors of the plan for achieving these goals.
- Effectiveness of the decision-making processes in terms of quality, timeliness, and implementation.
- Organization integration, cooperation, and vitality: As a company, is the organization dynamic, healthy, and growing?
- Effectiveness of individual managers: How well do various managers use their subordinates and how well do they treat them?
- Degree of openness and trust: Are people encouraged to speak up and voice dissenting opinions, or is a premium placed on not making waves?
- Job satisfaction: To what degree do employees enjoy their work, pay, benefits?
- Opportunities for individual growth and development: Is there a chance to learn new skills that will develop the talents and potential of individual employees?
- Performance orientation and accountability: Are expecta-

tions and performance standards clearly spelled out? Does the system really reward results achieved?

- Team effectiveness and problem solving: Are work goals for the department or the work unit clear to all and shared by all?
- Overall confidence in management: Are the employees comfortable with the way the organization is being run?

In order to determine just what the management style of a company is, the management climate survey is designed to measure both the effectiveness of individual managers and the overall leadership effectiveness. To guarantee anonymity and confidentiality, the survey results should go directly to an outside consultant and feedback should be reported in cohesive work units of no less than five to ten people.

Here are some representative questions that deal with the effectiveness of individual managers. Survey participants are asked to give their honest and frank opinions by selecting one of five choices in response to each question: definitely agree, inclined to agree, undecided/don't know, inclined to disagree, or definitely disagree.

The person to whom I report . . .

- Thoroughly understands my job
- Deals fairly and objectively with everyone
- Periodically lets me know how well I am doing
- Is relatively easy to see when I have a problem
- Goes out of his or her way to solve problems with tact and diplomacy
- Gives me all the information I need to do a good job
- Respects me as an individual
- Listens patiently to what I have to say
- Encourages suggestions and input from me
- Coaches me in my personal development
- Appraises my performance fairly
- Plans his or her work very well
- Shares decisions affecting my work and my future with me
- Supports me in my decisions
- Actively encourages communication and cooperation with other departments

- Encourages me to take reasonable risks
- Provides positive feedback to me when I perform my job well
- Communicates his or her expectations concerning my job performance

Suppose that your organization's managers and supervisors participated in a management climate survey. Imagine how your goals and productivity might be affected if 25 percent or more of the participants responded with the following kinds of written comments:

- What business plan? Everything around here is a crisis; priorities are constantly changing.
- Will someone please tell me what I'm responsible and accountable for? What are the performance standards for my job? On what basis am I being measured?
- No one ever asks my opinion or tells me what's going on.
- When my manager asks for suggestions, he seldom uses them.
- The best performers don't get the biggest pay increases.
- How does my work relate to that of others in the organization? I don't know.

These are actual examples of write-in comments from participants in management climate surveys. If real issues such as these can be resolved, a 20 to 30 percent increase — or more — in productivity may be achieved.

The Employee Opinion Survey

An employee opinion survey is designed to solicit feedback from employees at all levels of the organization concerning how they feel about their jobs, pay, benefits, working conditions, advancement opportunities, and recognition and respect received. This survey tells senior management how employees at every level feel about conditions that can both positively and negatively affect absenteeism, turnover, product and service quality, costs, and productivity. It also asks employees about the effectiveness

Table 6.1. Sample Action Plan.

Issue	Action Plan	Timing	Responsibility
1. Compensation and Benefits			
Need for more information	Publish explanations in employee publication	Quarterly	Personnel
Desire for recognition	Issue employee handbook	October implementation	Personnel
Need for competitiveness in compensation	Conduct service award ceremonies	Annually	Personnel
	Publish CAP reports more frequently	Quarterly	Benefits administration
	Conduct annual benefits surveys	Annually	Corporate benefits
2. Management-Employee Relations Review of process/results achieved at weekly staff meetings			
3. Supervisory Relations Need for better explanation for performance expectation/ standards	Identify training packages •Performance appraisal •Coaching/counseling	September implementation	Personnel
4. Career Development Poor new-employee orientation	Develop orientation program •History of company •Policies/procedures •Supervisory skills	June-September implementation •September •September •September	Personnel/managers

No coaching for career growth	Identify training needs for improved job performance	Complete	Personnel
Poor training on the job		Ongoing implementation	Managers/personnel
5. Working Conditions			
Inadequate space	Move some units out of Tower 1	September	R&D facilities
	Redesign floors 2, 3, 4	September	Personnel/facilities
	Move employees	December	Personnel/facilities
6. Management and Operating Effectiveness			
Inadequate staffing levels	Identify needs in resource plan	Annually (March-May)	All departments
Poor communications that inhibit productivity	Conduct state-of-the business speech	Twice annually	Vice president and general manager
	Issue newsletter	Monthly	Personnel
	Share departmental objectives and progress	January and June	Personnel/departmental managers
	Conduct staff meetings	Weekly	Departmental meetings
	Issue policy manuals	September	Finance/personnel
	Conduct (A) orientation and (B) training	(A) As needed (B) Quarterly	Personnel

Source: Adapted from G. D. Searle Consumer Products Division, a division of Procter & Gamble.

of their bosses as managers and measures people's feelings about the organization's effectiveness — for example, cooperation and teamwork, goals and direction. Further, it measures the impact of the performance appraisal process and its ties to the reward system.

Results should be reported down through the first line of supervision and reviewed with each work unit. A plan to address and correct weaknesses and areas of concern should be prepared, with responsibilities clearly assigned and target dates definitely established. A systematic, timely review of the progress made should be shared with all levels of management and all survey participants.

A suggested format for an employee survey is included in Appendix E. That survey focuses on employees' perspectives on management's commitment to service superiority. We can think of no more important focus for an employee survey because, as should be clear by now, the employees' opinions and feelings in this respect are critical if the company is to become a leader in customer service and satisfaction. (The focus of the employee survey can obviously be adjusted as necessary, however.)

The importance of employee surveys to the overall health of the company is illustrated by the example of a pharmaceutical firm that had no experience with employee surveys. During a focus group convened to address the lack of employee involvement, employees mentioned specific machine and layout changes that would reduce the need for many of the temporary workers that the firm was employing. When the focus-group leader asked why the idea had not been presented to the shift supervisor, a host of reasons emerged, all of which involved a general lack of trust in management and a specific perception that the shift supervisor was resistant to constructive change.

When the focus-group leader presented the idea to upper management, the plant engineer indicated that a similar idea had been considered earlier but had been abandoned in the rush to get the plant constructed and operating. At the plant manager's suggestion, the idea was explored further. The cost of implementation was projected at $78,000. Conservative annual material and labor savings were projected to be $118,000.

The change was implemented within ninety days, and the employees were recognized and rewarded for their contribution.

The plant manager later observed that the real loss was not a simple six-figure cost savings. Rather, he wondered, "How many of my 400 employees could make similar contributions if they were managed effectively?"

To capture this kind of information — general information and employee attitudes as well as specific suggestions for reform — many organizations use employee opinion surveys. If effectively conducted, these surveys supply organization managers with quantitative information to help them identify strengths and opportunities to improve their organizations.

A special kind of employee survey is the exit interview, given when employees leave the company for whatever reason. If handled with sensitivity, the exit interview can provide companies with particularly useful information from an insider's perspective. The goal is to find out why employees are leaving an organization in hopes of stopping the flow of blood. We might think of the exit interview as a postmortem on management effectiveness. A sample exit interview questionnaire, showing the main points that should be included, appears in Appendix F.

The Customer Satisfaction Survey

It is necessary to monitor customer service performance to determine how effective an organization's service policies, practices, and procedures are. A customer satisfaction survey tells the company where and how to take corrective action.

Many organizations already have available to them sources of information about customer satisfaction. The following kinds of systems should be monitored regularly, for they can provide insight:

Complaint logs
Records of product quality
Records of service quality
Billings
Credits

Accounts receivable
Returns and allowances
Delivery problems
Letters from customers
Comment cards and other suggestion systems
Records of time lapsed between receipt of a complaint
   and corrective action
Callbacks
Calls in on a toll-free number
Sales representative and merchandiser feedback
Service representative feedback
Direct solicitation for customer feedback

One characteristic of service leaders is that they regularly seek out customer feedback, analyze it, and use the results in decision making, to close the loop on internal measurements. There are many methods of soliciting customer feedback. The best and most innovative service leaders make use of a wide variety — from surveys, questionnaires, customer focus groups, customer appreciation days, toll-free numbers, personal visits, and direct phone contact.

We strongly urge you to have each of your top managers call four to five key customers to ask the following questions:

- Why did you start doing business with us?
- Why do you continue to do business with us?
- What do you like most about our relationship, products, and/or services?
- What do you like least about our relationship, products, and/or services?
- What (specifically) would you change to improve the relationship, products, and/or services?
- If you were to leave us and go to a competitor, what would your major reason be?
- Do you have any other suggestions for us?

Then summarize and pool the responses and hold a staff meeting, preferably off the premises, to develop an action plan based upon what your managers have learned in these calls.

Some companies base their ongoing customer surveys on the survey used to establish external customer standards in the first place. This method provides very detailed feedback and can be an accurate gauge of the company's performance in meeting its standards. You have probably encountered some of these surveys as a customer of hotels and airlines. Samples of such questionnaires are included in Appendix G, but these samples are just a beginning. An organization is limited only by its imagination if it really wants to find out what its customers think about its products and services.

Kampgrounds of America, headquartered in Billings, Montana, for example, uses an effective and innovative method. Every employee solicits guest feedback at social functions, at meals, and at check-in and check-out times. They keep what is called an "incident book" to record good and bad experiences. At regular staff meetings, the employees review these experiences and plan how to capitalize on and reinforce the good and eliminate the negative.

We cannot overstate the importance of tracking service quality and customer satisfaction. If you are in manufacturing, for example, you should track your missed shipments, your partial shipments, complaints, delays, and damaged goods. If you can discover the nature and the frequency of your problems, you can solve them. As an example, we know of an industrial rubber-goods wholesaler who was losing business. He decided to track his service quality and discovered a shipping-error rate of ten errors a month. The errors included missed shipments, partial shipments, delays, and damaged goods. To compensate for the inconvenience experienced by his customers as a result of the errors, he instituted a new policy. For every mistake (no matter how small) affecting a customer, that customer would receive $25 and an apology. The wholesaler set aside a monthly reserve of $250 to cover the ten errors. He told his employees that they could keep whatever was left of the $250 reserve at the end of the month. The errors quickly went down to two a month, and his business improved greatly.

Whether customers are polled, submit unsolicited comments, or respond to surveys, management should review the results very seriously to see how well their promise of service was fulfilled by the delivery and to what degree the organization performed according to its own exacting standards.

In the better hotels, for example, anything less than a 95 percent favorable response in customer surveys calls for immediate action. An investigation is conducted. Standards are reviewed. More training is given where necessary. A hard look is taken at operational details to determine where and how slippage occurred. No stone is left unturned until things are made right and action has been taken to prevent a recurrence.

The Internal Client Survey

The internal client (or customer) survey is designed to measure how effectively the various departments within an organization respond to each other's needs and requirements. This type of survey quantifies people's perceptions of how effectively their business needs are being serviced within the organization. Among other relevant aspects, a survey can measure the quality, timeliness, and responsiveness of the several departments or subsidiaries in terms of the products and services they provide for each other.

Each department should be asked to evaluate how well the departments that impact it satisfy its particular needs and to evaluate how well it meets other departments' needs. The evaluation is made according to standards for critical service encounters. Those standards that we find especially telling (see discussion in Chapter Five) are listed across the top in Table 6.2; you may substitute or add others. Departmental evaluations of how others are satisfying their needs and how they are satisfying other departments' needs are then compared with one another, and discrepancies and differences are noted and discussed.

A second style of internal client survey is included in Appendix H. Regardless of the form used, the idea behind the internal client survey is that it is not possible to service customers properly if the organization does not have effective teamwork and cooperation among the various subsidiaries that supply each other with products or services. Excellence in customer service begins at home. Specific areas surveyed include the degree to which other departments do the following:

Table 6.2. Determining Internal Client Satisfaction.

Departments	Standards for Critical Service Encounters										
	Quality	Quantity	Accuracy	Timeliness	Responsiveness	Problem Solving	Concern	Anticipation	Joint Standards	Planning Effectiveness	Overall Satisfaction

Select the departments that impact your ability to meet the applicable performance standards. Then rank each of these departments. Use a scale of 1 to 3, in which 1 = outstanding, 2 = satisfactory, and 3 = needs improvement.

- Fulfill your requirements for quality of service
- Jointly predetermine standards for quality of service
- Deliver service commitments in a timely manner
- Identify specifically who should be consulted to solve a service-related problem
- Understand your work, problems, obstacles, and requirements
- Take the initiative in identifying and solving service-related problems
- Are concerned with improving their own service effectiveness
- Plan their work to better service your needs
- Have clearly defined goals and standards for internal service
- Reward excellence in internal client service

Following up on surveys of external and internal customers involves a process similar to following up on employee surveys and management climate surveys—communicating results, establishing a game plan, setting specific responsibilities, and making provision for monitoring and recording progress.

The alternatives to measuring employee and customer satisfaction against the standards and goals the company has set are not very pleasant. Managers throughout the organization will likely allocate funds based upon poor decisions and wrong priorities. Tasks and activities will dominate over results. Financial results will not meet expectations. In addition, employee morale and motivation will decline so low that standards of excellence in customer service will go unmet. Total service quality will erode, and customers will be lost. Given that these results are in direct contradiction to what organizations want, the effort required to measure satisfaction is more than repaid by surveys. And as we will see in the next chapter, the cost of putting these surveys to work—by rewarding employees—is minimal compared to the benefits possible.

Chapter 7

RECOGNIZE AND REWARD EXEMPLARY SERVICE BEHAVIOR

*People are the most important asset in our delivery system. We have
excellence awards to recognize superior, exemplary service. Recognition,
participation, a sense of contribution are important.*
> —Thomas R. Oliver
> Executive Vice President,
> Worldwide Customer Operations,
> Federal Express

Why is it that even the best-managed organizations in
the United States can improve their productivity by at least 20
percent? The answer is really quite simple. Employees will perform better if there is something in it for them.

Yet few employees believe that performance and results
are appropriately linked to pay. Not surprisingly, then, they
are less than motivated. In fact, some estimates suggest that
workers spend up to 50 percent of their time on the job idle—
or at least not working at tasks that promote the business of their
employer.

If this is the problem, what is the cure? Richard Bunning
has put his finger on it: "We believe that behaviors that are outstanding need to be rewarded in some manner, and in turn,
more outstanding behaviors will be repeated in the future."

149

Briefly, by rewarding and recognizing the right behavior, this behavior tends to repeat itself and we get the right results. Yet organizations typically pay bonuses and incentive compensation to only a select few senior-level officers; the people who do the work that results in the profits are excluded.

The fact is that rewards and recognition do work. They shape and reinforce the behaviors we desire. One of the most powerful motivating tools available to managers is positive reinforcement. Yet few managers use this tool spontaneously. Their reinforcement is either nonexistent or negative. Rarely having received positive reinforcement themselves, they find it difficult to give.

Positive reinforcement can take the form of either rewards or recognition — or better yet, both. *Rewards* deal with cash incentives such as bonuses, pay-for-performance systems, merit increases, and cash prizes. *Recognition,* on the other hand, deals with those management practices and systems that personally and publicly recognize the importance of the employee and employee contributions over and above the call of duty.

In this chapter, we outline methods of positive reinforcement and see how it is used in successful companies. In addition, we give some practical tips on how to give positive reinforcement and how to help make sure it exists throughout your company.

What Behaviors Should You Reward or Recognize?

The kinds of behaviors that should be rewarded are the job-related behaviors described in previous chapters. In other words, employees who consistently demonstrate above-standard performance in dependability, initiative, motivation, cooperation and teamwork, enthusiasm, integrity, honesty, flexibility, adaptability, sensitivity, interpersonal skills, effective communication, ability to work under pressure, and judgment and decision making should be rewarded handsomely.

Any reward system for individual contributors should also take into account such matters as speed, quality, and timeliness of service; improvements to quality, productivity, or safety;

cross-training; employee referrals; attendance; longevity with the organization; internal and external customer satisfaction; cost savings; and job knowledge.

A reward system for managers should take into account how well a manager models the behaviors rewarded in individuals. In addition, the following factors should be considered: effectiveness of planning, organizing, and measurement; staff motivation; employee development and retention; innovation and personal contributions to the organization's goals; a participative management style; and financial and operating results.

Rewards

Ron Zemke tells us that great service organizations often pay above-average wages for their industry. Our own extensive research base solidly confirms this fact. This distinction enables an organization to hire and retain better-quality people. It actually builds quality into the organization and into the product, thus reducing service calls and service issues and increasing customer satisfaction.

As an example, Zemke discusses the First National Bank of Charlotte, North Carolina. The branch employees are "shopped" (and rated) by mystery shoppers as frequently as three times a quarter. Employees who score a perfect 6 according to predetermined criteria are awarded instant cash of up to $200. As another example, on our visit to Federal Express, we were surprised to learn that part-time employees can earn over $9 an hour. In addition, there are incentives in the form of a profit-sharing bonus. Small wonder that Federal Express continues to outperform its competitors.

Stated simply, the principle is this: take good care of your people, and they will take good care of your customers. As a detailed example of this principle in action, we look at a supplier of machined parts for the automobile industry.

Rewards in Manufacturing

In today's manufacturing environment, quality and customer service are nearly one and the same. The customer simply will not accept a product that does not meet increasingly exacting standards. We looked at an organization — a supplier to the automobile industry — that meets that need for near-perfection with an employee gainsharing plan that returns a portion of the company's profits to eligible employees. (Unlike profit sharing, which remains a paper profit for most employees until retirement, gainsharing puts extra cash in employee pockets on a regular basis — generally quarterly, semiannually, or annually.) The firm's more than 800 employees are directly rewarded through this plan based on their ability to meet quality production targets. Although the cap on payouts is theoretically unlimited, employees who are participants in the gainsharing plan regularly receive an additional 9 to 10 percent of their total annual hourly wages in gainsharing installments. Gainsharing payouts are made on a quarterly basis to regularly reinforce the need for quality production.

Because parts that do not meet quality standards are *deducted* from production targets, managers and employees have a strong disincentive for running imperfect parts. Thus every employee feels directly responsible for stopping imperfect production.

This company also recognizes that employees contribute differentially to quality production targets. As a result, the extent of employee participation in the company's gainsharing plan is based in part on a "peer and superior" performance management system. Each employee is rated by three selected peers as well as the individual employee's supervisor. Nominations for peer review are submitted by each employee and approved by the employee's supervisor. Ratings are conducted quarterly by the selected employees and the supervisor, who then conducts an individual feedback session.

When an employee receives the company's highest rating, the behaviors that motivated the rating are recognized, recorded, and communicated to the individual. When an employee receives less than the highest rating, that person's opportunities for improvement are similarly recognized, recorded, and communicated.

The performance rating determines each employee's degree of participation in the gainsharing program. There are five rating categories: a 1 (outstanding) is the highest rating and entitles an employee to 110% of his or her gainsharing share; a 2 (excellent) entitles the employee to 100 percent; a 3 (expected) entitles the employee to 80%; a 4 (below expectations) or a 5 (provisional) entitles the employee to no share at all.

The system serves to make individual performance and the maintenance of quality standards of consequence to each employee and the group. Performance ratings that carry no tangible reward generally mean very little to employees, and directions associated with these schemes generally produce little in the way of constructive change. At this firm, on the other hand, the performance management system focuses employees on performance and how it can be improved.

In addition to offering each employee the opportunity for significant rewards based on individual and group performance—a valuable end in itself—this company reports significantly reduced waste, rework hours, machine repair downtime, and raw materials costs, as well as significantly increased motivation and productivity in employees and significantly increased satisfaction in customers. And this organization is not alone: in our experience, a justly conceived and properly communicated participative gainsharing program inevitably increases business results, reduces costs, and improves employee and customer satisfaction.

It may also be important to note that this firm, like other suppliers to the automobile industry, is regularly reviewed by its customers not only on the basis of the quality and timeliness of the end product but also on the basis of systems in place to reduce the cost of production. Thus service to the customers means more than on-time delivery of a quality product; it also means effective cost management and new ideas to improve quality and reduce cost that the customers can utilize elsewhere in their own operations or with other vendors.

Rewards in the Service Sector

Because it is so labor-intensive, the service sector is an even better candidate for gainsharing solutions than other sectors of the economy. And yet Robert Doyle tells us that salaries and wages in the service sector are generally determined not by contribution or performance but by competitive pressures, employee tenure, and across-the-board pay adjustments in response to complaints.

When Desatnick was corporate vice president of human resources of McDonald's, all of the officers had a large discretionary cash fund from which to award anyone in their department at any time with no preapproval. He fondly recalls awarding $300 to the woman who was home-office personnel manager, who had received three thank-you letters from rejected job applicants complimenting her for her courteousness, the opportunity to present their credentials, and the chance to make the right decision — which was not to join McDonald's. These three rejected applicants were — and undoubtedly remain — customers of McDonald's. They will tell at least five other people, who, if they are not already, might well become customers or employees. The treatment these applicants received builds loyalty in the customer and in the employee population. The award was further warranted because all of the interviews took place at the applicant's convenience, before or after the manager's scheduled hours.

Reward Options

We noted earlier that service superstars pay well above average wage and salarics. In addition, they vary their system of rewards and recognition to avoid complacency and to keep employees enthusiastic and motivated.

Rewards that are very effective at encouraging superior service include the following:

- *Cash bonuses.* The bonus for exceptional behavior just described is a good example.
- *Gainsharing.* With improved service and/or productivity, employees share the gain.
- *Profit sharing.* As organizations earn more, they contribute more to profit-sharing retirement funds for employees.
- *Ownership.* This option includes employee stock ownership programs and 401(k) plans.

- *Incentive pay.* Extra monies are awarded for extra performance.
- *Commissions.* These can be used to encourage behaviors as
  well as to increase sales. For example, we have seen commissions used with very positive results for customer service personnel who get a customer to increase the size of
  the order or who defuse a situation so that a formerly angry
  customer places an order.
- *Promotions accompanied by significant pay increases.* An appropriate
  pay adjustment for someone who has been promoted is 10
  to 15 percent. The increase should not be tied in with the
  basic merit increase. At McDonald's, for example, this works
  so effectively that half of the senior managers started on as
  crew kids and, because of rapid advancement, stayed to build
  their careers there.
- *Merit increases.* We recommend merit increases of up to 14
  percent for top performers and 0% for marginal performers.
  Do not get trapped into a bell-shaped distribution. If your
  organization is performing significantly above the average
  of your industry, your average employee pay should be significantly above the average in the industry.

Recognition

People in an organization do those things that they perceive will
provide them with the greatest benefits. In other words, we get
more of the behavior that we reward and recognize. The manager's role in motivating employees to superior performance can
thus be helped by formal and informal company-wide recognition programs.

Clearly, people do or do not do things on a something-
for-something basis. The recognition system must therefore provide incentives for service superiority. The cornerstone of any
such system is the manager who thanks and compliments an
employee for each job well done. Beyond that, organizations
might sponsor internal contests (from the local level to national
competition for an all-American team), initiate employee-of-the-
month and unit-of-the-month recognition; display letters of appreciation from grateful customers (and grant accompanying

cash awards), and publish in company publications stories of employees who demonstrate outstanding customer-oriented behavior.

What are some of the other things that companies can do to heighten awareness of and to motivate exemplary service performance? To begin with, they must recognize that wages and salaries are not a sufficient stimulator. Because employees need more than money, companies must add a variety of recognition programs to reward outstanding customer service. Although the programs naturally differ from company to company, these are some typical features:

- Employee recognition programs run continuously and change periodically.
- A frequent theme used in employee incentives programs is "quality of service."
- The logical manager's bonus program is tied to the volume of complaints received.
- Supervisor-of-the-year competition is ongoing.
- Complimentary letters from customers qualify employees for outstanding service awards, which include such prizes as cash, gifts (for example, a television), paid vacations, and extra time off.
- All complimentary letters are placed in the employee's personnel file as well as sent to the home and posted on company bulletin boards.
- Special recognition for outstanding service performance is placed on the employee's name badge.
- Employees who have excelled in service to customers have their names published in bulletins and house organs for service beyond the call of duty.
- Instant rewards are given for superior performance.
- Mystery shoppers designate outstanding service employees, and these employees receive monetary awards.
- Similarly, mystery shoppers reward superior service with tokens that are then converted into dollars.

Over the years, we have observed a number of creative approaches to recognizing and rewarding service superiority.

As a detailed example, let us look at some of the techniques McDonald's has used over time to recognize exemplary service. We choose McDonald's as an example because recognition is particularly important in an organization such as this, where the pay of a large proportion of the hourly employees tends to be in the lower quartile based on wage surveys.

Recognition as a Motivator at McDonald's

McDonald's practices a variety of methods to foster exemplary service behavior. The goal is to encourage healthy internal competition and use rewards and recognition to maintain and constantly improve service performance. Here are some of the salient points of the methods used to recognize the importance of the employee.

Employee of the Month. Selection of the employee of the month (in each department of each restaurant) is based on multiple criteria defined by management, including various measures of service quality, productivity, and demonstrated use of job-related behaviors. Employees make the nominations, and management makes the final selection.

Department of the Month. Selection of the department of the month in each restaurant is based on a department's consistency in providing outstanding service to its internal customers, in recognition of the fact that there is an almost perfect correlation between internal customer satisfaction and external customer satisfaction.

McBingo. Because cross-training is an important part of McDonald's success, employees are encouraged to learn and master all stations in the restaurant. McBingo is a simple but effective way to generate enthusiasm for that mastery and to reward success. Managers prepare bingo cards with all the store stations included in separate boxes. For each station, the performance standard is clearly defined. As an employee meets that standard, the box is filled in. Five lines in any direction earn the employee an award; when the employee completes the entire card, he or she gets a raise.

McBucks. A simple reward for achieving customer service goals, McBucks can be earned by employees who demonstrate excellence in customer service. Nominations may be made by the employees, but the actual awards are the sole prerogative of management. Some of the criteria for the awards include cooperation and teamwork, going beyond the call of duty, dependability, number of employee referrals, and input from other employees. Monopoly money (or any other play money) can be used; at the end of the month it is converted into real dollars.

The Number 1 Club. The whole purpose of the Number 1 Club is to provide special recognition for exemplary customer service by individual employees. Eligibility requirements for this club are based on McDonald's precise quantitative performance standards. Other factors include, for example, length of service, performance appraisal ratings, examination scores, and peer review and input.

Rookie of the Month/Year. Among the most successful motivators at McDonald's is the selection of a rookie of the month and rookie of the year for each of the functional disciplines at each restaurant — the person hired within the past month or year who excelled in all aspects of job and behavioral performance. The individual may be nominated by management or fellow employees, although management makes the final selection. The awarding of the certificate is accompanied by appropriate ceremony and congratulations from the entire management team in the presence of the peer group.

The Top 1 Percent. Each year, across the entire McDonald's system, regional vice presidents and home-office staff directors nominate the top 1 percent of their employee population on the basis of all-around excellence in service quality. The nominating managers prepare a one-page brief on the candidate or candidates of their choice; the executive committee then makes the final decisions. The winners are treated to a weekend away with spouses, a formal dinner dance, and one week's vacation.

Customer Comments. All customer comments, both good and bad, are immediately forwarded to the recipient, and a copy is sent to the recipient's manager. Written compliments are placed on bulletin boards, and prizes are given to recipients of repeated or noteworthy compliments. Employees are motivated by instant feedback and are encouraged to correct mistakes.

Rewards from the Mystery Shopper. McDonald's uses management trainees from all over the country to shop McDonald's restaurants at randomly selected times and grade them on everything imaginable. The grading starts with driveway cleanliness, proceeds to the building's appearance, the condition of the shrubbery, and the cleanliness of the restrooms. The shoppers look at overall restaurant cleanliness and total customer comfort, food quality, and the courteousness and helpfulness of staff. Instant awards are handed out for exemplary service. Store managers receive immediate feedback, both positive and negative. All comments are shared with the entire crew and the management team. This continuing emphasis on all aspects of service behavior never lets up throughout the organization.

All of these things that McDonald's does to make employees feel important are significant because they recognize the importance of the employee not just once a year, at anniversary time, but throughout the year. And, as we have recommended, McDonald's is careful to vary the reward and recognition system to avoid predictability — what might be called the Christmas turkey syndrome. In addition, the company promotes almost exclusively from within, with the exception of certain positions requiring professional credentials and experience or an outsider's perspective.

Additional Recognition Options

Like McDonald's, the other service superstars take extra steps to make their employees feel important and to recognize and reward exemplary service behavior. In turn, their employees then make the customers feel important.

Here are some additional forms of recognition that we highly recommend as options for use from time to time:

- Using company publications to celebrate various employee special events, such as promotions, new hires, completion of orientation, birthdays, anniversaries, marriages, retirements, military service, civic recognition, public service recognition, service within the organization, changes in family composition, safety records, attendance records, and retention records
- Issuing awards — from merchandise gift certificates, to dinner for two, to time off with pay, to a vacation cruise — for exemplary service
- Arranging frequent, informal parties to say thank you
- Using newsletters, house organs, bulletin boards, and letters sent home to publicize service excellence
- Providing health-club memberships for the family or day-care benefits for those with children
- Providing third-party employee assistance programs
- Arranging arts-and-crafts competitions
- Allowing for flextime, glidetime, variable days, and a compressed work week
- Providing attractive trophies and other service awards, from stars for name badges to paper weights, lapel pins, jackets, shirts, certificates, and caps
- Offering challenging work and the chance to learn new skills and share in decision making

We also recommend giving the following awards annually:

- Most improved employee of the year
- Most improved manager of the year
- Most helpful person
- Best department in terms of providing overall satisfaction to department services
- Best department in terms of consistently good performance

From the time job candidates walk in the door until they retire, they should be made to feel valued. All the marks of recognition given by a company add up to one message to the employee: "You are important, and we treat you with respect." And if the employee feels important, the customer gets treated like a VIP.

Pay for Performance

In our discussion of rewards and recognition, we have thus far only touched on one of the most controversial of all the available options: pay for performance. The many issues and questions tied to pay for performance are likely to be debated for some time. Results of recent studies do, however, clearly point to its benefits. For instance, as Zemke reports, the National Science Foundation studied three hundred companies with respect to pay, productivity, and job satisfaction. It found that when pay is linked to performance, motivation and productivity are higher and employees are more satisfied with their work.

In another study of forty companies, also reported by Zemke, it was found that in those organizations that switched from a system that did not measure work to a system that measured work *and* included performance feedback and incentives, productivity increased by 63 percent, on average.

Not all experiences with pay-for-performance are as positive, however, and some surveys reflect this. For example, Peter Smith reports that the Wyatt Company surveyed 800 companies that had a pay-for-performance program. Less than one-third (only 31 percent) of the human resource executives in this company rated the programs as successful. The main reason cited for the low rating of pay-for-performance programs was inadequate training of managers and supervisors. Middle managers and supervisors have the tough job of making decisions as to who does and who does not get a pay increase, and how much, but very few are provided with the tools and the skills to differentiate effectively among exceptional, satisfactory, and mediocre performances.

In our consulting practice and in the literature, we have found some of the main issues and concerns about pay-for-performance to be the following:

- Managers have difficulty making fine distinctions among employees.
- Ninety percent of all employees think that they are above average.
- Employees prefer the security of automatic, tenure-based pay increases.

- Managers too often take the easy way out and give every-body the same increase.
- Most pay-for-performance systems reward individual instead of collective performance, yet work teams are becoming in-creasingly popular.
- Employees are suspicious of management's intent.
- Pay for performance is often used not to stimulate perfor-mance but to contain payroll costs.

Perhaps the concepts and potential benefits and drawbacks of instituting a pay-for-performance system are best understood by way of an example from our practice.

The Good Shepherd Experience

We worked with the Good Shepherd Medical Center in Long-view, Texas, to develop a pay-for-performance merit system. Good Shepherd's chair, Jerry Adair, recognized that if the hospi-tal achieved excellence in patient and employee relations, the bottom line would be properly taken care of. And it was. In one year, all financial and operating aspects of the hospital showed significant improvement.

As part of the program, we provided each employee with material explaining the pay-for-performance system. In this dis-cussion, we outline the salient points.

The objectives of the pay-for-performance merit system were focused on ensuring excellence in patient relations and in employee relations. As part of these objectives, the goals were as follows:

- Achieve a high-quality work force at all levels of the orga-nization through recruitment, retention, motivation, and re-wards.
- Provide for consistency in performance reviews and pay practices.
- Establish a competitive wage and salary program in rela-tion to survey data and market pricing.
- Develop clear, specific performance descriptions and spe-

cific performance standards for each position at every level of the organization.
- Objectively review an individual's performance and measure performance against established standards.
- Pay and promote employees according to demonstrated performance.

The performance descriptions mentioned as part of the objectives required some work. A separate performance description was developed for every job, prepared with the input of people actually performing the job. Each performance description included at least the following:

- A statement of the position's basic purpose — that is, what it contributes to overall objectives
- An orderly listing of the position's major responsibilities
- A listing of specific, objective, and measurable performance standards
- The behavioral characteristics that all employees are expected to exhibit
- Other position requirements, including education, training, experience, skills, and abilities

Performance standards — that is, a statement of the conditions that should exist when the responsibility is performed well — were developed for each of the position's major responsibilities. The standards were stated in clear, measurable terms and prepared with the input of people actually performing the job, with coaching from a manager or supervisor. (Standards may change from year to year.)

In some cases, a performance plan was also developed jointly between an employee and his or her supervisor. Such plans were based on the established standards and explained how the standards would be achieved. Specific goals and targets were set as needed.

A program and schedule for performance reviews was established. In accordance with that schedule, each individual's progress is now reviewed against established standards in a semiannual progress review with his or her manager. Plans and goals are discussed and additionally clarified (or modified, if necessary), in order to keep on track to achieve the standards.

An annual performance appraisal discussion between the individual and his or her department manager is held on or about the employee's anniversary date. Both the employee and the manager prepare a performance review independently, in advance of the discussion. At the meeting, the employee and the manager exchange their handwritten forms and discuss and resolve, in writing, any differences of opinion noted. The final document is approved by the next higher level of management.

The performance appraisal is the primary vehicle for determining the amount of the annual merit increase. The appraisal form for most employees consists of two major sections, although the forms for managers and supervisors may contain additional sections for evaluating job factors that relate to those positions.

In one section, the specific performance standards for the position are listed. The employee's performance is rated from 1 to 5 for each standard, with 5 representing outstanding performance and 1 representing unacceptable performance. A rating of 3 represents satisfactory performance — the minimum level expected for that standard. In the other section, each of the behavioral characteristics (such as dependability, honesty, cooperation, and enthusiasm) that employees are expected to exhibit is listed. The employee's demonstrated behavior is rated for each characteristic (using the same 1-to-5 scale).

Each of the performance standards and behavioral characteristics is assigned a point value. When an employee receives the top rating on a performance standard or on a behavioral characteristic, he or she receives the total points possible for that item; lesser ratings results in fewer points. The total score for the entire appraisal determines the percentage of merit pay increase to be given.

Throughout the year, management collects wage and salary data by conducting surveys at hospitals and other businesses in the local area and by reviewing other relevant surveys. Management then analyzes each position's worth to the hospital in terms of the skill and effort required, the responsibilities assigned to the position, and the working conditions in which the job is performed. These factors are combined with the market rate as indicated by the surveys to determine each position's overall value. Positions are grouped together with others of similar value into pay ranges (or pay grades); every position in the hospital, from those with the lowest overall value to those with the highest, is assigned to a pay grade. The pay range consists of a minimum (usually paid to newly hired or newly promoted employees with little or no prior experience), a midpoint, and a maximum (which can be attained by employees who consistently perform at or above the standards for their position).

An employee may earn annual merit increases, provided his or her base rate remains within the pay range for the position. Employees whose base rates are equal to or greater than the maximum of the grade are not eligible for a base-rate increase. However, provided their overall performance is rated as superior or outstanding, they are eligible for remuneration in a lump sum based on 2 percent of the maximum rate of the grade.

Good Shepherd's wage and salary program, including merit pay increases, is projected in the preparation of an annual budget each fiscal year. It is subject to change at any time if circumstances make a change necessary and warranted.

As part of Good Shepherd's program, all managers and supervisors, from the CEO on down, receive thorough training in preparing performance descriptions, establishing performance standards, developing performance plans, conducting progress reviews, planning for and holding annual performance appraisals, administering the compensation system, and conducting staff and information meetings.

Instituting Pay for Performance

In our experience, one-third of the people in service-related job classifications have not had a performance appraisal for more than a year. The other two-thirds *have* had, but (as we noted earlier) they often wish that they had not, in all likelihood because the appraisal was not conducted well or was conducted after too long a gap. Proper training and use of pay for performance can go a long way toward solving these issues.

We recommend that, in introducing a pay-for-performance merit system, you stress the following points:

- Money is an effective positive motivator.
- Superior performers resent automatic and indiscriminate across-the-board pay increases.
- Linking pay to performance puts teeth into the performance appraisal system.
- Well-managed pay-for-performance programs clarify the goals of the individual employee, because performance standards are predetermined.
- Good pay-for-performance systems increase the employee's sense of ownership in overall company performance.
- Instituting pay for performance helps to start the process of organization culture change.
- The subjectivity of performance reviews and unpleasant surprises at appraisal time are virtually eliminated.
- Employees are encouraged to track their own performance against predetermined targets.

The Alternatives to a Pay-for-Performance System

After reviewing our experiences and those of our clients, we asked ourselves, "What are the alternatives to a pay-for-performance merit system?" Here is a summary of our findings:

- All employees—including the best ones—feel insecure. With no performance standards on which to judge performance, no one is able to identify the exceptional employees to ensure that they will be retained if there are cutbacks.
- As we have mentioned, standard raises at the annual review— the birthday-increase syndrome—tend to drive out the best performers and encourage the worst ones to stay.
- The employees have no incentive to do more or better work. Why should superior performers work twice as hard, produce much better quality, and provide better service with no

difference in pay? As a consequence, the company's performance suffers.

- Similarly, middle managers whose pay is not based on performance have no incentive to improve; they do only enough to hang on.
- The wrong people get promoted. It is difficult to assess promotability in the absence of standards and compensation systems that reward results.
- People disappear into their job descriptions; they come to work and attempt to look busy rather than be productive.
- An authoritarian management style is encouraged. The best way to manage in the situation that does not recognize individual excellence is to criticize people. Consequently, the intimidation factor is quite high in organizations that give across-the-board increases.
- The customer suffers. Without the incentive to deliver service excellence, employees offer inconsistent external and internal customer service.

Resistance to Rewards and Recognition

Getting productive behavior from employees takes both rewards and recognition, as we have stressed. Successful managers create and maintain winning teams by multiplying, strengthening, reinforcing, and rewarding exemplary behavior — by not being afraid to give thanks for a job well done. It takes a secure manager to praise and continue to praise.

It also takes patience and understanding to institute change. Managers must realize that many people are resistant to change and that *any* change — even positive change — creates stress up and down the organization. In focus-group sessions we have held around the issue of pay for performance, we encourage people to identify their areas of concern. There was considerable resistance to the idea of pay for performance for a variety of reasons, including the following:

- Fear of failure, of possible job loss, of criticism; fear of being evaluated

- Fear of the unknown and acceptance of things as they are
- Distrust of the administration due to its past inconsistencies
- Questions as to whether the rewards would be worth the additional effort
- Lack of staff understanding of the pay-for-performance approach
- Doubts about obtaining management support up and down the line
- Concerns about finding time to do it right when time is at a premium
- Questions as to whether performance standards would be designed properly and be realistic

Issues such as these, however disturbing to those who raise them, are surely not new. Back in 1776, Adam Smith lauded the economy of high wages in his book *The Wealth of Nations.* He stated that productive behavior should be rewarded and not have a ceiling placed on it. Over eighty years ago, Frederick Taylor, often considered the father of scientific management, told us that the objective of management should be to secure maximum prosperity for both the employer and the employee.

Are these pronouncements equally valid today? What happens to those organizations that, having addressed the difficult issues raised in this chapter, go on to take all possible steps to recognize and reward exemplary service behavior? In the next section, we will look at a variety of service superstars that have done just that.

Reaping the Benefits

Throughout this chapter, we have emphasized the importance of recognizing and rewarding exemplary service behavior. To underscore that importance and illustrate how positive reinforcement works in the real world, we now present examples of organizations that practice these principles — and that are service superstars as a consequence. We cover a range of small, medium, and large organizations that share both a devotion to service excellence and a willingness to be innovative in their pay practices and recognition of employees.

Federal Express

The first recipient of the Malcolm Baldrige National Quality Award for excellence in customer service, Federal Express has consistently outperformed its competitors. It is a benchmark not only within its industry but for superstars outside of the industry, such as Motorola and Xerox.

The motto and goals of Federal Express coincide with the Baldrige criteria of continuous improvement. Briefly, Federal Express excels and continuously improves in each of the seven categories for this award: leadership, information and analysis, strategic quality planning, human resource utilization, quality assurance of products and services, quality results, and customer satisfaction.

Wal-Mart

Wal-Mart is one of the fastest-expanding retail chains in America. Delegation of responsibility and scholarships of up to $2,500 to help defray college expenses for part-time workers could be the main reasons for its success. Forty percent of its store managers began as hourly part-time employees. Like other successful role-model organizations, Wal-Mart believes in and practices promotion from within.

American Express

The outstanding success of American Express during an era in which credit-card companies are not doing very well makes its practices especially noteworthy. Every month, American Express monitors how its employees are performing on a wide range of customer service criteria, from speed in processing bills, to accuracy in billing processes, to thoroughness, to new applications. Employees receive results of these surveys every year. More important, employees benefit from the more than 100 programs that American Express uses to reward outstanding service.

Sutter Health Systems

As Sutter Health Systems has demonstrated, not-for-profit organizations can make use of strategies used by for-profit organizations. In January of 1988, Sutter installed a gainsharing program at two of its hospitals. Its 3,000 employees were asked to come up with cost-saving and time-saving ideas that would allow the company to finish the year well under budget. To ensure that the highest standards of patient care were maintained despite these savings, each department head had to meet rigorous standards for overall quality of patient care and for patient satisfaction.

Of the savings that resulted from the ideas generated, the hospital received 50 percent, the employees received 40 percent, and 10 percent was set aside as a reserve fund in the event that the budget was not made because of problems later in the year. As John Rude, vice president of human resources, reports, the result was startling. The first year's payout was $1 million. The typical nurse, earning about $27,000 a year, averaged an additional payout of between $125 and $160 a month (or between $1,500 and $2,000 a year).

American Airlines

Each year, passengers rate their airlines on the quality of service. This year, American Airlines ranked first in the United States. Key to this success is the fact that pay and performance are closely linked at American Airlines. The more than 100,000 employees are held to dozens of standards. For example, telephone calls to the reservations department must be answered within twenty seconds; 85 percent of all flights must take off within five minutes of the departure time and land within 15 minutes of the scheduled arrival time.

AT&T

An important part of AT&T's challenge is to protect its market share. As a key part of its strategy to accomplish this, it rewards employee behavior that retains customers. According to William

F. Blount, past president of the Network Operations Group, "To reinforce our customer focus, employee performance that helps achieve customer satisfaction objectives must be rewarded accordingly."

Lincoln Electric

Since 1945, Lincoln Electric has succeeded in establishing productivity levels that are twice those of its competition — and that show significantly improved quality. This 3,000-employee nonunion work force has virtually no employee turnover. The benefits work in both directions: factory workers can earn more than $40,000 a year, and the organization has remained profitable even during the worst recession.

Part of Lincoln Electric's success is due to the fact that each supervisor thoroughly evaluates each of his or her employees twice a year. Performance criteria as part of the evaluation include quality of work, dependability, cooperation, ability and willingness to contribute ideas, and outout. Individual responsibility for work is built into the system: employees correct mistakes on their own time and at their own expense.

Four Seasons Hotels

As J. W. Young notes, the Four Seasons chain, based in Toronto, makes it clear that it wants employees in each of its twenty-one hotels to go that extra mile. Young tells of a customer who left a camera in a cab and then told a hotel employee of the loss. The employee promptly called every large cab company in town until he located the camera; he then drove his car to claim it and returned the camera to the guest. Why might an employee go to such lengths? The employee incentive plan, developed over the past several years, has been credited with encouraging this kind of behavior.

At Four Seasons, rigorous service standards are upheld by even the lowest-ranked employees in order to provide full value and satisfaction for the customers. Peer-group pressure maintains the standards of excellence in customer satisfaction.

The annual bonus for front-line employees can range from 3 percent to 5 percent of pay, and it is tied directly to the hotel's financial results. Management incentives are tied to people, product, profits.

In addition to its financial results, an indication of the hotel's success is that Four Seasons's annual turnover rate is less than half that of the industry. The fact that Four Seasons provides extensive training for all employees, emphasizes the development of managers' personal skills, and offers base salaries higher than comparable hotels clearly benefits its bottom line.

The Manager's Role

In June 1985, the U.S. Chamber of Commerce and the Gallup Organization conducted an extensive poll involving a cross section of the United States. They asked, "What changes would bring about the largest improvements in performance and productivity in most companies?" Over 80 percent of the respondents cited worker attitudes and abilities and managerial attitudes and abilities. A very small percentage noted that computerized facilities or more modern plants and equipment would make a significant difference. The exact same responses apply to the achievement and maintenance of customer service superiority.

Corporate America has drastically deluded itself on the impact of capital investment versus the potentially greater impact of investment in people. The real problem for business organizations — and for the millions of bored, underutilized, insufficiently challenged, and poorly rewarded employees — is poor management.

Successful managers use motivation, training, communication, and recognition as their key management tools. They make the right things happen most of the time. Lee Iacocca believes that things are even simpler; he says that the job of a manager requires but two basic talents: motivating and communicating.

What it comes down to is this: a good manager unleashes people power. Tom Peters suggests that effective leaders orchestrate the band, wooing their employees, selling them dreams, and then helping them to realize and fulfill those dreams. To be able to accomplish all this, the manager must believe in the dignity and worth of every human being. The manager who trusts employees is self-confident and secure enough that employees do not merely perform jobs; instead, they help to create and define them.

The best managers are cheerleaders as well as coaches, and they live up to their own standards. For example, one senior manager at Procter & Gamble works the second shift at least once a week, believing that those employees are also members of the team and deserve the same amount of coaching and cheering as the first shift.

The manager is the key to creating the kind of positive environment that encourages people to produce. No matter which emphasis is chosen to improve productivity and customer service, certain attitudes are common to all the successes: establishing good communication between managers and service personnel, making each employee feel involved, and training management and employees to do their jobs.

Consistent excellence is the only proven formula for success in the service industry. The key to such consistency is developing each management team in depth. Good managerial practices, effective supervision, and sensitivity to individual aspirations are all inexpensive to adjust, and they can greatly improve employee morale (and hence productivity and service) and lower employee turnover. This latter result is particularly significant: high turnover is expensive, and it can kill any standards of service superiority. Raising the poor quality of supervision can help immensely in lowering the turnover rate.

Over the years, a great deal of attention has been paid to management style, but too little attention has been paid to building trust. If employees can rely on their bosses to behave in a consistent and predictable manner, they can and will modify their own behavior to be more consistent, particularly in their relationships with customers and each other. And that is what creating and perpetuating service superiority is about. It is built on a relationship of mutual trust and openness between management and employees.

One supervisor of a midwestern dairy is a shining example of this attitude. He has a glass office in the middle of the dairy plant and is available to all. People stop in freely to see him when they have job-related problems, and he helps them solve those problems. His role is clearly that of a coach building a winning team.

Once a week he takes a small group of employees out for breakfast — a different group each time. He uses that occasion to pose such questions as, "What can we do to help you do a better job, and how can we make this dairy a better place to work?"

This particular manager considers himself an enabler: he enables his people to achieve their fullest potential through removal of obstacles in the pathway to success. And *everyone* benefits. His dairy business is healthy and profitable, and a profit-sharing program shares the results of the company's success with those who contributed to that success. And best of all, there are virtually no service problems: no returns, allowances, shortages, or customer complaints.

Trust is built into any organization through the honesty and consistency of its management teams. If certain promises to employees cannot be kept, for example, managers owe affected employees a thorough explanation. Similarly, if a budgetary allocation for additional staffing to provide better service must be trimmed, detailed reasons should be given to employees. That is the way to maintain the right attitude toward service.

Another key area for successful managers is building and maintaining high morale. Managers are usually loaded down with manuals of procedures and outlines of special employee programs. But the finest manuals in the world are a poor substitute for a manager's own enthusiasm. A supervisor's enthusiasm is a healthy form of contagion; other people catch it.

Successful managers and supervisors also use happenstance encounters to reinforce the pivotal role of the customer. These one-on-one interpersonal events are viewed as developmental opportunities to motivate employees, because motivated employees motivate customers to come back. Every meeting, however informal, is used by management as an opportunity to practice leadership skills and to express appreciation or recognition when it is warranted. If the employee is recognized and appreciated, so is the customer.

In the next chapter, we will look at how to maintain service superiority once having achieved it. Being rated at the top in your industry for one year does not automatically guarantee your slot for life.

Chapter 8

MAINTAIN ENTHUSIASM, CONSISTENCY, AND PREDICTABILITY FOR THE CUSTOMER

As managers, you can create an attitude and spirit within your own unit that supports empowerment and peak performance. Share information, share control, and encourage participation. Empower and support your people, who support our customers.

> —John S. Bubolz
> President and CEO
> Secura Insurance

In previous chapters, we have discussed how to develop service superiority through various methods, including recognition and rewards. But how does a company maintain a level of enthusiasm for the customer so that customer service always comes first? How does a company continuously and constantly strive for perfection in customer service?

In the first edition of this text, the seventeen role-model organizations that were identified by Citicorp in 1981 were highlighted. Somewhere, somehow, between then and now seven of those service superstars faded from glory. What happened? All of our research indicates that customer satisfaction had lost its standing as a top priority in each of these seven organizations. Other goals and priorities, such as cost cutting, financial restructuring, and downsizing, became more important.

When an organization loses sight of its customer-focused value system, slippage creeps in and mediocrity becomes an accepted standard of performance. To prevent this, there must be continuing emphasis on customer service and satisfaction — from the top down. We have observed the tremendous effort that it takes to *become* a service superstar. It requires that same effort, that ongoing commitment to meet and exceed customer expectations, to remain on top.

Ray Kroc of McDonald's, who turned a few California hamburger stands into an international empire, exemplified the commitment required: he set a standard for the company and backed it up. To maintain the driving focus on the customer, he would often say, "My way or the highway." His ideals of quality, service, cleanliness, and value became like religious tenets to many of his followers, his associates, and his employees. Employees and managers who chose not to live by and with those values had to seek employment elsewhere.

As at McDonald's the task of maintaining superiority must be addressed from the top of the organization on down. In the following sections, we outline a number of practices that the service leaders have in common.

Emphasize Top Management's Customer Orientation

There is no substitute for firsthand, face-to-face managerial contact with employees and customers. As an example, at McDonald's, each member of the management committee is charged with the responsibility to make frequent field trips to "stay in touch" with employees and customers. These visits go a long way toward furthering management's understanding of employee and customer needs and expectations and toward increasing the degree to which these expectations are being satisfied. It is for these same reasons that members of the Domino's Pizza executive team visit two stores a week. Similarly, executives at Levi Strauss take time to sell blue jeans to the customers at the retail level, and Ryder System executives ride along with drivers on their routes.

Hold Regular Staff Meetings

In our study of service organizations, we found that the weakest link by far was the communication system. We firmly believe that average employees receive less than 50 percent of the information that they need to be fully effective. Perhaps that is one of the reasons that employees waste so much of their time daily.

At McDonald's, every manager and every supervisor in every office and in every restaurant conducts a weekly staff meeting. During these meetings, the number-one goal — customer satisfaction — is reemphasized. Ideas are solicited on how to improve customer satisfaction and how to make McDonald's a better place to work. The suggestions of employees, supervisors, and managers are acted upon to create win-win situations.

Unfortunately, in many organizations, meetings are neither well organized nor effectively run. In fact, in our observation, too many meetings are a colossal waste of time. In workshops that we facilitate on conducting staff meetings, we recommend and emphasize the following points for effective results.

You should hold regular weekly or biweekly staff meetings. Have employees contribute to the agenda for each meeting before you finalize it. Make sure that you know your audience and your subject matter thoroughly. Allow plenty of time for advance notification, arrange for physical comforts, and be punctual in your starting and ending times.

When you convene the meeting, first state all of the facts. In the clearest way possible, show that your proposition or solution will achieve the goals of both parties and that one group will not gain at the expense of the other. This will help avoid conflict and minimize any conflict that does arise. By underscoring the fact that cooperation is essential, you work toward a win-win situation. Be sure to share common likes, dislikes, and associations, involve participants as much as possible, and avoid any form of threat or coercion. As the meeting is winding down, obtain consensus on key points and close with a call for action.

The question-and-answer session presents slightly different demands than a standard staff meeting. For a successful Q-and-A session, be sure to solicit questions and invite participation. Have participants address you rather than each other, but take care to avoid being authoritarian and/or dictatorial. Learn to handle the difficult questions gracefully, bypassing only those that you absolutely cannot address, and restate questions as necessary. Respond positively and calmly to any negative input or hostility. Through it all, remember to protect participants' pride and their feelings.

In both staff meetings, and Q-and-A sessions, make sure that each person is given an opportunity to express his or her own needs and feelings. The parties involved — moderator as well as audience — must accept the responsibility to be open and honest about facts, opinions, and feelings. They must also agree to resolve conflict without personal threats, judgments, or defensiveness. Discussion should deal with things that can be changed; there is no point in protracted haggling over the immutables. The language of problem solving should be descriptive and factual rather than normative; feedback to questions should thus be specific rather than general and descriptive rather than judgmental.

With these guidelines, you are on your way to win-win conflict resolution — to results that achieve each party's goals and are acceptable to both parties.

Train Employees in Service Commitment

At the risk of being repetitious, we must reemphasize that every service superstar that we have studied and worked with invests heavily in training. Training is the key tool to building and maintaining a customer focus and to keeping your customer base. Training helps develop the skills, knowledge, and attitudes that keep the customer first and foremost in the mind of the employee and that maintain the organization's service goals.

In a recent client assignment with a courier service in New York, we asked 152 employees in twenty-nine focus groups the following question: "If you were to leave the organization and go to work somewhere else, what would be your main reasons?" Among the many responses, the two most important — and frequent — were these:

- I would leave if I felt I was not growing and developing new skills or using my talents.
- I would leave if my boss didn't treat me with dignity and respect.

We could not have said it better!

Motorola, the first Malcolm Baldrige National Quality Award winner in manufacturing, still devotes considerable resources to training, in part to maintain its excellence. As Therrien reports, Motorola spends $75 million on employee education each year. This represents 3.6 percent of its payroll and is more than twice what the average company spends on training. Motorola's education program teaches job-related skills to its 103,000 employees, starting with the chairperson and including the broom pusher.

One of the primary objectives of this training is to transform the entire corporate culture to focus on customer satisfaction. The training and incentives have paid off in a variety of ways. As just three examples, Motorola's new cellular telephones have 70 percent fewer components, workers are now able to build a telephone in four hours (versus forty hours three years ago), and product defects have been reduced by 400 percent.

Management authority George Odiorne (1987) suggests that top management should play an active role in improving training effectiveness. He tells us that if training does not change behavior and thus improve business results, we are wasting our money. To help ensure that training succeeds, top managers should be the first people to be trained. When we custom-design training classes for our clients, we insist that the CEO attend. Beyond that, we structure the CEO's participation and make specific plans as to how the CEO will role-model what he or she learned upon going back to the office.

Organizations need to think of training as a long-term process versus a series of individual courses. In fact, the most effective training programs are integrated multicourse curricula designed to build skills step by step. Organizations should ensure that each phase of the training contains specific objectives and lesson plans.

Training must be participative and should simulate real-world situations. Feedback to participants is important, as is follow-up to determine whether changes have actually occurred.

Training may sound expensive — and it is. But because the costs of doing without training are even greater in the long term, training should be viewed as a profit center rather than a cost center.

In fact, the companies that Patricia Sellers cites as the best companies to work for from a service perspective — Four Seasons Hotels, Domino's Pizza, American Express, Motorola, Rubbermaid, and Land's End Direct Merchants — each spend large portions of their budget on training. These organizations train every employee and every division to focus on the customer (including the internal customer, because workers who treat each other well will treat customers even better). They then monitor service at every level of the organization. And these efforts pay off in both market dominance and profit dominance.

To stay close to the customer, management and employees must be trained and encouraged to do the following:

- Think of what satisfactions you would want as a customer.
- Measure internal customer satisfaction periodically.
- Pay attention and listen to everyone in the distribution chain.
- Prune and eliminate bureaucracy; make it easier for customers to talk to you directly.
- Stay in touch after the sale; follow up.

To evaluate how well its employee training program contributes to efforts to maintain service consistency, the company must ask the following questions:

- What are the company's current service goals, and what is their degree of attainment?

- Is the service budget adequate and properly used?
- What is the productivity per employee?
- What are the sales per employee?
- What is the profit per employee?
- Are employment costs as a percentage of total costs increasing? Decreasing? Stable?
- What are the costs of service complaints? Are they increasing? Decreasing? Stable?
- What is the interval between the time a customer registers a complaint and the time it is satisfactorily settled?
- How frequent — and expensive — are grievances, strikes, sabotage, absenteeism, sitdowns, slowdowns, and walkouts?
- Do the best performers receive the highest pay increases? Is the margin of difference significant?
- Are performance appraisals on time and effective?
- How is customer service excellence rewarded?
- Are field service and field sales reports reviewed in a timely manner?

If the answers to these questions are disturbing, the training program may be one of the culprits.

Continuously Improve Service Performance

We have taken Odiorne's (1988) keys to performance improvement and applied them to *service* performance improvement:

- Have the CEO signal his or her intentions to the entire organization.
- Assume that you can do more and you can do better.
- Set demanding goals and make constant improvement one of those goals.
- Keep making small improvements, using consistent and constant effort.
- Create systems that support and encourage excellence in all that you do.
- Invest heavily in performance-oriented training.
- Remove all barriers to total team effectiveness.

- Empower your people to make decisions regarding customer satisfaction.
- Use your most outstanding performers as role models: highlight what they do and how they do it.
- Make a habit of regularly scanning both your internal and external environments.

Keep Close to the Customer

John Guaspari suggests that keeping close to the customer requires us to seek answers to four basic questions.

1. How do we get information from our customers?
2. Who in the organization receives that information?
3. What is then done with that information?
4. What conclusions may we draw from the previous three responses?

He goes on to list the three most effective means of gathering data and/or soliciting feedback: the toll-free number (this rated 4.08 on a scale of 5.0 for effectiveness); focus groups (3.89 on a scale of 5.0); and mail and/or telephone questionnaires (3.75 on a scale of 5.0).

Our experience in working with toll-free numbers indicates an equally high level of customer satisfaction and responsiveness. Customers feel perfectly free to talk about anything on their minds when they are not footing the bill. The operator of the customer service representative should be one of the best salespeople in your organization. In this way, customer service can also be a profit center.

Typically, customer information goes to the customer service department or the consumer affairs office, and there it stops. We strongly urge that this information, in summary form, be shared at least monthly (if not biweekly) with the entire organization, from top to bottom. Maintaining awareness of the customer helps to keep the total organization focused on customer satisfaction.

As one example of creative and effective use of information from customers, consider the experience of Techsonic Industries, a small manufacturer of depth finders. The chair of the company, James Balk, personally interviewed twenty-five groups of sportsmen across the U.S. They told him that they wanted a depth gauge that could be read in bright sunlight. He listened to his customers and produced the product. Sellers reports that, as a direct result of this responsiveness, Techsonic maintains 40 percent of the U.S. market for depth finders ($80 million in sales in 1988), despite competition from twenty Japanese companies.

Maintain Morale for Service Superiority

It is the CEO of an organization who sets the tone and is responsible for the overall commitment to customer service. But it is the rank-and-file employees who are out there on the front line, responsible for carrying out management policies. A big question for all those in senior management is how to keep morale high among employees, especially when problems are being worked on. How does a company keep its service team committed and enthusiastic when things go wrong?

Before we address that question, a reminder: enthusiasm is no guarantee. Consider the case of John, a minimum-wage employee at a messenger service. He was considered an ideal employee — cooperative, committed, honest, and enthusiastic. Then one day, for no apparent reason, John threw his delivery down the elevator shaft and left the company without notice. He did not even return to pick up his final check.

What happened to John can also happen in your organization. People do have problems — personal and professional. However, if the work environment continues to be warm, comfortable, and friendly, if there is something exciting in the air, people will actively look forward to coming to work and giving the best they can to each other and to the customer. They will tend to forget their personal problems and immerse themselves in their work.

So what can managers do to put that "something exciting" in the air? What can they do to build and sustain enthusiasm? The Forum Corporation in Boston, a leading customer service consulting firm, outlines ways to maintain employees' enthusiasm for their job, their organization, their boss, and their customers. Forum's two primary recommendations are to identify and use the full knowledge and talents of the entire work force and to demonstrate a continuing interest in the employees as people. Let us look at each of these in turn, fleshed out with ideas gleaned from our experiences with a wide variety of organizations.

- *First, you must identify — and then be sure to use — the full knowledge and talents of your entire work force.* A colleague of ours, Robert Lewis, president of Resource Networks, inventories the collective brainpower of entire organizations in the following manner. He develops tailor-made inventory instruments that swiftly and deeply probe for hidden skills and knowledge, task-force or project experience, specific problem-solving successes or failures, people contacts outside the organization, and other "gray matter" resources that companies typically pay for fully yet use only partially. He then provides high-powered software tools and procedures to assist companies in harnessing and mobilizing the newly revealed aggregate wisdom, intelligence, and experience of their employees. Most important, he helps companies identify and reduce those organizational, structural, political, and cultural obstacles that impede the use of their combined brainpower and prevent the whole from becoming greater than the sum of its parts within their employee groups.

In all these steps, Lewis works with a specially selected employee task force to unearth specific knowledge resources important to the company. All employee resource data are loaded into a computer program, NETWORX, and key personnel within the company are trained in the maintenance of the program, as well as in how to use it to bring forth substantially higher levels of employee cooperation, collaboration, and resource utilization.

Whether through a program such as Lewis's or less formally, you must encourage suggestions, alternatives, and new ideas. Make it company policy to reward risk taking instead of risk avoiding. Place a premium on creativity, not on conformity. Many a maverick has made a fortune for his or her organization. As just one example, the Post-it product was created by a 3M employee who benefited from this type of attitude from top management.

Share decisions with others; seek their input. Earlier, we made reference to the beneficial aspects of a participative management style. We then related management style to an organization's customer-retention quotient. Remembering this, take positive initiative in seeking out and using the ideas of your entire work force and reward employees for suggestions that make your organization a better place to work. These steps address employees' desire to have a say in all aspects of the work environment that affect them.

• *Demonstrate a continuing interest in your employees as people.* This interest does not imply soft management but the running of a tight ship. Just as the captain of a ship shows concern for each and every member of the crew, so you should show concern for your employees. Be firm in your values. Intervene with problem employees. Practice constructive discipline. Give plenty of positive reinforcement for exemplary service behavior.

All of these suggestions may sound simple, but they mean changing the way we manage. As you will see, however, the effort is well worthwhile.

Provide Motivational Tools

McDonald's is one organization that effectively manages to maintain consistency, predictability, and enthusiasm. How does it do this? McDonald's management, recognizing that everyone is not "up" all the time, came up with a people-oriented cookbook of ideas on how to keep the job interesting and how to keep the crew motivated.

The activities in this cookbook are not intended to substitute for basic good human relations practices, of course. Solid day-to-day human resource management comes first, complemented by regular, upbeat performance reviews. Weekly informational meetings for employees are still as essential as ever, and above all stands the manager's own example of a pleasant demeanor, motivation, enthusiasm, and a service orientation.

One "recipe" from this cookbook encourages managers to select, every month or so, an activity appropriate to the season and reward employees for their successful participation. Information about the activity can be posted on the bulletin boards and discussed in the weekly informational meetings for employees. The key is to get everybody involved in each activity. The resulting team spirit promotes service excellence.

A selection of similar motivational tools—some from McDonald's and some from other service superstars—is presented in the pages that follow.

- *The all-American team.* Designed to upgrade quality, service, and speed, the all-American team is basically a healthy, head-on competition between units—for example, several branches or stores performing the same work. The underlying purpose is to establish management's criteria qualitatively and quantitatively and then to communicate these criteria. For example, typical criteria in a restaurant could include sales per person, delivery time, quality of service, accuracy of service, dependability of the crew, and versatility (in an organization where people work several stations).

- *Employee involvement.* A rotating committee of the better performers can be involved in a variety of special management projects. This participation will make employees more committed to the organization's goals. The group should be changed frequently to make sure that many people have an opportunity to participate, and all assignments should be relatively brief.

There are all kinds of activities and projects in which employee committees can be involved, from decorating for a party to reviewing service performance standards, the appraisal system, safety, and community relations. Let the employees' imaginations guide them, as long as they end up with specific suggestions to management. Management should then adapt and incorporate as many of these ideas as possible—in particular those dealing with service superiority and keeping the customer happy.

- *Employee social events.* As an organization grows, the feeling of closeness enjoyed in the earlier days is sometimes forgotten. The family atmosphere can dissipate to the point that employees feel no one cares about them. One proven method of avoiding this is to hold periodic social or sporting events. Many organizations sponsor such events, with great positive effect on morale.

A volunteer employee activity committee can be formed and given a budget, and these employees should create the appropriate calendar of social events. During the year these could include such things as a family picnic, a Christmas party, regular games for an employee athletic team, a bowling night, a family day, and an open house. Sponsoring such events is one of the best and least expensive ways to create a service team. A social event builds commitment and team spirit; this enthusiasm quickly reflects itself in service at the customer level.

- *Job rotation.* Boredom is one of modern industry's greatest challenges. Bored people atrophy or quit. But people who are challenged to master new skills rightfully feel that they are growing. Those people tend to stay around.

One way to give people adequate opportunity for growth is to rotate jobs. This has the additional benefit of giving an organization flexibility and providing backups for highly skilled jobs.

- *Employee of the month.* In industry in general (and in retailing in particular), the excellent practice of recognizing the employee of the month has become fairly commonplace. Sometimes a variation in the theme can help to keep it lively. For example, management usually chooses the recipient on the basis of predetermined criteria (perhaps from the existing appraisal system) that relate to an area such as customer service. One variation is to have the employees themselves determine criteria and then nominate and vote for the employee who has achieved the highest standards of customer service. This is an excellent way to build employee awareness of the service issue. Many companies regularly use this practice, and it inevitably gets good mileage from the crew.

The award for this honor need not be expensive, but be sure that it is accompanied by publicity—for example, notification on bulletin boards and in a letter to the home, a plaque, or temporary use of a special parking place. Whenever possible, the award should be given in the presence of the employee's peer group.

• *Informational meetings for employees.* It is important to hold informational meetings frequently and to make them an interesting and pleasant experience for employees. As one way to capture employee interest, you might begin a meeting by having the employees nominate the best employee of the week in a particular job category. Have the employees define their criteria, nominate three to four candidates, and take a vote; you can then give a prize or an appropriate reward to the winner in front of the group. Or you might begin informational meetings by offering special recognition to, for example, the top employee of the month, those who have received scholarships or made the honor roll, or those celebrating birthdays. The essential thing is to vary the meetings and the tone to keep them interesting and lively as well as informational.

• *Employee-set service goals.* Because employees achieve higher standards of performance for themselves if they participate in the process of setting their own goals, the management team should set goals for service improvement in conjunction with the crew. The basic premise of quality circles, for example, is to let employees participate in decisions that affect them. They can help to decide what is most important and come up with realistic game plans to achieve those goals. Management should not abdicate its leadership role, of course.

• *Employee trainers.* Exceptional employees who serve as part-time trainers are role models for other employees. Through their performance, and with the use of constructive criticism, patience, and enthusiasm, they can quickly acquaint the new employee with excellence in customer service. This more formalized approach is preferred to the old "buddy system." It helps build in quality, speed, and accuracy. And for a few cents an hour more (perhaps $.25 to $.50), a load can be taken off the busy supervisor's back.

• *Employee referrals.* People who were referred for employment by other employees generally seem to work out well.

To encourage referrals, give the employees an incentive to tell friends and neighbors about your organization: reward them for each referral. If you pay out half the cost of a newspaper ad as a reward, you have saved money as well as helped an employee. It is a good idea to tie part of that referral bonus into the retention of the new employee — say, for a period of three months or more. Some companies also tie part of the bonus back into the performance rating of the new employee.

• *Customer awareness techniques.* Just as advertising people strive to create top-of-the-mind product awareness, the organization must create and maintain top-of-the-mind service awareness in all employees. Nothing is more important.

Cleanliness as an important part of service can be emphasized through the white-glove inspection. This can be done by a mystery shopper or a regular management employee from another area. The mystery shopper runs a white glove over hard-to-see places — for example, above the door jamb in the restaurant. If the glove comes out dirty or greasy, the store receives an unfavorable write-up. If clean, the store receives a favorable citation.

All of these are just examples of ways to maintain employee enthusiasm and to keep the importance of the customer in the minds and actions of employees. Organizations can tailor these to their own needs and supplement them with techniques of their own. But all the enthusiasm generated will fade overnight if employees sense that management is not keeping its promises and commitments to employees.

Happily, we are witnessing beneficial changes in many organizations. They are not just paying lip service to customer and employee satisfaction; instead, they are fully committed. You too can emulate what the service superstars do and how they go about doing it. It may help to keep in mind the motto of Federal Express: "People, Service, and Profits." Martha Finney (1988) quotes Jim Perkins, senior vice president of personnel at Federal Express, as saying, "We believe in our philosophy that customer relations begin with employee relations." People are treated with dignity and respect at Federal Express; the company takes care of its people, and the people in turn deliver service in a courteous and efficient manner.

For those who think that the efforts described in these pages are excessive, consider the alternative. Without continuous reinforcement of customer-oriented values, complacency sets in. Like a cancer, it slowly eats away the vitals of an organization. The consequences of complacency are grim:

- Stagnation begins.
- Creativity and enthusiasm wane.
- Innovation declines.
- Contentment with the status quo grows.
- Service slippage creeps in.
- Change is resisted.
- The customer is forgotten.
- Obsolescence starts festering.
- All systems begin to fall apart.

Service Superstars Commonalities

Some of the management factors that the service superstars have in common — factors that help maintain the edge and keep service superiority as the top goal — are listed here. If the principles seem simple, remember that successful implementation requires concerted and nonstop effort.

- Stress the message that there is no such thing as acceptable quality. Quality can always get better.
- Make sure that quality is everybody's business, from the corner office to the shop floor.
- Develop a detailed implementation plan. Talking about quality is not enough.
- Help departments work together. The territorial imperative is your biggest obstacle.
- Keep your ears open. Some of the best ideas will come from the most unexpected sources.
- Take control of your process: you must know why something goes wrong.

- Analyze jobs to identify their elements and set quality standards for each step.
- Be patient. Do not expect gains to show up next quarter.
- Make extraordinary efforts in unusual situations; customers will remember these efforts best.
- Think beyond cutting costs. The benefits of improved quality should reach every part of the organization.

These principles are all focused on customer service: not *adequate* customer service, but *exemplary* customer service — service so superior that customers will not be motivated to take their business anywhere else. The principles can be applied to any business, from giant to neighborhood stores. To be sure that you do not think the principles apply only to megasystems with billion-dollar budgets, we offer a story about a succesful — and very small — dry-cleaning business.

The wife of one of the authors would drive fifteen minutes out of her way for dry cleaning because the proprietress of this establishment made her feel like an old friend. She carefully inspected each garment, making all the necessary repairs and replacing buttons — all at no extra charge. Occasionally the proprietress would even give Margo a small silk scarf. This delightful woman said, "I know that you do not live in the neighborhood. There are many places where you could take your cleaning, so I treat you special because I want you to come back."

And that is what service superiority is all about.

PART THREE

THE FUTURE
OF
SERVICE QUALITY

As we look to the future, we see that ensuring customer satisfaction will become ever more important to the success of businesses. Planning for that success must begin today, because changing a company's culture, training workers, and building in the flexibility necessary to meet the unpredictable demands of a fast-changing future are not short-term tasks.

In Part Three, we provide a glimpse of what the future may hold. What we see clearly underscores the need, today and every day, for focusing on the customer.

Chapter 9

SCAN TODAY'S TRENDS TO ENVISION TOMORROW'S SERVICE

The American work force is in grave jeopardy. We are running out of qualified people. If current demographic and economic trends continue, American businesses will have to hire a million new workers a year who can't read, write, or count. Today we need people who are not only proficient in the basic skills, but who know how to think and communicate what they're thinking. We need people who can adjust to change, who can absorb new ideas, and share them easily with others.
        —David Kearns
        Former Chair and CEO
        Xerox

In the United States today, more than at any other time in our history, the gap is widening between the skill requirements of jobs and the skills of job seekers. If we project this gap into the future via the trends that we see today, we realize that we must prepare for an ever-increasing disparity between job requirements and job seekers' skills.

To illustrate the reality of the steady shift from labor-intensive to knowledge-intensive industries, Peter Drucker (1987) cites a drop in jobs pouring steel and a rise in jobs making pharmaceuticals. Indeed, this shift is seen across many sectors. To understand it, we must look at current trends in demographics as well as in industry and at trends in competition for market share and for qualified workers.

The Labor Shortage and Service Quality

Demographic changes will result in a work force slightly older than the present one. The proportion of youths (those sixteen to twenty-four years old) in the labor force dropped from 24 percent in 1976 to 19 percent in 1988. That number is projected to fall to 16 percent in the year 2000. (The decline from 1976 to 1988 reflects the end of the baby boomers' entry into the work force. The projected decrease by the year 2000 reflects fewer births in the 1970s.) The proportion of workers aged twenty-four to fifty-four is projected to increase by 2 percent between 1988 and 2000, and the older population, which is growing in absolute numbers, is projected to account for the same share of the labor force in 2000 as in 1988.

Aside from the changing age of the workers, we must factor in their education — or lack thereof. We cannot ignore the fact that our school system is providing an army of illiterates. Perry (1988a) provides these facts: of the 3.8 million eighteen-year-old Americans in 1988, 700,000 had dropped out of school and another 700,000 could not read their high school diplomas. An estimated 25 million adult Americans cannot read past the fourth-grade level; another 60 million cannot read past the eighth-grade level.

Illiteracy among minorities is even more alarming — in some groups, as high as 40 percent. Disturbing as these figures are today, they take on even more significance as we look to the future. Dale Feuer notes that, according to the Bureau of Labor Statistics, African Americans, Hispanics, and other non-white groups will account for about 57 percent of the growth in the labor force from 1986 to 2000. Further, he reports that, according to WORK FORCE 2000, a joint project of the Hudson Institute and the U.S. Department of Labor (Employment and Training Administration), if legal and illegal immigration stay at current levels, immigrants will account for approximately one-half of the U.S. population growth by the end of this century. The fact that many of these new immigrants come from the poorest areas of Asia and Latin America — areas where there are no laws requiring children to attend school — must be recognized. As minorities and immigrants become an increasingly large part of the work force, we can expect a corresponding rise in work-force illiteracy.

The Committee for Economic Development, an independent research group of 200 business executives and educators, claims that our schools not only produce illiterate graduates but also send to the workplace a steady supply of unmotivated youths who are incapable of appropriate on-the-job behavior and who are unable to solve problems, make decisions, or set priorities.

In light of these trends, businesses are seeing that they must encourage education of teachers in the school systems, students in the schools, and workers in the workplace. If businesses do not get involved in education — by contributing money to attract more and better teachers into the schools, for example — they will find that in the future they must make drastic accommodations for illiteracy in the work force (or do without workers).

By way of overview, let us look at the workers of the new millennium. Who will these workers be? The overall labor force — 83 million people in 1970 — is projected to be 70 percent larger in the year 2000. This increase disguises the fact that the growth of the labor force has been decelerating over the years; the rate of increase is projected to slow to 1.2 percent annually over the 1988-to-2000 period. The components of the labor force and the changes to it are of particular interest to businesses.

- The number of women in the labor force is projected to grow by 12 million (or 22 percent) from 1988, totaling 67 million in 2000. Women will account for 47 percent of the labor force in 2000, up from 41 percent in 1976 and 45 percent in 1988.
- Men will remain a majority of the labor force. The male labor force is projected to grow by 7.4 million (or 11 percent) over the 1988-to-2000 period.
- The youth labor force, both male and female, is projected to be at the same levels in 2000 as in 1988.
- It is in the percentages of minorities that we are likely to see significant changes. By 2000, African Americans are expected to make up 12 percent of the labor force, up 1 percent from 1988; Hispanics, 10 percent of the labor force, up 3 percent; Asians and others, 4 percent of the labor force, up 1 percent.

And what will these workers do? Most predictions agree that the fastest-growing job categories will be in professional, technical, and sales fields — the fields requiring the highest educational and skill levels. More specifically, the five occupational categories expected to experience faster-than-average growth are technician, service worker, salesperson, professional worker, and executive/manager. There will be continuing demand for workers in unskilled and semiskilled jobs, of course, but the mismatch will grow between the emerging jobs, which call for increasingly higher levels of skill, and the people available to fill them.

Richman notes that the U.S. Bureau of Labor Statistics expects the fastest growth to come from high-skill fields such as engineering, medical technology, computer programming, and systems analysis. Automation will lift many workers, such as bank tellers, out of menial jobs and transform them into true customer service representatives, responsible for a much broader range of challenging tasks. Occupations requiring postsecondary education will account for 30 percent of the growth in the new service-sector employment.

An overall summary of these Bureau of Labor Statistics projections is reproduced in Figure 9.1.

As Figure 9.1 indicates, substantial growth is expected in the service sector. Indeed, according to some estimates, by the year 2000 nine out of ten people employed will work in service jobs. Many of those employees will work in home health care, home nursing, retirement communities, and retirement homes for the elderly. In fact, it is expected that addressing the needs of and caring for the elderly will become one of the fastest-growing career opportunities in the next decade. Simple demographics are behind this prediction: by the year 2000, almost one-half of the American population will be fifty-five years old or older. An increased demand for service from industrial and commercial manufacturers is also expected.

All these service jobs, as we have already noted, will require increasing levels of skills and education. The employee who is not learning new skills and the organization that is not teaching new skills will very quickly become obsolete.

Clearly, finding, attracting, and retaining knowledgeable

Figure 9.1. The Employment Picture in 2000.

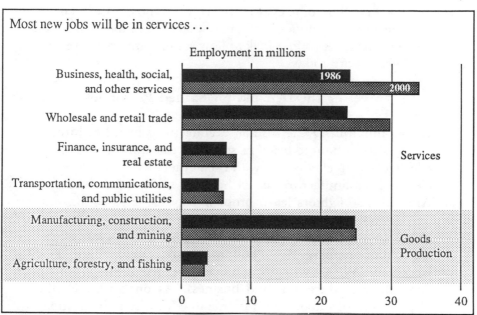

Most new jobs will be in services . . .

Employment in millions

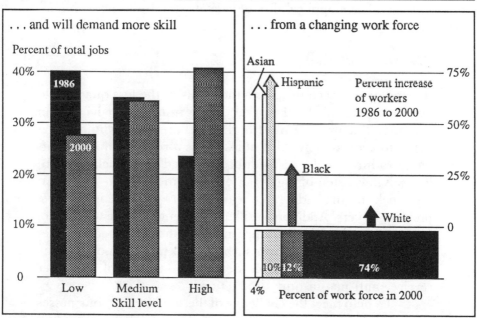

. . . and will demand more skill

Percent of total jobs

. . . from a changing work force

employees will become ever more critical to businesses. To determine what techniques companies might adopt today to adapt for tomorrow, let us first look at how some companies are successfully coping today.

Meeting the Demand for Skilled Personnel

In Washington, D.C., a small architectural firm has hired a training consultant to teach its staff how to communicate more effectively with clients and with each other. In Texas, a major electronics manufacturer is teaching the skills of teamwork. In Arizona, fire fighters learn problem-solving skills.

From the government and military, to the Fortune 500 group, to the small company, employers are aggressively soliciting valuable employees and building a core of new skills in their work force. We are witnessing much closer partnerships among government, education, and business. As one example, the Department of Labor issues grants to educational institutions to research the applicability of various skill-building technologies and techniques.

The New Skill Set

As employers reach deep into the ranks of the less qualified to obtain their entry-level workers, they must invest heavily in training. The workers most in demand are those who are prepared to acquire new skills quickly. As a result, employers attempt to hire employees with broad-based skills such as problem solving, listening, negotiation, and knowing how to learn; they seek mature, adaptable team players who are innovative problem solvers. Additional skills can be taught in the workplace.

A survey of the literature indicates that on-the-job courses presently being offered cover such areas as new technology, participative management, sophisticated quality control, customer service, and just-in-time production.

To help meet the challenge of the semiliterate, businesses are using new learning technologies in the workplace, including interactive videos and new software systems to support new hardware, and relying on theories about how adults learn.

A Training Success Story

Mazda Motor of America took a forward-looking approach to training when opening its first U.S. plant in Flat Rock, Michigan. When the plant opened, Mazda had a complete work force and a detailed training plan for each employee. Its courses covered constant improvement, group processes, problem solving, decision making, safety and health, creative thinking, interpersonal skills, and statistical quality process control.

Mazda's blueprint for success was the following eight-step program:

1. Identify job changes or problems related to basic workplace skills.
2. Build management and union support to develop and implement training programs in workplace basics.
3. Present strategy plan to management and unions for approval.
4. Perform a task analysis of each selected job or job family.
5. Design the curriculum.
6. Develop the curriculum.
7. Implement the training program.
8. Evaluate and monitor the training program.

Any organization, regardless of its size, could benefit from such a program.

Adapting to the New Employee and New Economy

Organizations are significantly changing the criteria applied for entry into the full-time work force and for upward mobility within it. Although the presence and maintenance (normal upgrading) of linear technical skills will remain important factors, interpersonal and decision-making skills are acquiring increasing importance at all levels within the organization.

The reasons for this increased emphasis on interpersonal and decision-making skills range from increasingly rapid changes in technology, many of which make existing skill sets obsolete, to new team-oriented approaches to corporate organization that

require interpersonal and decision-making capabilities at all
levels and within most functions in the organization, to higher
expectations of increasingly scarce qualified workers, to an increased level of awareness of available avenues for redress of
grievances.

Indicators of this trend include spectacular growth in consulting services related to measuring these qualities in prospective candidates and internal use of more sophisticated tools and
techniques to predict whether or not potentially costly investments in training and/or career development are indeed worthwhile. A few examples indicate the breadth of this trend:

- The new CEO of a regional property and casualty insurance company retains the services of a clinical psychologist
  to assess the CEO's capabilities with respect to the "critical
  competencies" he believes are required to successfully implement his strategy. The clinical psychologist is also to assess those who report directly to the CEO to determine their
  capabilities in the "competency areas" required to support
  the CEO's initiatives and then to provide recommendations
  regarding the career development of these managers and
  (where useful) provide plans for individual development.
- A gas utility hires a clinical psychologist to assess selected
  members of its hourly work force and develop career-path
  plans leading to supervisory roles and beyond.
- An international oil company hires a clinical psychologist
  (reporting directly to the CEO) to assess the capabilities of
  the organization's entire management work force against
  criteria believed to be required for effective competition in
  the next decade. Key among these criteria are interpersonal
  and decision-making skills and the ability to learn and apply
  new work styles and methods.

Such analyses of the members of the work force are relatively new. Their effectiveness will determine whether or not
they are continued.

In addition to these changing patterns of employee training and evaluation, there are also changes in the terms of em-

ployment. There is, for example, a trend toward flexible staffing levels and the broader use of part-time employees. These approaches have already been shown to be successful and are expected to continue into the future.

Increasingly, organizations are adhering to the principle that employment is contingent on business conditions. Competitive cost pressures no longer permit organizations to absorb the cost of maximum staffing levels during times of decreased revenue-producing activities. This principle has long been practiced in such industries as hospitality, food service, health care, and agriculture, which have reasonably predictable swings in their revenue-producing activities. What seems to be growing are methods of staffing and organization designed to take "normal" business cycles into account.

One indicator of the growth of "cyclical" employment methods is a nationwide growth in the number and size of part-time employment services for professionals. In addition to the traditionally part-time hourly workers, increasing percentages of nurses, medical technologists, lawyers, engineers, analysts, programmers, architects, accountants, and marketing, advertising, and human resource professionals are being employed by firms that offer their services to the marketplace at a rate that falls well below the cost of maintaining these services internally on a permanent basis. Firms utilizing these professional services note that the cost of acculturation is generally more than offset by the financial benefits of the term-employment concept. Further, the firms often benefit from the new ideas introduced into the environment by temporary personnel who have not "learned" that a particular concept is "not accepted here."

An increasing percentage of new hires in both manufacturing and service industries carry the designation *part-time*. Examples of the growth in part-time employment include the following:

• A regional health care network of twenty-two hospitals and extended-care facilities reports that 38 percent of its registered nurses are temporary. This percentage is double that of 1985.

- A growing auto parts manufacturer has an hourly part-time work force of 42 percent, up from less than 10 percent in 1985.
- An international food-processing organization maintains a part-time hourly plant work force of 48 percent in the United States. The percentage of part-timers in its hourly work force has grown from less than 8 percent in 1985.
- An international restaurant organization, with total domestic employment of more than 500,000 people annually, reports its systemwide part-time employment as 95 percent. This percentage is *down* slightly over the past ten years. (This slight downward trend is due in part to increasingly fierce competition within the firm's smaller traditional labor markets.)

New subscribers to the part-time labor concept cite the following primary reasons for their increased use of part-time labor:

- Decreased annual labor costs of an increasingly part-time work force
- Introduction of new ideas from part-timers with experience in diverse organizations
- Preference among many (although not most) of their hourly workers for more flexible hours
- Opportunity to test potential full-time employees through experience in the part-time pool

The trends discussed on preceding pages are indicators of ways in which companies are adapting to fit the new economy and the new employee. Companies are also adapting to the needs of the new customer. The lessons that businesses have learned about the customer's need for quality — in service, in products, and throughout the organization — are finally penetrating the U.S. economy and can be expected to continue to do so in the years ahead. Customers will no longer tolerate shoddy products that do not work, defective merchandise, poor service after the sale, or mediocre, inattentive service in a service industry. We are seeing that organizations — public and private;

for-profit and not-for-profit; small, medium, and large — are committing to total quality in everything that they do.

Success stories in the quality arena are appearing with increasing frequency. As just a few examples, Dreyfuss tells us that Florida Power and Light attacked a lightning problem and drastically reduced power outages; Whistler, one of the largest sellers of radar detectors, improved its manufacturing pass rate from 75 percent to 99 percent; and Corning Glass saved its TV factory by dramatically reducing the defect rate of new picture tubes.

Gilbert Fuchsberg reports another indicator of this trend toward service excellence: extension of the Malcolm Baldrige National Quality Award program to include hospitals, universities, and other nonprofit organizations is under consideration. Many nonprofits already request Baldrige applications; health and educational organizations use the contest criteria to help review their operations. Some of these organizations are now interested in competing as a way to further encourage excellence in service.

Successfully Competing for Talented Employees

Obviously, demographic trends must be taken into account by employers competing for talented people in today's job market. In our consulting business, we often hear the complaint that companies cannot afford to be as selective as they might like in their hires. Many employers say that they cannot yet use behaviorally oriented interviewing because they do not have significant numbers of job candidates from which to choose.

Now is the time to look for more creative ways to find employees and to tap pools of potential employees who might otherwise be overlooked. We have mentioned many of these methods throughout this book; by way of overview, in the following section we present our recommendations for locating and attracting quality employees. These methods are typically less costly, less time-consuming, and more fruitful than the traditional method of placing newspaper ads for vacancies, and they tend to increase the number of candidates from which a company can choose.

• *Pay employee referral bonuses.* Pay a bounty to employees who refer their friends or relatives for employment. The amount will vary depending on the level of the job that you are trying to fill. Our experience suggests $100 at sign-up for an hourly job and an additional $100 at the end of the probationary period (typically ninety days) if performance is satisfactory.

We have found several beneficial effects of employee referral bonuses. Employees making referrals tend to get more involved in the organization; they feel a vested interest. As a rule, only the better employees make referrals, and they then act as mentors for their friends and help them to succeed. We have also found that turnover is reduced significantly.

• *Hold open houses.* Run an ad in local newspapers inviting people to come visit your plant and offices and meet with your management. In the ad, highlight the success stories of people who started at the bottom and made it to the top. Make the open house a pleasant, informal affair with nice refreshments. Talk about career opportunities with the people who respond. Be prepared to make job offers on the spot, subject to checking on references and employment history.

A CEO of a small sausage manufacturer in Wisconsin told us that people still talk about an open house that he held several years ago, at a time when he was unable to get enough applicants through other means. In addition to gaining positive publicity, he filled fifteen key jobs that day.

• *Host job fairs.* A job fair is similar to an open house in its community outreach. Take out an ad in local newspapers and/or send invitations to the homes of people near your plant or office. You can offer free professional job-counseling services while presenting your organization's opportunities. Candidates will see this combination as a demonstration that your organization cares about them and their career; this gives a potential job added value.

• *Make yourself known to schools and youth organizations.* In a similar light, personally visit all the schools in your area, including high schools, vocational and technical schools, two-year schools, community colleges, and universities, and meet with each president, dean, and career guidance counselor. Also visit recreational and youth organizations, including the YMCA and YWCA. Soon you will find the best students heading your way.

•   *Visit local organizations.* Periodically visit religious, cultural, social, fraternal, and civic organizations in your community. If you cultivate relationships with these groups, your contacts will swell in numbers as time goes by.

•   *Contact military discharge centers.* A number of smaller organizations report a very high degree of satisfaction with military discharge centers as sources for new employees. These organizations find that former military personnel are disciplined, responsive, and eager to start new careers.

•   *Run advertisements.* We have said that traditional help-wanted ads are not particularly successful or cost-effective, but we would not rule out *all* advertising. We recommend preparing and distributing high-quality fliers and brochures that point up opportunities within your company. You can then have these available in the various places you recruit and in a host of other locales, from college dormitories to museums and libraries. You can also list employment openings with various offices, from career guidance centers in high schools and colleges to unemployment compensation centers.

Retaining Talent

After you have recruited the employees, how do you keep them on and keep them successful? Some of the tactics being used today by the service superstars point the way to actions that will need to be taken in the future.

Earlier, we talked about the job offer of the future. The future is *now,* and organizations need to use more creativity in structuring a job-offer package with long-term benefits or they will find themselves empty-handed. We would like to elaborate on a few aspects of this package and its impact on employee retention.

Career Ladders

Because hospitality continues to be the fastest-growing employment arena in our country, a restaurant is an ideal place to install a career ladder. According to Hall, a career ladder can also be thought of as a *career development system,* because it has many inter-related components. Its structure consists of a visible sequence of jobs through which an employee can progress. It has supportive processes that predict job vacancies and inform people of these vacancies, and it contains a vehicle for planned advancement. Training and development opportunities are provided to qualified people seeking better jobs.

Career ladders reinforce the practice of promoting from within. Service superstars follow this practice and ensure that the entire system is highly visible and marketed to all employees via a strong commitment from the top. Figure 9.2 presents a model career ladder for a full-service restaurant.

In order for any kind of structured career ladder to work, the company must provide training in addition to direction. The increasing scarcity of truly qualified and adaptable workers at all levels of the organization further increases the need for lifelong learning and cross-training. Companies that hire at midcareer or from established professional or hourly part-time labor pools may not need to provide as much technical training, but they should still provide orientation as a way of quickly transmitting the organization's mission, strategy, values, and culture.

Corporate universities, such as those developed by McDonald's and Holiday Inn, are becoming a regular part of many organizations. The curriculum generally contains technical skill components, but a growing part of corporate students' time is dedicated to the study of the corporate mission and values, the key strategic components that are presumed to give the organization competitive advantage, and the models of management behavior that the organization perceives as valuable to its success. Even McDonald's highly regarded Hamburger University, which offers courses accredited by some colleges and universities, has shifted its curriculum markedly from technical to interpersonal and decision-making skills. While Hamburger University continues to play a role in determining career development and expansion opportunities for its managers and licensees, its primary role is to acculturate or "McDonaldize" employees.

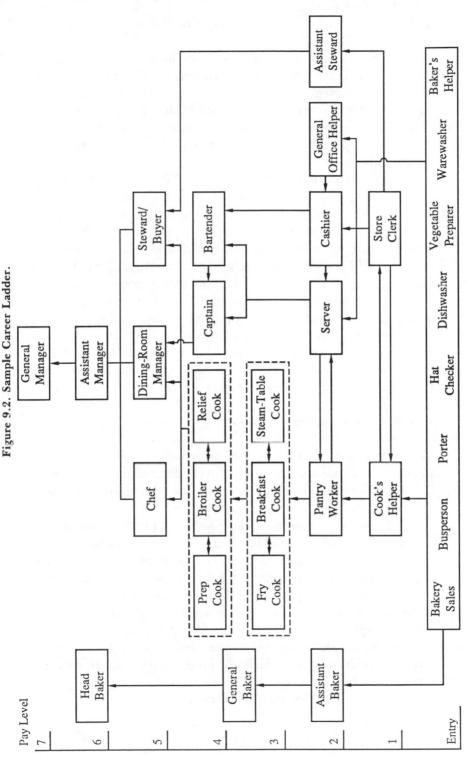

Figure 9.2. Sample Career Ladder.

Source: Adapted from Hall, 1989.

Other initiatives that organizations are addressing through large training investments include training employees (especially current line managers) how to train others, training employees with diverse backgrounds how to succeed in strong, unified, and frequently inhospitable organization cultures, and training employees how to understand and work with others with different values and styles.

Although it may not yet be identifiable as a trend, there is evidence that some business organizations are beginning to extend their training efforts outside the organization through participation in training and education programs in the community. More than fifty business organizations in Chicago, for example, offer industry education in insurance, banking, hospitality, and health care as curriculum components within the Chicago public schools. The Cosmopolitan Chamber of Commerce, a not-for-profit organization whose membership includes many large Chicago-area companies and more than 200 small minority-owned companies, offers business education courses to potential minority entrepreneurs and employees through the Chamber's Free School of Business Management.

Flexibility in Procedures and Pay

Organizations that want to keep their best people must learn to adapt to the new breed of employee. Part of the innovation is going to come in terms of how we pay people and what we pay people for.

As we have discussed, and as Perry (1988b) has documented, we are witnessing radical changes in pay systems. Perry notes that the American Productivity and Quality Center reported that 75 percent of employers now use at least one form of nontraditional pay plan — a radical surge in the last five years. Gainsharing plans, for example, reward improvements in productivity, quality, and service. Pay-for-knowledge systems pay workers for the skills they master, as well as the tasks they perform. Incentive pay is spreading rapidly into hospitals, banks, and other labor-intensive service providers.

As one example cited by Perry, Lincoln Electric has had

tremendous success with its incentive system (as we noted earlier). Factory workers are paid on a piecework basis; their bonuses average 97.6 percent of regular earnings, making them the highest-paid workers in the industry. The results for the company are astounding as well: fifty-four years without a losing quarter, forty years with no layoffs, and an average worker who is three times more productive than counterparts in other companies.

Expanded Benefits

The new and more competitive strategic marketplace, changing labor-force demographics, and corporate attempts to deal with the challenges posed are also promoting rapid change in the realm of benefits. Benefits have traditionally been provided for full-time employees only, but part-timers now have reason for optimism. Many Hay Group clients, for example, report that they expect some to offer core benefits to all (including part-time) employees. Universal core benefits have been needed for at least a decade, in part to facilitate the entry of the persistently under- or unemployed into the work force. Legislation requiring universal core benefits is now expected.

This direction in benefits will be accompanied by continued reductions in expensive benefits and perquisites for higher-level executives, increased contributions by all employees for benefits above a core level, and continuing movement toward a flexible benefits concept. Although many of the benefits trends are generated by cost considerations, there appears to be a strong interest in shifting the resulting savings over a larger employee base.

One major trend that impacts the area of benefits is the increase in numbers of dual-career couples and the consequent emphasis on the need for dependent care, day care for children, and financial assistance for such care. Indeed, child care may well be *the* challenge to society for the 1990s, with benefits reaching today's workers — and tomorrow's.

As Jaclyn Fierman reports, studies done by the High/Scope Educational Research Foundation in Ypsilanti, Michigan, indicate that just one year of high-quality preschool before kindergarten cuts the likelihood that a person will become a dropout by one-third! The organization that provides or contributes to preschooling thus helps ensure quality in the worker pool of the future. In addition, providing preschooling, day care, or daycare benefits eases the burden on today's workers and is a sound investment. Child care is not a luxury but a smart business response to the need to recruit, retain, and motivate the highest-quality people.

Other new additions to many corporate benefits portfolios are corporate wellness and employee assistance programs, along with corporate policies, equipment, and facilities designed to increase worker health and safety. Corporate exercise facilities, no-smoking work environments, confidential drug and alcohol referral and treatment services, improved CRT screens, family counseling, and other services are increasingly offered to corporate employees to reduce total benefits costs and retain personnel.

Participative Management

Another important business trend that is a positive factor in retaining employees is participative management (see Chapter Two). Rather than reiterate reasons for its importance here, we present a success story to illustrate its potential benefits.

Shenandoah Life Insurance is a 250-employee firm in Roanoke, Virginia, that has taken positive steps to keep its work force for life. These steps, according to the American Society for Personnel Administration (1989b), began with an employee attitude survey taken in late 1976 that showed that morale was low and communication was lacking. According to Dick Wagner, vice president of Industrial Insurance Services, management then took a tremendous leap of faith. Over the next decade, it involved employees in decision making at such high levels of management that the superior-to-employee ratio plummeted to 1:7 from 1:37. As part of this process, a consultant provided a quality program for all employees, involving forty hours of compulsory training in problem solving, brainstorming, and reaching group consensus. By 1989, the old ways of policy processing were gone. Today, each self-managing team handles all of its own policy processing itself and takes care of its own management and disciplinary problems. The traditional pyramid has been reversed: managers now work for the employees, instead of vice versa.

All of this additional responsibility requires additional skills, so Shenandoah Life installed a pay-for-knowledge program to reward its employees as they learn. Merit pay increases have gone from an average of 2 to 10 percent to an average of 12 percent annually.

The employees have benefited, both financially and in the satisfaction that they derive from their work. The company has benefited as well, in increased efficiency and speed and accelerated productivity. In fact, productivity is up by 42.7 percent since 1985; the average employee, who formerly processed 3,386 pieces of work yearly, now processes 4,833. In addition, Shenandoah Life is retaining valued employees and developing a loyal work force.

Meeting the Challenges of the 1990s

The trend toward change is clear, and it will continue. The bottom line is that the organizations to prosper into the year 2000 must begin to adapt now.

Human resource management and company competitiveness are more closely linked than ever before, and this tie will get even more close as the years go by. The American Society for Personnel Administration (1989a) has taken some very broad initiatives in meeting the challenges of the 1990s. It has reviewed future trends and patterns of more than 200 specific issues and identified five basic areas where change is occurring.

1. *Employer/employee rights.* There has been a shift in employer/ employee negotiating from the bargaining table to the courtroom as organizations and individuals attempt to define rights, obligations, and responsibilities. Among the many specific issues are job entitlement, privacy (as in testing issues), whistle-blowing, mandated benefits, and comparable worth.

2. *Changing demographics.* The aging of the work force has major implications for all aspects of human resource management. Among the issues in this area are the shrinking pool of entry-level workers, funding for retirement health benefits, increasing numbers of nonpermanent and contract employees, and plateauing and motivation.

3. *Work and family relationships.* Due in part to the rapid increase of women in the workplace, as well as to growing interest in and concern for the family, there is increasing demand for recognition and support of family-related employee concerns such as day care, child-care leave, alternative work plans, elder care, and parental leave.

4. *Productivity, quality, and competitiveness.* The calls for increased productivity, quality, and competitiveness will grow in intensity over the coming years. Among the issues in this area are productivity improvement, worker participation, quality programs and measurement, globalization, and downsizing.

5. *Education, training, and retraining.* As organizations trim personnel and gear up for competition within the global economy, the skills and competence of the available pool of employees are becoming a pivotal issue. Among the key issues in this area are literacy, employee education and training, management development, plant closings, and industry obsolescence.

Turnover: Causes, Costs, and Cures

The recommendations described thus far in this chapter are all directed at retaining employees in a changing world and workplace. In various ways, they all address the issue of avoiding a major cause of backsliding: turnover. High employee turnover and the shortsightedness of businesses that think they can make money without customer service are, according to Thomas, the major causes of poor service. In our opinion, turnover leads the way and can logically be expected to do so in the future.

Our research indicates that high employee turnover (which often results in staffing shortfalls) costs the average service business between 5 and 10 percent of its customer base annually. This lost business often cannot be made up. In addition, the business faces the costs of hiring and training new personnel. Given these costs and today's demographic situation, what business can afford high levels of turnover?

In our analysis of turnover, we have found the major causes to be poor or inappropriate selection processes, inadequate orientation, unclear expectations (on the part of supervisor and employee alike), ineffective supervision, unsatisfactory personnel performance reviews, and the fact that rewards are not linked to performance and results. In general, the cures involve training managers in management and supervisory skills (starting with behavioral interviewing) and establishing good orientation processes. There is no panacea; these cures require commitment and diligence. But given the effort required to locate and hire the right employees, companies should be willing to expend extra effort to retain them.

Setting realistic expectations at the outset is a good place to start. Management needs to tell prospective employees what it can and cannot deliver in terms of salary, bonuses, and other resources. Although some people are likely to feel disappointment (and will perhaps turn down your job offer), that disappointment will not be as great as the disappointment resulting from unkept promises based on unrealistic expectations.

Being creative with rewards may help to reduce staff turnover. Pay and promotion are far from the only tangible incentives that we can offer employees to stay on the job and work effectively. For example, one potentially effective reward that costs nothing is the opportunity to work for an understanding and challenging manager. If employees find satisfaction in working for a boss who gives them professional respect and autonomy on the job, that "hands-off" style may be a reward in itself and can make the employees less willing to take jobs elsewhere. (See Chapter Seven for a more detailed discussion of rewards and recognition.)

There are many other nonmonetary rewards that can give an employee second thoughts about leaving the company. They include:

- *Flexible scheduling that gives employees a measure of control over their work hours*. This is especially useful for people struggling to balance the demands of home life and work life (for example, working parents).

- *Recognizing good job performance.* This can range from saying thank you for a job well done to granting a spontaneous afternoon off.
- *Recognizing positive employee attitudes and effort.* Too often we focus only on results and neglect to recognize the effort needed to obtain them. We can reward attitude and effort by, for example, sending a letter of commendation to an employee (and adding it to his or her personnel file).
- *Providing a choice of job assignments.* Satisfaction with one's work is a major factor in employee loyalty.
- *Improving information flow and communication.* Seeing the bigger picture can make an employee's job seem easier and more successful.
- *Allowing input into decision making.* A participatory climate can make employees feel that they are a valuable asset to the company.

Do not make the mistake of assuming that you know what is best for your staff in the way of rewards. Instead, go directly to your people and ask them what rewards they value. (You might use the list of suggestions above as a starting point for this exchange.) In order to keep your share of top-quality people, you must discuss with them their needs and wishes. Your survival over the next decade may well depend on it!

Chapter 10

CREATE STRATEGIES FOR CONTINUOUSLY IMPROVING SERVICE QUALITY

To survive and grow in today's global market, a business must satisfy its customers by providing them with quality goods and delivering quality services. This requires a continuous reassessment of customers' needs and an unswerving commitment to change when necessary to meet or exceed customers' expectations.

— Paul A. Allaire
President and CEO
Xerox

Even a careful analysis of the current trends cannot fully prepare us for the unknown — and unknowable — changes of the future. How, then, can a company prepare for the future? The first step, on recognizing that change will come quickly, is to prepare the organization to adapt with similar speed.

Look, for example, at how quickly technology has changed in the past decade. Paper communication is giving way to electronic mail; communication from car, plane, home, or the street-corner by voice or fax is becoming commonplace; the science of robotics is altering labor; materials are becoming more durable; transportation and shipping options have increased. These have been rapid changes, but we may well see ten times as much technological progress in the next decade as we have experienced in the past decade.

217

Technological Innovation

What sort of progress might we see? In his article on "Technology in the Year 2000," Eugene Bylinsky tells us that many of the changes that will affect the business world stem from what is expected to be enormous proliferation and miniaturization in the field of computers. Miniaturized computers will respond to handwritten or spoken queries and commands. In addition, corporate supercomputers a thousand times more powerful than today's fastest computers will be used to create new materials. Electronic books will become travel companions; we may carry as many as 200 novels on trips with us.

Telecommunication networks will link the world. Computerized networks will process voice, printed data, and video images with equal ease. As part of this process, we might assume that the strongest growth markets of the future will include cellular telephones, facsimile machines, high-definition televisions and VCRs, and home satellite dishes.

Technological changes have significantly altered the mission and structure of industry sectors such as manufacturing, health care, telecommunications, and trucking. In addition to raising the expected standards for product quality and service delivery, technological innovations have dramatically changed the knowledge and skill requirements for effective participation in the labor force.

We (and many others) believe that technology may bring with it a variety of ways to alleviate the critical labor shortages of highly skilled workers we are now experiencing. As one example, robots are being used not only in traditional manufacturing jobs, where they were first introduced, but also in the service sector. In "Invasion of the Service Robots," Bylinsky explains that robots are being used in tasks as diverse as picking oranges, taking care of handicapped and elderly people, cleaning office buildings and hotels, guarding commercial buildings, and helping police officers and brain surgeons.

In U.S. laboratories, more than 1,200 robots already perform such intricate tasks as weighing, measuring, and mixing minute quantities of chemicals, medications, and even DNA.

Other identified fields for robot applications include building and maintaining off-shore oil rigs, working on construction sites, assembling space stations, pumping gasoline, preparing fast foods, fighting fires, and inspecting high-tension electric equipment.

Even with the help that robotics may provide, the critical shortage of highly skilled workers, coupled with growth in the economy, will make it even more necessary to do more with less.

We visualize a series of continuous reductions in force at all levels of white-collar employment. These reductions in force will primarily affect marginal performers, who will be identified through more sophisticated approaches to performance standards and performance measurement.

American Businesses in the Global Economy

For the past several years, our national economy has been stagnant. In turn, minimal to slow growth has assisted in creating a more competitive business environment, forcing organizations to vie more effectively for more limited and more highly valued consumer dollars.

Meanwhile, the international situation has changed radically:

- Through political pressure and/or economic necessity, traditional foreign markets are more receptive to American products and services as well as American-owned production facilities. Despite continuing problems with the trade balance, American exports have *increased* dramatically since 1985.
- The increased need for more competitive domestic business activity mentioned above, combined with the willingness of traditionally "debtor nations" to more effectively participate in business processes, has created increased consumer and production opportunities.
- New market opportunities are opening up at breathtaking rates. The falling away of walls, barbed-wire fences, and iron curtains is creating access to vast new markets and redefining "pent-up demand." Similarly, newly participating

populations offer significant opportunities for overseas production and impact domestic labor-force demography through immigration.

These radical changes in domestic and international strategic market conditions — as well as other changes in demography, economics, domestic and international political contexts, technology, social trends and values, and market opportunities — are challenging American business organizations. Successful businesses are responding by making revolutionary changes in the systems and processes of their organizations. Performance data from those organizations that have survived the "change gauntlet" seem to indicate that these changes have had a revitalizing impact.

Data from the Hay Group's organization effectiveness survey data base indicate that, for the most part, these organization changes seem to be having an encouraging impact on management personnel. Perceptions of the conditions of rank-and-file employees, however, suggest that benefits of constructive organization change may not have yet trickled down. If these observations are valid, most of the rewards of new organization systems and processes may not yet be realized. It is essential that these changes reach the rank and file and that they be well received there; otherwise, the process of adaptation may falter.

Competitive strategy will, Kupfer tells us, include an emphasis on global challenges. Businesses will need to know more and sooner about competitors, customers, technology, economy, and their own organizations. Any organization that does not put customer and employee satisfaction first will come out second-best in a competitive race. Our prevailing concern is that there will be too much preoccupation with strategy and not enough hands-on leadership and management.

As a general summary of worldwide trends, Sadler and Barham tell us that we are witnessing the movement in management from the old world order of efficiency, productivity, optimism, conformity, and authority to a new order emphasizing enterprise, marketing, change, initiative, and leadership. This fundamental transition in the global business environment is dominated by the shift to a service economy, wherein the scarce resource will be knowledge.

Preparing for the New Work Force

Pierre Goetschin, of the Management Development Institute in Lausanne, Switzerland, notes that since the 1970s, the management of human resources has become one of the key components of business strategy. He discusses the internal and external pressures of the past two decades that have motivated the attention of a number of business establishments. Consider the trends that Goetschin identifies:

- Increased competition puts a premium on intelligence, skills, creativity, and entrepreneurship.
- Higher levels of education produce people with a greater sense of their own worth; as employees, these people demand more autonomy and independence.
- Corporate structures are flattening, leading to increased delegation of responsibilities and power.
- Technologies are changing the patterns of work.
- The number of scientists and highly trained specialists employed by companies is growing.
- New reward systems have been developing.
- Corporate values, cultures, and images are being integrated into policies.

Hervé Serieyx, a French management consultant, advises us on the need to quickly identify environmental shifts and respond with change as necessary. He too predicts intense competition, accelerated technological change, and continuing turbulence and uncertainty. Serieyx adds that, because of changes affecting customers and employees, the need is greater than ever for quality management. Companies must continuously improve the quality of products and services to satisfy customers' increasing demands.

Quality performance can be obtained only through constant effort and innovation at all levels of the organization, starting with the shop floor. The widest possible participation is necessary throughout the organization for everything from developing mission statements and plans for their fulfillment to creating alternative scenarios and intelligent systems. Serieyx challenges business and industry to put into practice the adage that human resources are an organization's most important strategic weapon. Indeed, this is valid advice: the enterprises of the year 2000 that prosper will do so by mobilizing the intelligence and effort of all their personnel.

Further, given the tremendous shift in the composition of the work force, Badi and others remind us that tomorrow's supervisors and managers will need to effectively monitor, motivate, and manage employees of increasingly wide variety. Companies will need to recruit, orient, teach, and train men and women of all races, cultures, ages, religions, physical abilities, sexual attitudes, and life-styles, and adapt to their needs. They will need to evolve ways to view the range of diversity as an asset and use it as a strength in developing the organization. The managerial skills necessary for these tasks will be extraordinary.

Looking to the Future

In addition to the trends that we can extrapolate from today's trends and therefore plan for, we must prepare ourselves and our organizations for the probability that many — some estimates are as high as 80 percent — of tomorrow's jobs will be in fields for which we do not have training today. The need for new skills and talent will be ever shifting and may well tax managerial creativity and adaptability.

The future of American industry will rely in large measure on our human resource management. To succeed in the future, businesses have no choice: they must adapt to new technologies, and they must learn how to manage work-force diversity constructively and efficiently.

APPENDIXES

A RESOURCE TOOLKIT

A. Outside Change Agents

In this appendix, we will give some clues to determining when a change agent from outside the organization is needed, characteristics to look for in a change agent, and ways to help ensure that the chosen change agent is successful in meeting the organization's goals.

The basic conditions that mandate strategic change are usually accompanied by a need for a senior-level executive to introduce and implement those changes. Much as we believe in promotion from within, very often the changes required are so drastic that an outside executive is necessary. The reasons for bringing in an outside change agent can generally be divided into four categories, as described here.

- *Business environment.* When changes in the business environment — whether a slip in profits, a decline in sales, the entry of new competition, or some other factor — demand a new approach, an outside change agent is sometimes needed to initiate and superintend this approach.
- *Diversification and growth.* Existing management may not be capable of a sufficiently rapid response to needed changes. In that case, an outside change agent can provide the initiative.
- *Technology.* If the right people to lead and manage changes in the existing and required new technology are not on board, new skills and abilities must be introduced into the organization by an outside change agent.
- *People.* If it is anticipated that current management will have difficulty seeing new perspectives, adapting to a highly participative management style, or strengthening the organization, an outside change agent is needed.

The characteristics that one should look for in an outside change agent include the following:

Action orientation	Dynamism
Results orientation	Conceptual skills
Persistence	Commanding presence
High energy level	Broad business orientation
Demonstrated leadership	Excellent communication
Exceptional intelligence	skills: oral and written
Sense of urgency	Sense of vision and perspective
Creativity	Analytical abilities
Willingness to risk	Resistance to intimidation
Self-confidence	

Not all change agents possess all of these characteristics, but most share a restless dissatisfaction with the status quo. Simply stated, they have a need to achieve and the ability, knowledge, and self-confidence to make their plans happen.

In the process of interviewing and selecting a change agent, management should put time and effort into learning about the agent's approach. Our experience suggests that successful change agents share a common approach in new situations. They

- Develop an understanding of the business and its culture
- Address the most important strategic business considerations
- Merchandize and market themselves in their disciplines
- Measure and evaluate their own effectiveness

In other than the most pressing turnaround situations, the successes we have worked with ease into rather than plunge into their jobs, aware that an organization can absorb and digest only a limited amount of change at any given time or over any period of time. Before prescribing specific changes, they take time to learn the business: they lunch regularly with the executive officers individually and collectively; they study the business, strategic, and marketing plans and the financial statements; and they carefully cultivate and nourish relationships above, below, and at their own level. In the process, they quickly assimilate and evaluate the real situation. They also learn the real values of the organization, in terms of what goal-seeking behaviors are rewarded or discouraged, how decisions are made, and how problems are solved.

In addressing the most important business needs, the change agents who succeed do so by encouraging a variety of senior-level executives, including the CEO, to voice their priorities, goals, and plans. They anticipate obstacles and take preventive action to win others to their point of view. They take whatever action is necessary to position themselves and their expertise. In the process of managing relationships, they successfully market themselves and their ideas.

Not content to merely gain acceptance, they frequently pause to reflect, to sense, to listen, and to evaluate. They ask themselves the following questions: Where can I contribute added value to the existing systems in a manner totally compatible with the cultural norms? How well am I doing? They constantly analyze their own efforts, measure their own effectiveness, and ask others to suggest improvements.

To hire a change agent halfheartedly is to invite defeat.

To help ensure that the change agent will be successful, the CEO and other top managers must be ready to pay the full price — and not just in dollars. A new chief marketing officer, for example, will impact and perhaps drastically change the way you conduct your business and even your daily interpersonal transactions. The shift from conservative to dynamic leadership has similarly profound implications for the entire organization.

The hiring of a change agent implies subscription to the three conditions necessary for behavioral change:

1. Recognition of the need to change, coupled with knowledge of what to change and why, based on appropriate diagnosis
2. Capacity and willingness on the part of the CEO and the CEO's direct reports — that is, the next layer of management — to make the needed changes
3. Skills and competencies, corporate-wide, to manage and implement the needed changes

The second of these conditions is a major stumbling block. Unfortunately, too often neither the CEO nor the CEO's direct reports have the capacity or the willingness to make the needed changes. This is particularly true when a change agent has responsibilities that cut across all functional lines — responsibilities, for example, in such diverse areas as finances and human resources. An outsider's changes in management style and behavior, work methods, standards, and priorities may threaten the very foundation on which a few senior executives have built their careers. Regrettably, it takes only one or two managers to ensure that the newly hired change agent fails. To forestall failure, the CEO might carefully position the individual coming into the organization through involvement of the executive team in the definition of what needs to be done, the position description, and the selection process itself.

Assuming that a competent executive search firm can find you a change agent, will you and your organization support the newly hired executive in both introducing and implementing the needed changes? As a litmus test of how supportive you and your organization might be, ask yourself these questions:

- Does a position description exist for the change agent? Is this description comprehensive?
- What is the real purpose of this position? Why does the job exist? What contribution to the business is expected?
- Consider the senior management team's expectations as to the position. Are these expectations realistic? Consistent?
- Is there a plan for orienting the agent? What support is expected as far as budget, staffing, authority, and backup? Have you established appropriate office space and secretarial support?
- Have you determined how the agent is expected to relate to superiors, peers, and subordinates?

The bottom line is a recognition that the management team must be totally committed to the change — and to the idea that their own behavior must change. Otherwise, the new executive stands a high probability of failure no matter how many successes have gone before.

Unless a special effort is made to integrate the new person into the management team and to discuss and highlight the organization's cultural norms and values, there is great risk of failure. Management can assist that integration by allowing the change-agent two or three months to get acquainted with the job and the people before he or she assumes the other responsibilities of the position.

Because the arrival of a new executive, particularly a change agent, sends a message throughout the company, people's expectations are raised. Even so, change is not easy. In fact, it is sometimes downright painful, but often there is no other alternative.

B. Management Climate and Leadership Effectiveness Survey

Please circle the number corresponding to the response that most accurately reflects your attitude toward each of the following statements:

	Strongly Agree	Tend to Agree	Doesn't Apply to Me; Don't Know	Tend to Disagree	Strongly Disagree
1. Members of my work unit receive regular feedback about their performance in relation to goals.	1	2	3	4	5

	Strongly Agree	Tend to Agree	Doesn't Apply to Me; Don't Know	Tend to Disagree	Strongly Disagree
2. There's more independent effort than teamwork in my work unit.	1	2	3	4	5
3. Members of my work unit are encouraged to think for themselves and suggest ways to improve the work environment.	1	2	3	4	5
4. Major decisions affecting our work unit require group consensus before they are adopted.	1	2	3	4	5
5. Management often makes decisions without explaining the rationale.	1	2	3	4	5
6. Members of my work unit are committed to achieving our group's goals.	1	2	3	4	5
7. When a problem needs to be solved, members of my group usually work together.	1	2	3	4	5
8. Members of my work unit are seldom asked for their opinions before decisions are made.	1	2	3	4	5
9. My co-workers and I help make the decisions about the important issues affecting us.	1	2	3	4	5
10. The rumor mill is often a better source of information than our managers.	1	2	3	4	5
11. Members of my work unit meet regularly to review how we are doing on our goals.	1	2	3	4	5

	Strongly Agree	Tend to Agree	Doesn't Apply to Me; Don't Know	Tend to Disagree	Strongly Disagree
12. There is little sense of "groupness" in my work unit.	1	2	3	4	5
13. Management appreciates and uses our suggestions for improving the work unit.	1	2	3	4	5
14. The authority and power for decision making clearly rests with management in this organization.	1	2	3	4	5
15. I feel free to go to management to find out about decisions that are being made.	1	2	3	4	5

C. Employee-Based Service Performance Standards

	Above Standard	Standard	Below Standard
Communication Skills	Listens attentively and avoids interruptions	Listens most of the time; occasionally interrupts	Frequently interrupts
	Clearly and accurately transmits messages in a timely manner	Usually transmits messages in a clear and accurate manner	Has difficulty transmitting messages in a clear, accurate, and timely manner
	Is rarely misunderstood by others	Is occasionally misunderstood by others	Is frequently misunderstood by others
	Allows for feedback and acts on it	Occasionally fails to allow for or act on feedback	Seldom asks for feedback
	Is concise and to the point	Sometimes overstates oral and written messages	Embellishes oral and written messages; is frequently verbose
Cooperation	Pitches in to help others without being asked or told to do so	Pitches in when asked most of the time to help others	Complains about being asked to help others
	Puts the good of the department first	Puts the good of the department first most of the time	Puts the good of self over that of the department
	Completes unpleasant tasks without complaint	Completes unpleasant tasks with occasional complaint	Complains about unpleasant tasks
	Works with other departments, providing assistance or information necessary for the other departments to function well	Assists other departments if it does not interfere with own work	Frequently says, "That's not my job," particularly when help is needed by other departments
Dependability	Is steady and reliable; can be counted on consistently	Is steady and reliable most of the time; honors most commitments	Tends to forget commitments on occasion; is not totally dependable
	Is consistently on time; is seldom (if ever) absent	Is seldom late for work; phones in well in advance if unable to come in	Comes in late for work without reason
	Comes in early and stays late; does whatever it takes to get the job done	Gives a fair day's work for a fair day's pay	Is absent one day a month or more; does not carry fair share of the load
	Meets responsibilities; does not need to be prompted	Occasionally requires reminders to get responsibilities completed	Requires frequent reminders or assistance to complete responsibilities

Enthusiasm	Eagerly completes fair share and usually goes beyond	Seldom complains about workload; completes fair share	Frequently complains about workload; does not complete fair share
	Is cheerful and friendly in all situations	Is pleasant in most situations	Is unpleasant in some situations
	Is consistently encouraging; coaches other employees (peers)	Sometimes encourages and coaches others	Frequently discourages others by comments
	Rarely complains; if does so, provides a solution	Voices legitimate complaints on occasion	Often complains
	Consistently has positive comments about others and the organization	Gives positive feedback when asked	Rarely has anything positive to say about others or the organization
Initiative and Motivation	Performs job responsibilities with minimal direction/supervision	Performs job responsibilities with moderate supervision	Requires frequent supervision to perform basic job responsibilities
	Seeks additional responsibilities	Performs additional responsibilities if asked to do so	Handles additional responsibilities with difficulty (or not at all)
	Identifies and offers solutions to problems/issues	Identifies problems/issues	Rarely identifies problems/issues
	Offers suggestions on alternative methods to improve the job, department, or organization	Suggests alternative methods to improve the job, department, or organization when asked	Makes little or no contribution to finding alternative methods for improving the job, department, or organization
Integrity and Honesty	Willingly admits mistakes and takes initiative to correct them	Admits mistakes when asked and agrees to correct them	Denies mistakes; blames others
	Avoids malicious rumors and takes steps to stop them	Does not spread rumors	Starts or participates in rumors or gossip
	Does not betray a confidence	Occasionally betrays confidences	Is indiscreet with confidential information
	Always does what has been promised	Will do what is promised most of the time	Does not do what is promised
	Consistently upholds policies/procedures	Usually upholds policies/procedures	Knowingly violates policies/procedures

	Above Standard	Standard	Below Standard
Interpersonal Skills	Is able to establish and maintain harmonious relationships with almost everyone	Occasionally has difficulty establishing a harmonious relationship with another individual	Frequently has difficulty establishing harmonious relationships
	Is frequently praised by others for ability to get along (or receives no complaints)	Is occasionally praised by others for ability to get along (or receives few complaints)	Is often complained about by others
	Lightens a situation through humor or positive comments	Does not contribute to making a situation less tense	Often contributes to making situations uncomfortable
	Listens with empathy and responds in a manner that makes the other person feel good	Demonstrates empathy most of the time; occasionally puts self before others	Is rarely empathetic; puts self first most of the time
Judgment and Decision Making	Considers the majority of facts and implications before acting	Occasionally acts before considering all the facts or implications	Frequently does not recognize when a decision is needed or procrastinates in the implementation of decisions
	Makes decisions quickly and accurately and implements them right away	Occasionally procrastinates on tough decisions; implements most decisions right away	Seldom considers all the facts or implications when making decisions
	Invariably has good outcomes from decisions	Has good outcomes most of the time	Frequently has poor outcomes from decisions
	Involves the appropriate people in the process	Occasionally forgets to involve some key people in the process	Rarely involves appropriate people in the process
Ability to Handle Pressure and Priorities	Consistently maintains sight of long-term objective while dealing with the immediate stressful/difficult situation	Sometimes loses sight of long-term objective when challenged by a stressful/difficult situation	Frequently loses sight of long-term objective when challenged by a stressful/difficult situation
	Thinks and responds quickly; is able to improve situation to successfully achieve results	Occasionally has difficulty thinking and responding quickly or improvising; has results that are not always successful	Has difficulty thinking and responding quickly; rarely can improvise to ensure successful results
	Remains calm and is able to keep others under control during a crisis or stressful situation	Remains calm most of the time; occasionally has difficulty controlling others during a crisis or stressful situation	Rarely remains calm; contributes to others' losing control during a crisis or stressful situation
	Completes responsibilities with a high degree of quality even under pressure	Occasionally allows quality to slip with pressure	Frequently has difficulty maintaining standards of quality under pressure

D. Telephone Techniques for Service Leaders

The telephone is, without question, a critical part of every business. How courteously and how rapidly telephone requests are answered gives customers an impression of the company at large. How well employees use the telephone in all tasks, from selling products to setting up appointments, affects the company's bottom line. In this appendix, we provide some tips for effective use of the telephone.

Answering the Phone

A funny thing about business calls: callers expect businesses to "be home" during business hours. Callers do not like to feel that

Note: The material in this resource was contributed by Eileen Montgomery. The authors gratefully acknowledge her generosity in allowing us to use it.

someone is there but not answering the phone. And callers will not wait forever for their calls to be answered; eventually they will simply hang up and call another company.

To alleviate that problem, answer incoming calls within three rings (preferably two). If this is not now possible, make some changes, whether by adding operators or automatic equipment, so that callers can reach their desired party quickly.

When the phone rings, it is always an interruption to the work in front of you. Under no circumstances, however, should you let callers know that they have interrupted you. Before answering the phone, allow yourself a moment to compose yourself and to prepare to devote your full attention to the call.

Answer the phone with a cheerful greeting: "Good morning" (or afternoon or evening). As a matter of courtesy, identify yourself to the caller.

Remember that on the telephone, your words and your voice are your only tools for making an impression; you do not have the benefit of, say, a friendly handshake. If you are angry, you will sound angry; if you are bored, you will sound bored. Enthusiastic, positive people convey that impression on the phone. Your physical posture, general attitude, and personality all influence your tone of voice.

You can control the speed of your speech, the volume and brightness of your tone, the clarity of your pronunciation, and your vocabulary. If you want to improve your voice, you might start by reading *Change Your Voice, Change Your Life,* a book by Morton Cooper, perhaps America's best-known voice specialist. He feels that a "magic voice" is a trait shared by almost all great people. Experiment a bit, and you will prove to yourself that a good telephone voice is a definite asset in conducting business on the telephone.

Using Hold

There is absolutely nothing as frustrating to a caller than being put on hold. Therefore, use hold *very* sparingly. Never put a caller on hold without permission. Offer the caller a choice: "Would you like to hold for a few minutes, or could I call you back?"

When you absolutely must use hold, give the caller an estimate of the length of the wait. Check back with the caller sooner, even if only to say, "I haven't forgotten you; I'm still checking." When you return, be sure to thank the caller for waiting.

Transferring Calls

A poorly handled transfer is sure to alienate a caller. If every employee understood the corporate structure, most calls could be correctly transferred the *first* time.

The best way to transfer an incoming call is to have the operator/receptionist stay on the line to pass the caller to the next employee. On-line introductions are ideal, but the volume of incoming calls often makes this impossible.

Before transferring any call, explain the transfer to the caller. At the very least, announce the name of the department to which you are transferring. Even better, announce the name of the person to whom you are transferring, that person's title, and the department. This gives the caller the chance to correct what might be an inappropriate transfer. If you do not know who can handle the call, ask the caller to hold briefly while you find out. Then return to the call, provide the transfer information, and complete the transfer.

Screening Calls

If you are able to have your calls screened, by all means do so. One significant advantage to call screening is the potential to schedule your calls. You can work without interruption while incoming calls are screened and stop later to return all calls at once. Call screening also gives you some extra time to pull your files, at least mentally, and prepare to offer some of the information the caller will request.

Screening calls is a delicate art, however. Be sure to set up a questioning system by which your screener can determine whether the caller is one you will want to speak to. Have your secretary use the truth in screening calls. Worded gently, the truth will discourage the callers you want to discourage and encourage those who are important to you. For example, if you do not intend to take a certain sales call, your secretary might say, "I'm afraid Ms. Smith will not have time to discuss that with you. She asked me to let you know." This saves the caller's time and allows the caller to move on to other calls that may be more productive.

Taking Messages

When we think of telephone messages, most of us think of pink, preprinted message pads. While these forms cover simple phone messages, they cannot always convey sufficient information. Professional secretaries might take better messages with a blank pad, recording any important information the caller gives.

If message forms are to be part of your company, design your own. Include a space for the caller's name, company or organization, phone number, and time of call. Then provide lines for the message, for the action you should take (return call, file information, and so on), for the approximate time to return call, and for impressions. A record of impressions of the call can be invaluable: Did the call seem urgent? Was the caller panicked? These perceptions can add a personal touch to your return calls.

It may also be helpful to provide space for a priority rating on your message form. This rating can be as simple or complex as you and your employees would like. Your secretary could simply number calls in importance, for example, allowing you to return the most important calls first.

Controlling Use of Telephone Time

Have you ever felt that your last call took up too much of your time? A commonly noted telephone problem is inefficient time management. We lose the benefits of the telephone's convenience when we let calls run on too long.

Get straight to the point in your conversations. Use the telephone to communicate as quickly as possible, within the bounds of politeness. You will save time for yourself and your caller. Monitor your call time. Whenever possible, keep calls to ten minutes or less.

Scheduling calls can also make you more time-efficient. Allocate a certain time during your business day to return phone calls. Mark these calls on your calendar just as you do in-person appointments. If you cannot make contact on your first attempt, schedule an appointment to call back, and keep the appointment.

The Winning Technique

To sum up, here are a few simple rules to help you improve your telephone communication:

- *Know what you are talking about.* Understand your company, your product, and your job. Avoid making promises that you are not sure you can keep.
- *Verify.* To make sure that you understand a caller's request, repeat the points discussed during the conversation. Make sure that you both have the same impression about the result of the conversation.
- *Keep a positive attitude.* Smile while on the phone. It may feel ridiculous at first, but it makes a difference in the way you react to callers. Word your statements in a positive manner. Studies have shown that people understand positively worded statements more quickly than statements worded negatively.
- *Stay calm.* If you hear that a caller is angry, disappointed, or mad, take a deep breath. Remind yourself that you represent your company as a professional. Do not let the caller drag you into a fight, or you will lose control of the call. Listen calmly. Do not interrupt until the caller tells the entire story. Once the caller has finished, ask questions to clarify the problem for yourself.

E. Sample Survey of Employee Opinion

Your management asks you to fill in this questionnaire to express how you feel about your job here. This information will aid management in addressing employee needs and in trying to run this operation more efficiently.

The statements in the questionnaire (that is, its "questions") have been constructed so that your response will reflect your attitudes and opinions. There are no right or wrong answers. The proper answer for you, therefore, is the one that best shows how you feel about the matter. Record your attitude toward each statement by drawing a circle around the number of the response you choose.

Please answer every item; do not skip any. If you are not sure of the meaning of a statement, please ask the person in charge of the survey to explain it to you.

The statements express a wide range of feelings that people might have about their jobs. In recording your feelings, please indicate what *you* think about *your* job — what you like about it and what you dislike.

Please do not discuss the statements with anyone until after the meeting. We want you to express your individual opinions without being influenced by your fellow employees.

This survey is only as useful to you and to your management as you make it. In other words, it can be valuable only if you express your attitudes honestly and frankly in response to each statement.

The answers will be scored by machine according to each *group* of employees. No *person* can be identified in this survey. The questionnaires will be destroyed as soon as the scores for each group are completed.

	Strongly Agree	Tend to Agree	Doesn't Apply to Me; Don't Know	Tend to Disagree	Strongly Disagree
A. Style of Management					
1. My management treats me the way it wants me to treat our customers.	1	2	3	4	5
2. I get regular feedback on the quality of my service performance.	1	2	3	4	5
3. My supervisor helps me solve my work problems.	1	2	3	4	5
4. My management works to create a positive work climate.	1	2	3	4	5
5. My management is interested in me and my work.	1	2	3	4	5
B. Management's Concern for Customer Satisfaction					
1. My management places top priority on customer satisfaction.	1	2	3	4	5

	Strongly Agree	Tend to Agree	Doesn't Apply to Me; Don't Know	Tend to Disagree	Strongly Disagree
2. My supervisor regularly discusses the importance of customer service with me.	1	2	3	4	5
3. I am encouraged to suggest ways to improve customer service.	1	2	3	4	5
4. My management insists on the highest standards for customer service.	1	2	3	4	5
5. My management recognizes and rewards excellence in customer service.	1	2	3	4	5
6. In my job, goals for improving customer service are clearly defined.	1	2	3	4	5
7. Cooperation and teamwork are encouraged.	1	2	3	4	5

C. Quality of Service

	Strongly Agree	Tend to Agree	Doesn't Apply to Me; Don't Know	Tend to Disagree	Strongly Disagree
1. The quality of customer service is excellent in my department.	1	2	3	4	5
2. High-quality service is expected and demanded.	1	2	3	4	5
3. My department has goals for customer service.	1	2	3	4	5
4. We accomplish our goals for customer service.	1	2	3	4	5
5. My management does all that is possible to improve customer satisfaction.	1	2	3	4	5
6. In my department, we help each other to improve customer service.	1	2	3	4	5

	Strongly Agree	Tend to Agree	Doesn't Apply to Me; Don't Know	Tend to Disagree	Strongly Disagree
D. Corporate Leadership					
1. I am proud to work in this organization.	1	2	3	4	5
2. Management does all it can to improve customer service.	1	2	3	4	5
3. Management will act on results of this survey.	1	2	3	4	5
E. Effectiveness of Communication					
1. I get the information I need to do my job.	1	2	3	4	5
2. I'm kept informed about changes that affect my job.	1	2	3	4	5
3. The importance of customer service is regularly communicated to me.	1	2	3	4	5
4. I get worthwhile information from the organization's newsletter.	1	2	3	4	5
5. The organization's newsletter emphasizes the importance of customer service.	1	2	3	4	5
F. The Following Provide Me with a Great Deal of Useful Information:					
1. "Grapevine" (that is, other employees).	1	2	3	4	5
2. Bulletin boards for memos.	1	2	3	4	5
3. One-on-one conversations with my manager or supervisor.	1	2	3	4	5
4. Group meetings with my manager or supervisor.	1	2	3	4	5
5. The organization's newsletter.	1	2	3	4	5
6. Other communications from corporate management.	1	2	3	4	5

F. Exit Interview Questionnaire

To be completed for each employee who has resigned.

Name _____

Office _____

Job title _____

Date interviewed _____

By _____

Termination date _____

Supervisor _____

We want to make this organization a better place to work, and we need your help to do so. Would you please spare five or ten minutes of your time to answer a few questions?

1. If you accepted another job, what does that job offer that your job here did not?
2. What factors contributed to your accepting a job with this company? Were these expectations realized? If not, why not? If you are no longer in the job for which you were initially hired, were subsequent expectations raised?
3. Was the job that you held accurately described when you were hired? To what extent do you feel that your skills were utilized?
4. What constructive comments would you have for management with regard to making our organization a better place in which to work?
5. What are some of the factors that helped to make your employment enjoyable for those parts that you liked?
6. Would you recommend this company to a friend as a place to work? If yes, why? If no, why not?
7. Was your decision to leave influenced by any of the following? (Please check all those that are applicable.)

    * Leaving the city   _____
    * Returning to school   _____
    * Poor health   _____
    * Family circumstances   _____
    * Retirement   _____
    * Better position elsewhere _____
    * Dissatisfaction with:
        Type of work   _____
        Working conditions   _____
        Salary   _____
        Supervision   _____
        Other (please specify) _____

8. What did you think of the following factors in your job or your department? (Please rate each one *excellent, good, fair,* or *poor.*)

	Excellent	Good	Fair	Poor
Orientation to job	—	—	—	—
Physical working conditions	—	—	—	—

	Excellent	Good	Fair	Poor
• Equipment provided	—	—	—	—
• Adequacy of training	—	—	—	—
• Fellow workers	—	—	—	—
• Cooperation within the department	—	—	—	—
• Cooperation within other departments	—	—	—	—
• Workload	—	—	—	—

9. How would you rate your supervisor/manager in each of the following areas?

	Excellent	Good	Fair	Poor
• Demonstrates fair and equal treatment	—	—	—	—
• Provides recognition on the job	—	—	—	—
• Resolves complaints and problems	—	—	—	—
• Follows consistent policies and practices	—	—	—	—
• Informs employees on matters that directly relate to their jobs	—	—	—	—
• Encourages feedback and welcomes suggestions	—	—	—	—
• Expresses instructions clearly	—	—	—	—
• Develops cooperation	—	—	—	—

10. How would you rate the following?

	Excellent	Good	Fair	Poor
• Your salary	—	—	—	—
• Opportunity for advancement	—	—	—	—
• Performance appraisals	—	—	—	—
• Company policies (If fair or poor, explain why.)	—	—	—	—

G. Examples of Customer Opinion Surveys

Passenger Survey

Section A: Some Facts About This Flight

1. In which section are you traveling?
   - ☐ First class
   - ☐ Coach
2. Who paid (or will pay) for this ticket?
   - ☐ Company, client, business associate, or government
   - ☐ Yourself
   - ☐ Relative or friend
3. The primary purpose of this trip?
   - ☐ Business
   - ☐ Personal

4. Could you have made this trip on another airline?
    ☐ Yes
    ☐ No

5. If so, why did you choose our airline?
    ☐ Price   ☐ Reputation
    ☐ Convenience of time   ☐ Frequent-flyer program
    ☐ Quality of service   ☐ Other _____
                                         (Please specify.)

Section B: Your Opinion About Our Service

6. Please rate the service you have received from us. *(Circle one number for each area listed.)*

	Out-stand-ing	Good	Aver-age	Poor	Does Not Apply
A. When making reservations:					
Efficiency of personnel	5	4	3	2	1
Friendliness of personnel	5	4	3	2	1
B. At the airport:					
Efficiency of personnel	5	4	3	2	1
Friendliness of personnel	5	4	3	2	1
Boarding process	5	4	3	2	1
Baggage claim	5	4	3	2	1
C. On the airplane:					
Efficiency of personnel	5	4	3	2	1
Friendliness of personnel	5	4	3	2	1
Cabin cleanliness/comfort	5	4	3	2	1
Meal/beverage service	5	4	3	2	1
In-flight magazine/audio selection	5	4	3	2	1

7. How would you describe our airline? *(Check as many words as you feel apply.)*
    ☐ Reliable   ☐ Convenient
    ☐ Efficient   ☐ Affordable
    ☐ Friendly   ☐ Competent
    ☐ Innovative   ☐ Responsive

8. How would you rate the value of your flight today based on its cost?
    ☐ Excellent   ☐ Poor
    ☐ Good   ☐ Very poor
    ☐ Average

9. All things considered, what is your overall opinion of this flight?
    ☐ Excellent   ☐ Poor
    ☐ Good   ☐ Very poor
    ☐ Average

10. Compared to other airlines, our airline's . . .

	Better	Same	Worse
Overall service is	3	2	1
Value for the money is	3	2	1

11. Name the airline that would be your first choice if all airlines had the same schedules and fares.

    _____

Section C: Some Facts About Your Travel

12. About how many flights have you made in the last twelve months, including this one? *(Count round trips as one flight.)*

    _____

13. How many of these flights were primarily for business purposes?

    _____

14. How many of these flights were made on our airline?

    _____

15a. Are you a member of any frequent-flyer program — that is, a program that offers free trips for accumulating mileage?
     ☐ Yes *(Please answer questions 15b, 15c, 15d, and 15e.)*
     ☐ No *(Please skip to question 16.)*

15b.   In which airline's mileage programs do you most actively participate? *(List the two that you most frequently use.)*

_____

_____

15c.   Other than flight schedules and destinations, why did you join the frequent-flyer program you use most often? *(Check all reasons that apply.)*
  ☐   First-class upgrades for joining
  ☐   First-class upgrades for a nominal charge over the full coach fare
  ☐   First-class upgrades on the reward chart
  ☐   Reduced air fares
  ☐   Free trips
  ☐   Mileage bonus for joining
  ☐   Hotel tie-ins
  ☐   International airline tie-ins
  ☐   Rental car tie-ins
  ☐   Other _____
                         (Please specify.)

15d.   Considering the benefits of frequent-flier programs, how much would you be willing to spend for memberships?
  ☐   Nothing
  ☐   Up to $20
  ☐   Between $20 and $30
  ☐   Between $30 and $50
  ☐   Between $50 and $75
  ☐   Between $75 and $100

15e.   Please rate our frequent-flyer program compared to others in the following areas:

	Better	Same	Worse
Program administration	3	2	1
Awards	3	2	1
Award-redemption procedures	3	2	1
Problem resolution	3	2	1
Promotional materials	3	2	1
Monthly statements	3	2	1
Application procedures	3	2	1

Section D: Just So We Can Classify Your Answers

16. Your occupation:
- ☐ Executive or managerial
- ☐ Professional
- ☐ Government or military
- ☐ Sales
- ☐ Student
- ☐ Homemaker
- ☐ Retired
- ☐ Airline or travel industry employee
- ☐ Other _____
  (Please specify.)

17. Are you self-employed?
- ☐ Yes
- ☐ No

18. Your annual income:
- ☐ Under $10,000
- ☐ $10,000-$19,999
- ☐ $20,000-$29,999
- ☐ $30,000-$39,999
- ☐ $40,000-$49,999
- ☐ $50,000-$59,999
- ☐ $60,000-$74,999
- ☐ $75,000-$99,999
- ☐ $100,000 or more

19. Your education *(check highest level attained):*
- ☐ No formal diploma
- ☐ High school diploma or GED
- ☐ Bachelor's degree
- ☐ Master's degree
- ☐ Doctoral degree

20. Your age:
- ☐ Under 18 years
- ☐ 18-24 years
- ☐ 25-34 years
- ☐ 35-49 years
- ☐ 50-64 years
- ☐ 65 or over

21. Your sex:
- ☐ Male
- ☐ Female

22. Which of the following publications do you read regularly?
    (Check all that apply.)
- ☐ Your local newspaper
- ☐ *Wall Street Journal*
- ☐ *USA Today*
- ☐ *New York Times*
- ☐ *Time*
- ☐ *Newsweek*
- ☐ *Sports Illustrated*
- ☐ *Savvy*
- ☐ *Inc.*
- ☐ *Forbes*
- ☐ *Working Woman*
- ☐ *Business Week*

☐ *U.S. News & World
    Report*
☐ *People*

☐ *Money*
☐ *Frequent Flyer Magazine*

Thank you very much for your time and cooperation! Please use the space below for any additional opinions or comments that you would like to share with us.

Guest Survey

1. How would you rate our hotel on an overall basis?
   ☐ Excellent ☐ Good ☐ Average ☐ Fair ☐ Poor

2. Was your room reservation in order at check in?
   ☐ Yes ☐ No

3. How would you rate the following?

	Excellent	Good	Average	Fair	Poor
Check-in speed efficiency	☐	☐	☐	☐	☐
Cleanliness of room on first entering	☐	☐	☐	☐	☐
Cleanliness and servicing of your room during stay	☐	☐	☐	☐	☐
Decor of your room	☐	☐	☐	☐	☐
Check-out speed efficiency	☐	☐	☐	☐	☐
Value of room for price paid	☐	☐	☐	☐	☐

4. Was everything in working order in your room?
   ☐ Yes ☐ No
   If you checked *no*, would you please tell us what was not in working order?
   ☐ Room air-conditioning
   ☐ Room heating
   ☐ Bathroom plumbing
   ☐ Television
   ☐ Light bulbs
   ☐ Other _____

5. How would you rate the following in terms of their friendly and efficient services?

	Excellent	Good	Average	Fair	Poor
Reservation staff	☐	☐	☐	☐	☐
Front desk clerk	☐	☐	☐	☐	☐
Bell staff	☐	☐	☐	☐	☐
Housekeeping staff	☐	☐	☐	☐	☐
Telephone operators	☐	☐	☐	☐	☐
Gift shop staff	☐	☐	☐	☐	☐
Engineering staff	☐	☐	☐	☐	☐
Front desk cashier	☐	☐	☐	☐	☐

If any members of our staff were especially helpful, please let us know who they are and how they were helpful so that we can show them our appreciation.

Name _____

Position/Comments _____

_____

_____

6. Please rate any of the following that you have used on this visit.

A. Restaurant
   Please indicate name of restaurant

   _____

   ☐ Breakfast   ☐ Lunch   ☐ Dinner

Were you seated promptly? ☐ Yes ☐ No

Was your order taken promptly? ☐ Yes ☐ No

Was your food served promptly? ☐ Yes ☐ No

	Excellent	Good	Average	Fair	Poor
Friendly service	☐	☐	☐	☐	☐
Quality of food	☐	☐	☐	☐	☐
Menu variety	☐	☐	☐	☐	☐
Value for price paid	☐	☐	☐	☐	☐
B. Room Service					
Prompt service	☐	☐	☐	☐	☐
Friendly service	☐	☐	☐	☐	☐
Quality of food	☐	☐	☐	☐	☐
Menu variety	☐	☐	☐	☐	☐
Value for price paid	☐	☐	☐	☐	☐
C. Cocktail Lounge					
Prompt service	☐	☐	☐	☐	☐
Friendly service	☐	☐	☐	☐	☐
Quality of drinks	☐	☐	☐	☐	☐
Value for price paid	☐	☐	☐	☐	☐
D. Banquet/Convention Event					
Prompt service	☐	☐	☐	☐	☐
Friendly service	☐	☐	☐	☐	☐
Quality of food	☐	☐	☐	☐	☐

7. Did you use the "Hot Line" to register any dissatisfaction with our hotel?

☐ No
☐ Yes, problem was resolved
☐ Yes, but problem was not resolved

Please explain any problem that remains unresolved.

_____
_____
_____
_____
_____
_____
_____
_____
_____
_____
_____
_____

8. What was the primary purpose of your visit?

☐ Pleasure
☐ Convention/group meeting or banquet
☐ Business (other than above)

9. Have you stayed at this hotel previously?
   ☐ Yes   ☐ No
10. If in the area again, would you return to this hotel?
    ☐ Yes   ☐ No

Please print the following information:

Departure date _____

Length of stay _____ days. Room number _____

☐ Mr.   ☐ Mrs.   ☐ Miss   ☐ Ms.

Name _____

Home address _____ Zip _____

Company or organization _____

Business address _____ Zip _____

Thank you very much for your response. Your evaluation will make a difference.

H. Sample Survey for Internal Clients

The internal client (or customer) survey is designed to measure how effectively the various departments within an organization respond to each other's needs and requirements. It quantifies people's perceptions of how effectively their business needs are being serviced within the organization. For example, the survey measures the quality, timeliness, and responsiveness of the several departments or subsidiaries in terms of the products and services they provide for each other.

The internal client survey is based on the fact, proven by outstanding leaders in customer service industries, that it is not possible to service customers properly if the organization does not have effective teamwork and cooperation among its various subsidiaries that supply each other with products or services. Excellence in customer service begins at home.

Questions 30 through 47 relate to earlier questions. In analyzing the data, you may want to have the answers to the related questions set side by side to help make any differences in the perception of service, quality, timeliness, and responsiveness immediately clear. The following questions are directly related:

1 – 30	8 – 36	14 – 42
2 – 31	9 – 37	15 – 43
3 – 32	10 – 38	16 – 44
4 – 33	11 – 39	19 – 45
6 – 34	12 – 40	20 – 46
7 – 35	13 – 41	21 – 47

1. Please indicate, by circling your choice, the degree to which the following departments/subsidiaries are responsive to your business needs:

Department	To a very great extent	To a reasonably satisfactory extent	To a less than satisfactory extent	To a limited extent	Not applicable
a. _____	1	2	3	4	5
b. _____	1	2	3	4	5
c. _____	1	2	3	4	5
d. _____	1	2	3	4	5

Comments:

2. To what extent does the quality of services/products of each department/subsidiary meet your requirements?

Department	To a very great extent	To a reasonably satisfactory extent	To a less than satisfactory extent	To a limited extent	Not applicable
a. _____	1	2	3	4	5
b. _____	1	2	3	4	5
c. _____	1	2	3	4	5
d. _____	1	2	3	4	5

Comments:

3. To what extent does each department/subsidiary jointly predetermine standards for the quality of services/products provided to you?

Department	To a very great extent	To a reasonably satisfactory extent	To a less than satisfactory extent	To a limited extent	Not applicable
a. _____	1	2	3	4	5
b. _____	1	2	3	4	5
c. _____	1	2	3	4	5
d. _____	1	2	3	4	5

Comments:

4. To what extent are service commitments delivered to you in a timely manner?

Department	To a very great extent	To a reasonably satisfactory extent	To a less than satisfactory extent	To a limited extent	Not applicable
a. _____	1	2	3	4	5
b. _____	1	2	3	4	5
c. _____	1	2	3	4	5
d. _____	1	2	3	4	5

Comments:

5. When you have a problem with another department/subsidiary, you know who to go to for a solution.

Department	Definitely agree	Inclined to agree	Inclined to disagree	Definitely disagree	Undecided; don't know
a. _____	1	2	3	4	5
b. _____	1	2	3	4	5
c. _____	1	2	3	4	5
d. _____	1	2	3	4	5

Comments:

6. To what extent do you understand the workers of the departments/subsidiaries—for example, how they affect you and your work and how you affect their work?

Department	To a very great extent	To a reasonably satisfactory extent	To a less than satisfactory extent	To an extremely limited extent	Not applicable
a. _____	1	2	3	4	5
b. _____	1	2	3	4	5
c. _____	1	2	3	4	5
d. _____	1	2	3	4	5

Comments:

7. To what extent do you feel that other departments/subsidiaries understand you and your problems, difficulties, and obstacles?

Department	To a very great extent	To a reasonably satisfactory extent	To a less than satisfactory extent	To an extremely limited extent	Not applicable
a. _____	1	2	3	4	5
b. _____	1	2	3	4	5
c. _____	1	2	3	4	5
d. _____	1	2	3	4	5

Comments:

8. To what extent do you feel that other departments/subsidiaries are concerned with helping you solve your problems?

Department	To a very great extent	To a reasonably satisfactory extent	To a less than satisfactory extent	To an extremely limited extent	Not applicable
a. _____	1	2	3	4	5
b. _____	1	2	3	4	5
c. _____	1	2	3	4	5
d. _____	1	2	3	4	5

Comments:

9. When a problem does arise, to what extent is a joint effort made to solve it by both parties (for example, your department/subsidiary and others)?

Department	To a very great extent	To a reasonably satisfactory extent	To a less than satisfactory extent	To a limited extent	Not applicable
a. _____	1	2	3	4	5
b. _____	1	2	3	4	5
c. _____	1	2	3	4	5
d. _____	1	2	3	4	5

Comments:

10. To what extent do other departments/subsidiaries take the initiative in identifying and preventing possible problems from occurring?

Department	To a very great extent	To a reasonably satisfactory extent	To a less than satisfactory extent	To a limited extent	Not applicable
a. _____	1	2	3	4	5
b. _____	1	2	3	4	5
c. _____	1	2	3	4	5
d. _____	1	2	3	4	5

Comments:

11. To what extent do other departments/subsidiaries plan ahead with you to avoid potential problems?

Department	To a very great extent	To a reasonably satisfactory extent	To a less than satisfactory extent	To a limited extent	Not applicable
a. _____	1	2	3	4	5
b. _____	1	2	3	4	5
c. _____	1	2	3	4	5
d. _____	1	2	3	4	5

Comments:

12. How well satisfied are you, overall, with the services provided by other departments/subsidiaries?

Department	To a very great extent	To a reasonably satisfactory extent	To a less than satisfactory extent	To a limited extent	Not applicable
a. _____	1	2	3	4	5
b. _____	1	2	3	4	5
c. _____	1	2	3	4	5
d. _____	1	2	3	4	5

Comments:

13. Please rate how valuable the work of other departments/subsidiaries is to you in the achievement of your business objectives.

Department	Of considerable value; critical	Of noticeable value; necessary	Of little or no value	Is a retardant	Not applicable
a. _____	1	2	3	4	5
b. _____	1	2	3	4	5
c. _____	1	2	3	4	5
d. _____	1	2	3	4	5

Comments:

14. To what extent do you feel that other departments/subsidiaries really work at improving their own internal service effectiveness?

Department	To a very great extent	To a reasonably satisfactory extent	To a less than satisfactory extent	To a limited extent	Not applicable
a. _____	1	2	3	4	5
b. _____	1	2	3	4	5
c. _____	1	2	3	4	5
d. _____	1	2	3	4	5

Comments:

15. To what extent do you feel that communications with other departments/subsidiaries are effective and meaningful to you?

Department	To a very great extent	To a reasonably satisfactory extent	To a less than satisfactory extent	To a limited extent	Not applicable
a. _____	1	2	3	4	5
b. _____	1	2	3	4	5
c. _____	1	2	3	4	5
d. _____	1	2	3	4	5

Comments:

16. To what extent do you feel that other departments/subsidiaries plan their own work to better service your needs?

Department	To a very great extent	To a reasonably satisfactory extent	To a less than satisfactory extent	To a limited extent	Not applicable
a. _____	1	2	3	4	5
b. _____	1	2	3	4	5
c. _____	1	2	3	4	5
d. _____	1	2	3	4	5

Comments:

17. In terms of overall service to your department/subsidiary, which three departments consistently provide the best service?

a. _____   b. _____   c. _____

18. In terms of overall service to your department/subsidiary, which three departments consistently provide the worst service?

a. _____   b. _____   c. _____

19. To what extent do you feel that other departments/subsidiaries have clearly defined goals and standards for servicing their internal customers?

Department	To a very great extent	To a reasonably satisfactory extent	To a less than satisfactory extent	To a limited extent	Not applicable
a. _____	1	2	3	4	5
b. _____	1	2	3	4	5
c. _____	1	2	3	4	5
d. _____	1	2	3	4	5

Comments:

20. To what extent do you feel that decisions involving internal customer services are effectively implemented in other departments/subsidiaries?

Department	To a very great extent	To a reasonably satisfactory extent	To a less than satisfactory extent	To a limited extent	Not applicable
a. _____	1	2	3	4	5
b. _____	1	2	3	4	5
c. _____	1	2	3	4	5
d. _____	1	2	3	4	5

Comments:

21. To what extent do you feel that managers of other departments/subsidiaries are free to make their own decisions with regard to servicing your internal client needs?

Department	To a very great extent	To a reasonably satisfactory extent	To a less than satisfactory extent	To a limited extent	Not applicable
a. _____	1	2	3	4	5
b. _____	1	2	3	4	5
c. _____	1	2	3	4	5
d. _____	1	2	3	4	5

Comments:

22. The structure of the organization is clear and facilitates improved internal customer service among departments/subsidiaries.

Definitely agree	Inclined to agree	Inclined to disagree	Definitely disagree	Undecided; don't know
1	2	3	4	5

Comments:

23. In this organization, we all share responsibility and accountability for what happens in other departments/subsidiaries. For example, if one of us fails, we all fail.

1   2   3   4   5

Comments:

24. I clearly understand the interrelationship of my job with the jobs of others in other departments/subsidiaries in servicing our internal client needs.

1   2   3   4   5

Comments:

25. People in my department/subsidiary are urged to provide the highest standards of service excellence to other departments.

1   2   3   4   5

Comments:

26. The quality, timeliness, and effectiveness of internal client services are reflected in the reward system.

1   2   3   4   5

Comments:

27. The rank-and-file employees in other departments/subsidiaries are as concerned with servicing my business needs as they are with servicing their own needs.

1   2   3   4   5

Comments:

28. In this organization, cooperation among departments/subsidiaries is actively and visibly encouraged by senior management.

Definitely agree	Inclined to agree	Inclined to disagree	Definitely disagree	Undecided; don't know
1	2	3	4	5

Comments:

29. Top management will take specific actions to effectively address the issues and concerns resulting from this survey.

Definitely agree	Inclined to agree	Inclined to disagree	Definitely disagree	Undecided; don't know
1	2	3	4	5

Comments:

In this next section, please rate your own department on the same basis that you rated the other departments. The two sets of perceptions will then be compared to determine if there are any significant differences in the levels of services and products provided and to identify opportunities for improvement.

30. Please indicate the extent to which your department/subsidiary is responsive to the business needs of other departments.

To a very great extent	To a reasonably satisfactory extent	To a less than satisfactory extent	To a limited extent	Not applicable
1	2	3	4	5

Comments:

31. To what extent does the quality of your department's/subsidiary's services meet the needs of those departments to whom you provide the service?

1	2	3	4	5

Comments:

32. To what extent does your department/subsidiary jointly predetermine the standards for the quality of service you provide to others?

1   2   3   4   5

Comments:

33. To what extent do you deliver your service commitments to other departments/subsidiaries in a timely manner?

1   2   3   4   5

Comments:

34. To what extent do you feel that other departments/subsidiaries understand the work of your department—for example, how you impact them and affect their work and how they impact you and affect your work?

1   2   3   4   5

Comments:

35. To what extent do you feel that your department/subsidiary understands the work of other departments and their problems, difficulties, and obstacles?

1   2   3   4   5

Comments:

36. To what extent do you feel that your department/subsidiary is concerned with helping other departments solve their problems?

1   2   3   4   5

Comments:

37. When a problem arises with another department/subsidiary, to what extent do you make an effort to reach a jointly satisfactory con-
clusion?

To a very great extent	To a reasonably satisfactory extent	To a less than satisfactory extent	To a limited extent	Not applicable
1	2	3	4	5

Comments:

38. To what extent does your department/subsidiary take the initiative in identifying and preventing service-related problems from occurring with other departments?

1	2	3	4	5

Comments:

39. To what extent does your department/subsidiary plan ahead with other departments to anticipate potential problems?

1	2	3	4	5

Comments:

40. On an overall basis, to what extent do you feel that other departments/subsidiaries are satisfied with your services?

1	2	3	4	5

Comments:

41. Please rate how valuable you feel your department/subsidiary is in the achievement of the business objectives of other departments?

Of considerable value; critical	Of noticeable value; necessary	Of little or no value	Is a retardant	Not applicable
1	2	3	4	5

Comments:

42. To what extent do you feel that your department/subsidiary really works at improving your internal service effectiveness?

To a very great extent	To a reasonably satisfactory extent	To a less than satisfactory extent	To a limited extent	Not applicable
1	2	3	4	5

Comments:

43. To what extent do you feel that your department's/subsidiary's communications with other departments are effective and meaningful to them?

1	2	3	4	5

Comments:

44. To what extent do you feel that your department/subsidiary carefully plans its work to better service the needs of other departments?

1	2	3	4	5

Comments:

45. To what extent do you perceive that your department/subsidiary has clearly defined goals and standards for servicing your internal clients?

1	2	3	4	5

Comments:

46. To what extent do you feel that decisions involving service to your internal customers are effectively implemented?

1	2	3	4	5

Comments:

47. To what extent do you feel that managers/supervisors in your department/subsidiary are free to make their own decisions with regard to serving the needs of your internal customers?

1	2	3	4	5

Comments:

I. Some Suggestions for General Management Skills

Running a Good Meeting

- Carefully prepare the agenda.
- Thoroughly know your audience.
- Thoroughly study your subject matter.
- Allow plenty of time for advance notification.
- Arrange for physical comforts.
- Follow the five steps (below) for making a successful presentation.
- Involve the participants.
- Manage conflict.
- Obtain consensus.
- Be punctual.
- Close with a call for action.

Making an Effective Presentation

- Determine your objective.
- Plan your strategy.
- Organize your ideas.
- Evaluate the impact on the audience.
- Practice.

Planning Employee Performance Reviews

Goal: To make sure that all employees know exactly what is expected of them and feel that the expectations are fair and reasonable.

Matters That Need to Be Communicated	*What Supervisors Need to Do to Ensure Communication*
• Work required	• Make sure employees understand the job
• Goals, plans, and programs	• Keep employees informed regarding goals, plans, and programs
• Importance of the employee's job; its relationship to others	• Explain organization of unit
• Day-to-day problems and emergencies that arise	• Review regularly with group
• Reasons for changes	• In advance, review changes affecting the group
• How well the employee is doing	• Conduct performance reviews periodically
• How the employee feels about objectives, plans, goals, and so on	• Seek out employee attitudes

Holding Compensation Discussions

Goal: To make sure that all employees know exactly what they are receiving as compensation for their efforts and feel that these rewards are fair, considerate, and in line with their desires.

Matters That Need to Be Communicated	*What Supervisors Need to Do to Ensure Communication*
• What is realistically possible as fair reward	• Make practical limitations clear
• How pay is determined	• Make sure employees understand how pay is set
• Employee benefit plans	• See to it that employees understand and appreciate employee benefit plans
• Management's efforts to provide good working conditions	• Conduct individual and group discussions regarding working conditions
• Management's efforts to provide good bosses	• Explain what you think makes you a good boss
• Management's efforts to provide steady work	• Keep employees informed of steps to provide steady employment
• Opportunities for self-development and promotion	• Discuss with employees opportunities and prospects ahead
• Efforts to treat employees with respect	• Demonstrate through word and deed the value of treating employees with respect
• How well the employees think management is doing	• Seek employees' opinions

REFERENCES

American Society for Personnel Administration. "Adapting Your Business to Fit the New Employee." *Personnel Administrator,* Jan. 1989a, pp. 38–39.

American Society for Personnel Administration. "Learning Is a Job for Life." *Personnel Administrator,* Jan. 1989b, p. 48.

Badi, F. G., and others. "Work Force Diversity in Business." *Training and Development Journal,* Apr. 1988, pp. 38–47.

Below, P. J., Morrisey, G. L., and Acomb, B. L. *The Executive Guide to Strategic Planning.* San Francisco: Jossey-Bass, 1987.

Blount, W. F. "AT&T Service, Quality, and Renewal." *AT&T Technology,* June 1988, pp. 3–4.

Bowen, D. E. Quoted in Schneider, B., and Bowen, D. E. "Employee and Customer Perceptions of Service in Banks: Replications and Extension." *Journal of Applied Psychology,* 1985a, *70* (3), 423–433.

Bowen, D. E. "Taking Care of Human Relations Equals Taking Care of the Business." *HR Reporter,* Nov. 1985b.

Bruce, M. "Managing People First: Bringing the Service Concept to British Airways." *ICI,* Mar./Apr. 1987, pp. 25-26.

Bubolz, J. S. Quarterly Team Meeting address to all managers and supervisors of Secura Insurance, Aug. 1, 1990.

Bunning, R. L. "Rewarding a Job Well Done: Recognizing Employee Productivity Will Create Job Satisfaction for You and Your Workers." *Personnel Administrator,* Jan. 1989, pp. 60-64.

Bylinsky, E. "Invasion of the Service Robots." *Fortune,* Sept. 14, 1987, pp. 81-84.

Bylinsky, E. "Technology in the Year 2000." *Fortune,* July 18, 1988, pp. 92-98.

Carnevale, A. P., Gayner, L. J., Meltzer, N. S., and Holland, S. "The Skills Employers Want Most." *Training and Development Journal,* Oct. 1988, pp. 23-30.

Cherrington, D. "Managers Lead by Example." *Chicago Tribune,* June 14, 1984.

Cincinnati Institute for Small Enterprise. *CEO's on Hiring.* Cincinnati: Chamber of Commerce, 1988.

Cooper, M. *Change Your Voice, Change Your Life.* New York: HarperCollins, 1985.

Davies, K. R. "Is Individual Responsibility a Radical Idea?" *Training,* Nov. 1988, pp. 64-65.

Denison, D. R. "Bringing Corporate Culture to the Bottom Line." *Organization Dynamics,* Autumn 1984.

Doyle, R. J. *Gainsharing and Productivity.* New York: AMACOM, 1983.

Dreyfuss, J. "Victories in the Quality Crusade." *Fortune,* Oct. 10, 1988, pp. 79-84.

Drucker, P. F. *Managing in Turbulent Times.* New York: HarperCollins, 1980.

Drucker, P. F. Interview. *Wall Street Journal,* Apr. 23, 1987.

Feuer, D. "The Skill Gap: America's Crisis of Competence." *Training Magazine,* Dec. 28, 1987, pp. 27-30.

Fierman, J. "Child Care: What Works and What Doesn't." *Fortune,* Nov. 21, 1988, pp. 163-176.

Finney, M. I. "Talents of a Team Player." *Personnel Administrator,* Nov. 1988, pp. 44–47.

Finney, M. I. "Planning Today for the Future's Changing Shape." *Personnel Administrator,* Jan. 1989, pp. 44–45.

Forum Corporation. *Building, Using, and Sustaining Influence.* Boston: Forum Corporation, 1987.

Fuchsberg, G. "Managing." *Wall Street Journal,* Mar. 14, 1991.

Fullerton, H. N., Jr. "New Labor Force Projections, Spanning 1988 to 2000." *Monthly Labor Review,* Nov. 1989, pp. 3–12.

Goetschin, P. "Reshaping Work for an Older Population." *Personnel Management,* June 1987, pp. 39–41.

Guaspari, J. "Keeping Close to the Customer." *Trainer's Network,* Winter/Spring 1988, pp. 6–7.

Hall, C. G., Jr. "How an Investment in People Increases Profit." Speech given at the National Restaurant Association convention, Chicago, July 1989.

Kearns, D. Quoted in Kearns, D., and Doyle, D. P. *Winning the Brain Race.* San Francisco: ICS Press, 1988.

Koehn, H. E. "Corporate Loyalty: Missing in Action." *New Management,* 1987, pp. 44–46.

Kupfer, A. "Managing Now for the 1990s." *Fortune,* Sept. 26, 1988, pp. 44–47.

"Managing Values." *Inc.,* Sept. 1987, p. 110.

Melone, J. Quoted in *Building Customer Satisfaction.* Chicago: Dartnell Corporation, 1990. Audiotape.

Miller, L. *American Spirit: Visions of a New Corporate Culture.* New York: Morrow, 1984.

Morrisey, G. L. "Who Needs a Mission Statement? You Do." *Training and Development Journal,* Mar. 1988, pp. 50–52.

Naisbitt, J. *Megatrends.* New York: Warner, 1982.

National Institute of Business Management. *Personnel Report.* New York: National Institute of Business Management, 1987.

Odiorne, G. S. *George Odiorne Newsletter,* May 2, 1986.

Odiorne, G. S. "Senior Executives in Government and Industry Play an Important Role in the Area of Training." *George Odiorne Newsletter,* June 19, 1987.

Odiorne, G. S. "Eleven Keys to Performance Improvement in Your Organization." *George Odiorne Newsletter,* Feb. 5, 1988.

Odiorne, G. S. "Seven Deadly Sins of Supervision for the 90's."
George Odiorne Newsletter, Feb. 10, 1989.

Oliver, T. Quoted in *Building Customer Satisfaction.* Chicago: Dartnell Corporation, 1990. Audiotape.

O'Toole, J. *Vanguard Management.* New York: Doubleday, 1985.

Perry, N. J. "Saving the Schools: How Business Can Help."
Fortune, Nov. 7, 1988a, pp. 42–56.

Perry, N. J. "Here Come Richer, Riskier Pay Plans." *Fortune,*
Dec. 19, 1988b, pp. 51–53.

Peters, T. J. *A Passion for Excellence.* New York: Random House, 1985.

Richman, L. S. "Tomorrow's Jobs: Plentiful, but . . . " *Fortune,*
Apr. 11, 1988, pp. 42–56.

Rollins, T. "Pay for Performance: Is It Worth the Trouble?"
Personnel Administrator, May 1988, pp. 42–48.

Rude, J. "Sharing the Wealth at Sutter Health." *Personnel Administrator,* Jan. 1989, p. 46.

Rudia, E. "Seven Essential Elements of a Positive Work Environment." *Production Supervisors Bulletin,* Jan. 10, 1989.

Sadler, P., and Barham, K. "From Franks to the Future." *Personnel Management,* May 1988, pp. 48–51.

Schuler, R. S., and Jackson, S. E. "Linking Corporate Strategies with Human Resource Management Practices." *Academy of Management Executive,* Aug. 1987, pp. 207–219.

Sellers, P. "Getting Customers to Love You." *Fortune,* Mar. 14, 1989, pp. 38–39.

Serieyx, H. "The Company in the Year 2000." *Personnel Management,* June 1987, pp. 30–35.

Sherden, W. A. "Gaining the Service Quality Advantage." *Journal of Business Strategy,* Mar./Apr. 1988, pp. 45–48.

Smith, A. *An Inquiry into the Nature and Causes of the Wealth of Nations.* Oxford: Clarendon Press, 1976. (Originally published 1776.)

Smith, P. "Lack of Training Creates Pay for Performance Dilemma." *Personnel Report,* July 1988.

Taylor, F. *The Principles of Scientific Management.* New York: W. W. Norton, 1967. (Originally published 1911.)

Therrien, L. "Motorola Sends Its Workforce Back to School." *Business Week,* June 6, 1988, pp. 80–81.

Thomas, L. R. "Customer Service Going from Bad to Worse." *Knoxville News Centennial,* Business and Real Estate Section, Mar. 15, 1987.

Tichy, N. M. *Managing Strategic Change.* New York: Wiley, 1983.

Watson, S. Quoted in *Building Customer Satisfaction.* Chicago: Dartnell Corporation, 1990. Audiotape.

Young, J. A. Quoted in *Building Customer Satisfaction.* Chicago: Dartnell Corporation, 1990. Audiotape.

Young, J. W. "An Incentive System for All Seasons at Four Seasons." *The Human Resource Professional,* Nov./Dec. 1988, pp. 10–11.

Zemke, R. "Rewards and Recognition: Yes, They Really Work." *Training,* Nov. 1988, pp. 48–53.

Zemke, R., and Schaaf, D. *The Service Edge.* New York: Dutton, 1989.

INDEX